Endor.

I celebrate this book! Personal and autobiographical, the author shares important lessons from teachers, science, experiences, victories and defeats, integrating them into a narrative that many can relate to. Once a teacher of the author, I am excited to see her integrate Meister Eckhart and other mystics into her real-life experience as, for example, when she tells of "returning to the stable" of the church after many breakthrough experiences. The book is practical and lively with a critical questioning of the present-day church but her well-earned sense of hope outweighs the pessimism of our times. A genuine contribution for the march from stale religion to lively spirituality!

Matthew Fox, author of *Original Blessing* and *The Reinvention of Work*

This book is a treasure chest of spiritual gems. It's filled to the brim with evolutionary insight, wisdom for the crises we're facing, and rituals to celebrate the wonders of our planet, our lives and our communities. A helpful book for a troubled time.

Jan Phillips, author of *No Ordinary Time*

Transition and adventure capture the spirit of this eco-spiritual narrative, in which Carol Kilby traces her faith-story from that of conventional Church to creation-based spirituality. While for some this could mean an irreparable rupture, for Kilby it matured into a re-integration and a revitalization of Church and worship, with several valuable insights for the evolving global spirituality of our time.

Diarmuid O'Murchu, author of *Quantum Theology* and *Evolutionary Faith*

This book deserves a wide readership. Skillfully interpreting ecology and evolution in a soul-nourishing way, Carol Kilby invites religious folk to take prophetic responsibility for ushering humanity into a healthy relationship to the larger body of life. Weaving cosmic storytelling, biblical texts, and practical wisdom, she offers rituals, practices, and holidays that can be used in, out, and on the fringe of the church by those hungering for a worldview that inspires us to compassionate action in crazy and confusing times.

Rev. Michael Dowd, author of *Thank God for Evolution*, and host of "The Future Is Calling Us to Greatness" and "Post-doom conversations"

With honesty, humour and vulnerability, my former minister invites us on a journey of transformation guided by deep eco-spiritual wisdom. With updated stories and new holiday rituals, Kilby offers inspiration for any seeking an evolutionary path.

Rev. Lynn Harrison - Unitarian Universalist

Evolutionary Dancer

Out, In, and On the Fringe of the Church

CAROL KILBY

Ebook: 978-1-7753258-2-6
Paperback: 978-1-7753258-1-9

Other books

Cosmic Beatitudes
A Code of Being for this Evolutionary Moment
Carol Kilby with Peter and Caitlin Adair

Contents

Part 1
Out

Out of the Pulpit and into the Woods
Evolutionary Wisdom for a Climate of Uncertainty

Part 2
In

Out of the Woods and Back IN the Church
Evolutionary Stories for Climate-Conscious Pewsters

Part 3
On the Fringe

Evolutionary Rituals
Out, In, or On the Fringe of the Church

Resources and Rituals for Evolutionary Spirituality

Preface

We dance for laughter, we dance for tears ... we are the dancers, we create the dreams.

I'd never imagined such a day would come. But it did. Wakened by the planetary crisis, I walked away from the church. Nor did I imagine that same crisis would take me back. And I certainly never imagined that one day I would write a book from the fringe of the Christian culture. But then evolution, be it planetary or personal, isn't something one puts in a five-year plan.

Evolutionary Dancer is the story of what's been for me a three-step dance – first out, then back, and finally to the fringe of the church. The dance? Ah, that is the ongoing tango between belief and consciousness. In three sections, the book is an account of that dance as it's happening in me, and all around me, in these times.

Out. Stepping out of paid professional ministry, I stepped into a post-Christian world as director of an Eco-Spirituality retreat centre. It was the new millennium. Spiritual, social, and environmental consciousness was rapidly breaking through old paradigms. In Canada, 40% of the population identified as not religious, 9% as atheists, and almost 30% had left religion for another or no religion at all. The stories in this section tell of my dances with the shift-makers of our time, the teachers and their students who are the Evolutionaries among us.

In. Stepping back into a small rural congregation of sophisticated elders was an adventure. We engaged the church's seasons within the context of the planetary break-down. We read the old stories with evolutionary eyes. We included wisdom coming from the modern sciences. We saw there is an emerging belief system called Evolutionary Spirituality. The accounts of our adventure through Advent, Christmas, Epiphany, Lent, and Easter will surprise, affirm, or challenge you.

On the Fringe. In language that reflects the emerging Earth-community worldview, the last section offers Evolutionary Rituals, fresh practices and rituals relevant to these environmentally threatened times.

Glossary. Because entering the uncharted future requires innovative language, here are words and phrases to navigate, communicate, and co-create a never-before species for never-before times.

Thank you

To the many wondrous guests and leaders who came into the Gaia Centre, widened my world, and became my evolutionary teachers; and to those who served on the board of the Gaia Centre For Eco-Spirituality and Sustainable Work, thank you for creating a vessel of conscious evolution.

To the dear hearts and gentle people of Kinmount United Church who faced death, found another way to live as evolutionary elders, and welcomed me home, thank you for sharing in an experiment in evolutionary spirituality.

To the neighbours of Haliburton County who remind me daily what it means to love the Earth; to Grandfather Pine, Mother Lake, the four legged, winged, and finned that complete me; and to the Mississauga, Nipissing, Ojibwa, Huron, and Algonquin first peoples who blessed Gaia Centre's presence on these lands, thank you for deepening my faith in this experience called life.

To Paul who everyday is my supporter, and fan; to daughters Jill and Tanya who helped me grow up and are reason enough to protect Earth's future, thank you forever.

To my editors Lisa, Holly, Carolyn, Paul, and the Author Academy Tribe, thank you for your dedication to this project; no book is ever written alone.

And lastly, thank you to the Evolutionary Impulse for trusting me to do this work.

Gaia Farmhouse, 2005-2020.

One day we realized Gaia Centre wasn't a physical location but a spiritual destination from which to lead an Earth-centred life.

Introduction

The world mind, it seems, is forging a new container for its spiritual seekers ... something unprecedented is brewing in the Earth's spiritual continuum. Perhaps the most hopeful sign is just this: the grand company of mystic-minded adventurers, bent on exploring every room in the many-mansioned House of the Holy. Jean Houston

In the Beginning ...

Bright wide ribbons formed three large circles on the auditorium stage. A dancer moved from one to another like Goldilocks looking for the chair that fit her best. The red circle represented the Canadian Church, spiritual home to me and over half the participants. The blue symbolized the religious diaspora, those disappointed by Christianity's lack of rights for women, gays, and lesbians. The green circle, its edges touching the other two, acknowledged those who lived on the fringes of both. It was 1995 and the opening ceremony of a conference called, Women Waking the World. The dance was in honour of five hundred registrants who'd come from in, out, and on the fringe of a conflicted and evolving institution. I was that dancer.

That dance, as life would have it, turned out to be prophetic. In 2004 I made *la grand jeté* out of ministry in a vibrant urban congregation and into environmental education in the Algonquin Highlands. And though I would later return to offer occasional leadership in a rural congregation, I would find my place on the evolutionary edges, on the fringe of Christianity. This book is an account of that three-step dance.

The vision – Gaia Centre for Eco-Spirituality and Sustainable Work – refocused our lives. We sold the four bedroom home in the suburbs and purchased the old farmhouse on the edge of Little Cameron Lake. We didn't mind it was a renovation project or even that the attic was full of bats. When the shingled roof danced with the winds, the siding clapped its applause. Inside, neighbouring children made a game of moving the floor tiles like they were puzzle pieces. But that's the way with a vision, you don't fixate on what is, only on what can be. In the end, a carport became two bedrooms and a sitting room; an aluminum sunroom became a third bedroom; a mudroom turned into a hall closet and third washroom. The old walls stretched to be able to sleep seven guests, and feed a dozen or more, all without changing the house's footprint.

Gaia Centre, a not-for-profit, charitable organization, operated under the auspices of a Board of Directors. Its programs invited participants to fall in love with Mother Earth again and to reinvent their work to protect her. Its international guest teachers shared their genius in the areas of ecology, environmentalism, Creation Spirituality, Shamanism, Buddhism, alternative medicine, mysticism, Taoism, Cosmology, Conscious Evolution, and more. While most programs happened in the farmhouse and on the land, many were held in larger urban settings. One day we realized Gaia Centre wasn't a physical location but a spiritual destination from which to lead an Earth-centred life. Looking back, it was a vessel for my own, and I hope others', evolution of consciousness.

As a Gaia-conscious organization, the aim was to let green ethics govern our programming. To reduce the cost of fossil-fuels involved in bringing registrants to events, we took programs to the people, travelling to many centres around central Ontario. Following the cosmic law of co-creation, we found allies such as progressive churches and yoga studios to co-sponsor workshops. To honour body, mind, and spirit, each event included movement and centering, lecture and learning, Gaia-glorious food and nurture, art as meditation, time on and with the land. Later, we learned to add a co-creative community component. It was an experiment in conscious education.

When guests asked me why I'd stepped out of the pulpit and into the woods, the answer I learned to offer was, I followed the energy. By energy, I didn't mean my own physical strength but the larger energy that, according to Teilhard de Chardin, is part of a "vast process in which the whole mass of the universe is involved." My fresh-sprung passion for the planet was part of what he'd described as "the evolution of the world towards the spirit becoming conscious." In short, I left following that spirit-full, evolutionary energy that was leading so many others to reconnect with the Earth.

Another answer, equally true and too simple, was, I'd found a new story. The creation story, as told by modern science, wakened me to an undeniable fact – before I was a Christian, I was an Earthling and a cosmic being. Whereas Christianity was a worldview that was two millennia old, the cosmology offered by post-modern science was almost fourteen billion years old. Recognizing I'd emerged from this greatly expanded story of energy and consciousness, some shift in my life purpose, according to Theilhard de Chardin, was to be expected.

> "For the first time since the awakening of life on earth … we must address the fundamental problem of action" and "organize around us for the best maintenance, distribution and progress of human energy."[i]

Over a century ago, this priest, whose mysticism was inspired by twentieth century science, had foreseen the significance of the new story.

Why did I step away from Christianity? In a language befitting the new cosmology, my answer is this – I'd awakened to the Evolutionary Impulse.

To say I followed the energy seems a straightforward reply. But these are not, and cannot be made to be, simple times. They are times when our species is awakening to a Gaia-consciousness that's drawing many out of lives that today feel too small. That's not to say, the exodus is an easy passage.

Growing up in small-town Ontario in the fifties, Holy Trinity Church was my second-home – Explorers on Tuesday, junior choir on Thursdays, and of course, Sunday School on Sundays. So, when in my early forties my mother died, I turned to that home. Faith drew me to study for ordained ministry.

But it wasn't an easy fit for a gal who loved innovation more than tradition and Mother Earth more than Mother Church. Though leaving ministry introduced me to a vast world of evolving consciousness, it left a family-sized hole.

The shifts taking place, however, were not just in me. Other books explore in detail the varied reasons for the exodus from the mainline church at the end of the century. Here it is enough to share two sets of figures. In 1986, the year before I began seminary, 43% of Canadians were reported to attend church once a month. By the time I retired in 2004, those numbers had dropped to 27%. In my denomination, from 1991, the year I was ordained, to 2001, the number of people claiming an affiliation with the United Church decreased by 8%. As congregations shrunk, a clergy could sometimes feel there was more interest in growing the number of bums in the pews than the spirituality of a community. But the church's decline was all part of the rapid evolution of consciousness happening in the new millennium.

Five powerful social movements have made this time what history will call another axial moment. *Feminism,* which continues to expose the oppression of patriarchy, demand language, security, and rights for women, gays, lesbians, children, and Mother Earth. *Environmentalism,* better described as an ecological awakening to global warming and the extinction of mass numbers of species. The *New Cosmology*, that is the study of the 13.8 billion-year-old cosmos. The *Conscious Evolution* movement, that is the global awakening to how our one species will now determine the planet's future. And last, the *spiritual revolution* has taken many forms including Incarnational Spirituality and Creation Spirituality as humans sought the sacred in their midst. Together, these new-thought movements bear witness to the shift in social awareness.

And I was not oblivious. Absolutely, these emerging philosophies created a major shift in my North American, liberal Protestant belief system. In response to rapidly accelerating climate change, my values began to realign with the ways of Earth. A sense of sacred connection to life, that's to say, Creation Spirituality, was in bud. Worship of an omnipotent, unchanging deity in a distant Heaven felt passé. It was empowering to believe in divinity as the Creativity enfolded in everything. And this force of creativity, by its very nature, was no longer obedient to finite doctrines. Rather, it loved to dance; its preferred music was the music of the spheres, the vibrations of that first big bang. In short, it might be said, that which had led me into the pulpit to preach eternal love was now leading me out to live it now.

These pages are a response to the Evolutionary Impulse some call God that's leading the dance of becoming. Becoming what? Awake, conscious, mindful, Gaia-centred, love, a new kind of human – yes to all of these. This book's plea for an evolution in religious thinking, for the emergence of a Gaia-conscious culture, for faith in the future are my response to the death of life around me.

Who is the book for?

Do you identify as a spiritual seeker or an evolutionary thinker? Do you frequent farmers' markets, practice yoga, go to drum or dance circles? Perhaps this book is for you. If you've rejected oppressive dogma, exited a marinating mainline denomination, joined mindfulness or meditation classes, these stories are for you. If you count yourself a tree hugger, among the growing number of mystic-minded adventurers, a disciple of Darwin, one of the children of Star Wars – you may resonate with a chapter or two. If you feel passionate about the environment, are drawn to ecojustice groups, long for a spiritual community but won't commit to anything that smacks of hierarchy or patriarchy, these pages may ring true.

Certainly, here are a few thoughts for the "SBNRs." In Canada, the numbers of folk who identify as Spiritual But Not Religious went from 17 to 24% in a decade. By 2012, SBNRs and Nones – those professing to have no religion – made up 40% of our nation's census and 20% in the United States.[ii]

But this book is also for you in the pew and the pulpit. If, like me, you have so much gratitude for the wisdom teachings of Christianity and have dedicated your life to its study, but have come to understand it must evolve or drown in its own shadow, this memoir is certainly for you.

Why this primer on Evolutionary Spirituality?

Living in the end times, the end of the planet as we've known it, we're hungry to find ways to navigate the unknown. Such ways, however, are not only political, technological, or environmental. What is most important is that we find novel ways of thinking. Evolutionary Spirituality reflects such a new consciousness.

As a belief system, it redefines everything as sacred, engenders love for non-human and human alike, embraces the cosmic story as our story, and nature's creative processes as wisdom's ways. Going beyond the tenets of our former religious and cultural ideologies, this worldview holds the potential to foster a spiritually ethical, and ecologically sustainable human species capable of deep inter-dependence with the whole of things.

In an age when the Earth family is divided, broken, and much of it disappearing, Evolutionary Spirituality points to a universal experience of holy communion.

What is Evolutionary Wisdom?

At the end of each chapter, you will find what I believe to be tenets and ecological truths – I call these Evolutionary Wisdom. Learned from my own consciousness-stretching encounters and spirit-expanding experiences, these ideas have been like footprints on a dance studio floor guiding me into greater alignment with the Evolutionary Dancer.

The 3-Step.

Written in three sections, the book reflects my own spiritual adventure. It begins with my stepping out of the Church, then back in, and finally landing in this place on the cusp of a rapidly shifting social, ecological, and spiritual culture.

Out. Step out of the Christian culture with me to meet wonder-filled humans living awe-struck lives and working like Earth depends on us. Try on new frames for seeing – ecology, evolution, and awe. Gain evolutionary eyes. Meet Grandmother Universe. Her stories can empower us for life in this time of mass extinction.

In. Now step back into a gracious circle of Christian elders to re-interpret the Church's stories, seasons, and beliefs within the evolutionary context, and speak justice to the truth of global warming.

On The Fringe. These original rituals and unique practices reflect the principles of Evolutionary Spirituality. Better called spiritual dances, they celebrate both our cultural and Christian holidays while bridging the gap between our planet's dis-ease and our longing to make a healing difference.

In the End...

Dance, to me, is more than a metaphor. Before spoken language, there was dance, the articulate movement and intentional communication between human and divine, the hunter and the hunted, Earth and Heaven, sun and moon, rains and winds. It was and remains all dance. Since the beginning, there has been the dance of birth and death, death and rebirth. Existence itself is dance.

Modern science tells us the subatomic world, moving to the rhythms of creation and destruction, is a dance. An electron is not just an elementary particle but a dancer in the great cosmic sequence of moves and patterns. Vibrating and inter-connected, inorganic and organic, everything is a dance of energy. Parts of a holographic Universe, we ourselves are a reflection of the whole. Life is a mirror dance.

Dance to me is communication with and of Source. Before I was a clergy, I was first a liturgical dancer interpreting a Biblical story or spiritual theme. The round dance was part of the early church's tribute to the Cosmic Christ. Prayer is dance. At the University of Creation Spirituality, dancing was prayer. Life is a sacred dance and the embodiment of the sacred. Dance to me is a way of being. And so, this is the story of my dance with that sacred and evolutionary energy.

The stories and rituals you will find between these covers have been as a result of my dance with the Evolutionary Impulse I have called God. They are my contribution to the ongoing movement of human consciousness. May they, in some small way, contribute to yours. And most importantly, may they speed the end of planet abuse in our time.

I left the church following that spirit-full, evolutionary energy that was leading so many others to reconnect with the Earth.

PART 1

Out of the Pulpit and into the Woods
Evolutionary Wisdom for a Climate of Uncertainty

CHAPTER 1

The Mirror Dance

Aquinas sees creatures as a "mirror" or image of God. Every creature is for us like a certain mirror. Because from the order, goodness and magnitude which are caused by God in things, we come to a knowledge of the divine wisdom and goodness and eminence. And this knowledge we call a vision in a mirror. Matthew Fox

Turning to the stranger on my right, I met my partner for the Mirror Dance. Amy, according to her name tag, wore calf-high black Doc Martens, striped green tights, a fitted army jacket, and a top hat. A gazillion hoops and rings hung from various parts of her petite body. To middle-age-me, in my beige polyester dress pants and white blouse, she was the embodiment of strange.

"Welcome to Dances for Universal Peace." Sporting a guitar, ponytail, and more rings, the leader addressed a circle of forty-odd folks. Odd indeed for both women and men wore flowing skirts and dance-slippers. Standing in the dim gymnasium of a fortress church in the bowels of Toronto, having come in from the mix-and-match suburbs, what I felt was anything but peaceful.

"Now, stand face-to-face about two feet apart." A hundred reasons I had to leave came to mind.

"Like in a game of cops and robbers, put your hands up with palms facing but not touching your partner's." No problem. I already felt robbed of my comfort zone.

"Look directly and deeply into your partner's eyes." He might as well have told me to get naked.

"When the music starts, mirror each other's hand movements." But who starts? Who follows?

The music started. Our eyes locked. A gentle, swaying hand dance began. Self-consciousness fell away. Bodies, minds, and spirits synchronized. It was over when it was over, and when it was over, so was the world of separation, judgment, panic, and anxiety. We had danced into one-Earth consciousness and that future of non-judgmental relationship we all say we want.

As a child, I wanted to be a ballerina. I imitated my instructor's every step and gesture to learn what my own body could do. Truth be told, my whole childhood was spent mirroring others – at home, school, and church – to learn how to be an adult. As an adult, I continued to seek teachers who could show me the steps to take my place in the dance. As I approached my elder years, however, my heart did an unexpected pirouette that led me away from the life I knew, out of our elegant home in the suburbs, out of mainstream Christianity, and into a dilapidated farmhouse in the woods of Ontario's Algonquin Highlands.

The vision was a retreat house for these times. The goal was an educational centre in the lap of Mother Nature where ecology and spirituality were partners, where human could reconnect with humus, and where important wisdom teachers would offer programs for seekers longing to live and work within Earth's means. What was the driving force that made the dream a reality? The Evolutionary Impulse, leader of the cosmic dance itself.

The timing of this leap of faith wasn't my own. Five years away from professional and national pensions wasn't what anyone would call the opportune moment to reinvent one's lifework. But if you've ever watched loons in late August on a northern lake, you'll understand. One pair, then another and another gather together, laughing, flapping their wings, rising like so many ballerinas on point. It goes on for a few days until one morning they're gone. Attuned to Gaia's time, they leave, join the great migration in accordance with the turning of the seasons. Likewise, I found myself following some undeniable allurement and part of the global shift in human consciousness. The time to follow some nobler pragmatism than one's personal finances, professional training, social, or cultural loyalties for the sake of the whole hurting planet had come.

In this chapter, you'll meet some of Gaia Centre's guest teachers. Though they come from diverse disciplines, they agree this is the time to leave behind the world's myth of separation, to embrace the reality of oneness, and discover our species' potential and place in the planetary family. I name them Evolutionaries.

- Rev. Dr. Matthew Fox: Dancing Creation's Paths
- Geologian Thomas Berry: Dance to Tell A New Story
- Sister Miriam MacGillis: The Shell Dance
- Cosmologist Brian Swimme: Dance of the Cosmic Powers
- RN and Shamanic Practitioner Jeannette McCullough: Dance Like You're Not Alone
- Abbess Khenmo Drolma, author Dawn James, and mystic Joseph Rael: Raise Your Vibrations
- Futurist Barbara Marx Hubbard and Yogi Celeste Shirley: Dance For Conscious Evolution Now
- IT Developer Alice Miller: Dance Like You're Wired for More

Dancing Creation's Paths with Matthew Fox

> *Honouring all of Creation as Original Blessing, Creation Spirituality integrates the wisdom of Eastern and Western spirituality and global indigenous cultures, with the emerging scientific understanding of the Universe, and the passion of creativity. It is both a tradition and a movement, celebrated by mystics and agents of social change from every age and culture.* Creation Spirituality Communities

It was not climbing up the 48 steps that left me breathless but the walls of the stairwell. Unlike the dullard green of most educational institutions, they were the bright blue of a perfect day, the vibrant green of fecund vines, the rich golds of seed-full sunflowers, and the deep cobalt of a midnight singing with silver stars. Passing by those murals celebrating the original blessing of creation was an exhilarating ascent into postmodern consciousness. The spiritual climb into the adventurous new University of Creation Spirituality, that was breathtaking!

Creation Spirituality – that's what drew me 4,200 kilometres from home. A re-emerging expression of a lost ancient tradition, it is a hopeful worldview. Its teaching contradicts all that has brought society to the edge of self destruction: following nature's paths, we live not only aligned with the Earth, but aware of our original blessing. It's a belief system honoured by the mystics and prophets from every age and culture and it has resurfaced in this planetary moment to call us to spend our lives on the best of struggles – the conscious evolution of religion, economics, politics, education, and our species.

The classrooms at 4151 Broadway, a concrete corner of commerce in downtown Oakland, California, did not disappoint. Wherever I turned, art, mystical images, colourful tapestries, and prayerful sculptures from Hindu, Buddhist, Muslim, Indigenous, and Christian mythologies revealed deeper and novel interpretation of reality. I was like Alice in the kaleidoscope world of Wonderland.

I had come, once again, face-to-face with the strange. And once again I discovered what connects us all: four spiritual paths by which to encounter divinity. Referred to in Latin, the titles sounded foreign to my Protestant ears. Now, almost 20 years later, they are the points of my spiritual compass. *The Via Positiva* leads in the way of amazement. *The Via Negativa* describes the journey of loss. *The Via Creativa* points to the way of creativity. And the *Via Transformativa* indicates a path of justice and compassion. I know and teach them as those universal experiences in which we engage the Divine Intelligence and find our way home to ourselves as holy beings. It was to study these paths, the precepts of a just-crowning spiritual tradition, that I'd come.

At the top of the stairs, on the other side of massive glass doors, learning was never dull. Days began with teachers and students swaying and chanting, playing and praying together. Celebrating with eyes, arms, and hearts wide open was freeing. Not only of my body, but my love and joy. For the first time, I saw prayer not as submission to God the Judge but as dance in a spirit-filled Universe. Honouring creation as loving and each other as star-stuff at this University that actually taught about the Universe, I began to regard my tradition's practices with fresh eyes. The guilt-ridden prayers of confession, pleading petitions for healing, prosperity, or liberation I saw as an abdication of response-ability. That community's reinvented rituals encouraged me to befriend the godness in myself and the world around me. In this new paradigm, worship became celebration, a celebration of sacred existence. In that school of the sacred, boredom was the new sin, reconciliation was not with God in Heaven but the divinity in and around me, and prayer was dance.

My native tongue was dance. As a toddler, then a school girl, and a teenager, I danced to the tunes on the Nickelodeon in my Dad's restaurant. After school, I took tap and ballet at the Legion Hall. In this alternative quantum-age university, I found my tribe and they spoke my language, dance.

In the midst of this gyration of contemplation was the unassuming and controversial Matthew Fox. An evolutionary scholar called a prophet for our times, he is to Christianity what Rudolph Nureyev is to ballet – a risk-taker. The former Dominican priest makes unconventional leaps of theology, higher and further than his tradition allowed. His feminist teachings, interfaith alliances, the unorthodox schools he started, and writings of the Cosmic Christ cost him dearly. Deemed too wild and untamed, he was silenced by the Vatican, set adrift by his order, and consequently cast as a great soloist on the religious stage. In morning circles, Fox's movements mimicked a brave's war dance around a sacred fire. The heart of the Creation Spirituality community, the prophet of its ancient message, Fox dances to reawaken the Church's reverence for life. Reinvention – of religion, of work, and education – is his war cry. In his late seventies, he was and continues to be a spiritual warrior battling religious irrelevancy in environmentally threatened times.

From twenty to eighty, from California to Italy, the alumni of this wisdom school was post-generational and international. Protestant, Catholic, Buddhist, Muslim, Hindu, Indigenous, Wiccan, atheists, and more, the community is post-denominational and inter-spiritual. Religious leaders, engineers, psychologists, social, physical and cosmological scientists, corporate consultants, health-care professionals, and artists, everyone's work, according to Fox, can be a sacred ministry. The reinvention of creation-centred churches, businesses, lives, families, and communities – this is our lifework.

The teachings were evolutionary. As well as Fox's own post-religious reinterpretations of the Church fathers and mothers, we studied post-modern science. Core courses included the New Cosmology based on the writings of today's Father Thomas Berry and physicist Brian Swimme, and medieval mystics such as the twelfth-century German Abbess Hildegard of Bingen, the thirteenth-century Persian Sufi poet Rumi, and the Rhineland's Meister Eckhart of the fourteenth century. Together, these teachers called us home to our roots. I came to believe that only by learning to see the planet as our holy home and the Universe as sacred revelation will humanity refrain from totally destroying Starship Earth.

The result was the re-greening of my beliefs, even my vocabulary, underwent significant transformation. Like one needs to learn the Anishinaabe language to understand the worldview of the Mississauga First Nation, I needed to learn new terminology and redefine old in order to articulate the reality of a mystical cosmos. Words, that growing up had held little emotional value, burst with significance.

The universe I'd thought cold, impersonal, and negligible space, with a Creation Spirituality, was filled with Divine Intelligence. Now I capitalize it and speak of Universe with awe. Raised to think of creativity as the special gift of artists and creation as the completed handiwork of a heavenly Creator, I've come to know Creation as that divine process out of which I've come and of which I am part. God, who art in Heaven, according to every Sunday School teaching, became the Evolutionary Impulse and cosmic pattern of interconnection. Christ, no longer a synonym for Jesus of Nazareth, became the Cosmic Christ of Creativity that has been there since the beginning. Likewise cosmos, which had only ever been a scientific term, became Cosmos, my first and sacred home. I stopped referring to Sunday gatherings as worship of a great and distant benefactor. They became celebrations of all existence.

At first it was merely exciting to use new rhetoric to convey a deeper reality. But the reinvention of language, I now understand, is essential for the reinvention of a religion, society, and our species if we are to live with reverence in the Earth.

In time, stirred by Fox's vision of the reinvention of work, my own vocation shifted. Moving from inside to outside the institutional church, I stopped preaching Christianity and began teaching the Universe Story. I no longer offered Bible Study but a program called, Work Like You Don't Need the Money. It was designed for those longing to quit occupations and jobs by which they made a living at the expense of the environment.

The essence of this curriculum – earning a livelihood without compromising the vitality of the Earth-community – was a spirituality of work.

In the following chapter, you'll meet some of the women and men who took the reinvention of work program. Their stories illustrate what it means to follow Creation's compass, to find God in the woods, Christ in a caterpillar, and divinity within. They show what it is to name the work we do to make a living our lifework and become co-creators of the unfinished story.

The long and steep climb to dance with Fox was transforming. It not only introduced me to the world views of global cultures but also to the nascent creation story, the epic tale of the Universe. But more importantly, he showed me we can reclaim and reframe ministry for ourselves. Refusing to be silenced or stripped of his priestly life, he continued his lifework under the auspices of the Episcopalian Church and today is known as Rev. Matthew Fox. He gave me permission to leave the church, to return in my own way, and to find my unique ministry on the fringes.

In the rear-view mirror, I see how dancing among artists, mystics, activists, and green clerics of every stripe freed me from the bastardized belief that Christians had the only way, the only truth, and were the only ones to gain eternal life.

Today, I dance ecstatically. The word means freely with excitement. When there is not one way but many paths, when all wisdom traditions, science included, can be vessels of Divine Evolutionary Intelligence, it is freeing and invigorating. We move across a stage that spans the arc of the ages. Time, on a cosmic clock, moves from one axial moment to the next. Life is an ever-ascending dance of consciousness along four intertwining paths.

Evolutionary Wisdom

- All life is an ever-ascending dance of consciousness along four paths.
- The step of awe leads to wonder, gratitude, and the affirmation of all existence.
- The step of detachment, death, dying, and emptying is toward fecund nothingness.
- The step of creativity births more possibility and manifests more Universe.
- The step of compassion transforms separation into greater wholeness.

Dancing with a Geologian – Thomas Berry

We are in trouble now because we do not have a good story.
Thomas Berry

There are so many times I wish I'd had a "good story" to tell. But our cosmic origin story, the good story Berry was referring to, wasn't anything I'd been brought up to know.

For the times, the mid-twentieth century, Ontario's public-school education system was considered progressive. Each day began with the Lord's Prayer, God Save the Queen, and ended with O Canada. We were brought up to know ourselves as members of a Commonwealth nation, a Christian society, and a resource-rich economy. We studied reading, writing, and math, grammar and literature, British history, art, music, social studies and health. In High School, we were streamed for post secondary education or the work force. Boys took Shop and girls, Home Economics. In thirteen years of schooling, however, there was no ecology or cosmology.

When I attended seminary, the focus was God, the historical Jesus, and the institutional church. Ignored was what Thomas called the first revelation of the divine, Universe itself. There was no story that provided a realistic, deep time account of existence.

The lack of a comprehensive worldview, Thomas believed to be the root of the sixth mass extinction. The unnaturally rapid disappearance of countless numbers of species and their habitats, usually attributed to the urban, industrial, and technological revolutions, the cultural historian saw as a problem of story. Climate change, the sense of general fear, and the hopelessness it generated, he said, were symptoms of the spiritual crisis of our times caused by an inadequate story.

What story is that? The non-human reality – plant, animal, mineral – is inert matter, without spirit, and intended to serve as human resources. That story, Thomas believed to be the bane of our existence.

The story we needed, *The Universe Story,*[iii] he co-authored with a former student, Brian Swimme. Reading its unfamiliar scientific terminology was a hard go. Yet, being an account of creation that was scientifically accurate, spiritually inspiring, and inclusive of the Earth community, this text, more than any other, expanded my understanding of life and excited my hope. This narrative, as Thomas suggested, could enable the evolution of religion and society itself.

Thomas Berry was for me a new and relevant voice. Even while I trained at Emmanuel College, a wing of the ecumenical Toronto School of Theology, I didn't hear of his work on the relationship between ecology and theology. And yet, as part of the Passionist priest's work – to bring Catholicism into its cosmological stage – he was meeting with Canadians only an hour away.

For over 20 years, from 1979-2000, Holy Cross Centre in Port Burwell was an incubator of dialogue around his ideas. In 1982, when Thomas declared the Church's future to be dependent on its ability to pay attention and take responsibility for the fate of the Earth, I missed it. Only after I'd taken my first step outside mainline Protestantism and into an inter-spiritual community did I become aware of this mystic living in our times.

When I arrived in California, talk of Thomas and the New Cosmology was integral to the Creation Spirituality ethos. Professor Larry Edwards – a former physical chemist at the National Science Foundation in the United States – taught the Universe story as a creation story for our times. Not a better one, just the latest one, he made a point to say. I'd read many cultural and religious creation stories, but this being older and inclusive of them all was like no other. Galaxies, planets, sun, Earth, biological life, human life – each was a chapter in one sacred story. Learning science as sacred story, I wakened to the historic animosity between Christianity and science for the first time.

Today, this story and the new worldview it offers, challenges my despair at the climate future and stirs my faith in the evolutionary process.

Drawn to Thomas's story, I sought out his students as my teachers. At Genesis Farm in New Jersey, Miriam MacGillis taught earth-literacy. In Vermont, Sisters Gail Worcello and Bernadette Bosnick co-founded Green Mountain Monastery, the first Ecozoic monastery devoted to caring for the Earth. When they laid the Eucharistic bread and wine atop the 13.8 billion year timeline, they showed the Universe itself to be a sacrament, a revelation of the divine. Today Sisters of the Earth can be found in New Zealand, Thailand, Ireland, Hawaii, and right across North America in ecological and learning projects. So much innovation has been inspired by Thomas' hope for the integration of Catholicism with environmentalism.

The closest I came to meeting this thought-leader in person was at a conference dedicated to the world's wisdom traditions and The Great Work. Thomas, author of a book by the same name, was to be the honorary guest. Remarkably, it was hosted not by a religious group, but by the Centre for Transformation within the Ontario Institute for Studies in Education – a graduate school in the University of Toronto. Innovation! Where I found one, I found Thomas.

Too ill to attend, the 96-year-old sage spoke via live-stream teleconferencing. Even on the screen, his craggy visage and tremulous voice carried an impact.

> "What's needed is to carry out the transition from the current period of human devastation of the Earth to the future time when humans would be present to the planet in a mutually beneficial manner."[iv]

His call was for nothing short of a complete social metamorphosis, and though I didn't know it, mine had begun. The Great Work, according to Thomas, was for humanity to consciously move out of its destructive stage and emerge as a new kind of human, one capable of co-existing within Earth's community.

It was 2004. It would be only a matter of months before I left the pulpit to become director of the Gaia Centre. Offering programs and speakers who shared an Eco-Spirituality and inspired sustainable work, the organization was intended to play its part in 'the Great Work.'

The message of this Evolutionary was humbling. Like every other living being in Earth's bio-sphere, I too was part of a species. And my species was evolving. Like the caterpillar consuming the leaf, Homo sapiens in its destructive stage has the potential to evolve. Unlike that creature, however, our transformation in these times is more voluntary than involuntary. His ideas were as humbling as they were challenging.

To consciously accomplish this monumental shift, Thomas suggested three steps. Inner work – awakening to oneself as part of a species. Outer work – reinventing the work we do to make a living into work that sustains planetary life. And the Great Work which we participate in by consciously attending to the first two.

In the shaky voice of a weathered man via the advancements of technology, Wisdom spoke truth to my story at that conference. Clearly, the evolutionary process was happening.

Over the next 15 years, within the chrysalis of Gaia Centre, two things happened. I slowly became an advocate and storyteller of that good story. We hosted teachers who'd once been that elder's students to tell the cosmic story in their own way.

Earth Day, April 22, 2009. Our guest was children's author, Jennifer Morgan. A global Montessori consultant from Princeton, New Jersey, Morgan shared Thomas' dedication to children. Dressed in a midnight blue cloak wired with twinkling lights, she told of the birth of the Universe and planted the bazaar idea – we are star-stuff, expressions of the Universe. It was electric.

But that was small stuff compared to Morgan's present day work. As founder and president of the Deeptime Network website, she's become an international force for the new cosmology hosting scholars, religious, authors, and others offering programs, essays, and credit-courses for teachers.

Drew Dellinger is an international speaker, teacher of the new story, climate activist, and also a spoken-word poet. Standing before a dozen of our county's writing circle, then in a second engagement before a half-filled sanctuary, he recited his widely acclaimed and haunting work, *Hieroglyphyic Highway.*

> "It's 3:23 in the morning and I'm awake. My great, great-grandchildren ask me in dreams what did you do while the planet was plundered? What did you do while the earth was unravelling? ... What did you do once you knew?[v]"

Founder of Planetize the Movement, Dellinger is a professor of cosmology. Asking the piercing questions, he carries on Thomas' work.

In no small way did Thomas Berry, a radical religious who lived ever in search of what is real and worthwhile, influence education. In him, I found a mirror in which to reflect on my own faith and its relationship to the suffering planet.

Berry was ordained into the Passionist Order as a young man. He took not only his name from Thomas Aquinas, the 13th century mystic who believed a mistake about creation results in a mistake about God; seemingly, he took his lifework. A scholar in Eastern religions and director of the Riverdale Center of Religious Research for a quarter of a century, Thomas had no presumptions as to the infallibility of religious doctrine.

It is in this priest's reflection, I found the encouragement I needed to re-interpret key Christian stories within the evolutionary context.

Though history describes him as a priest and a cultural anthropologist, he was not a man limited by labels. Trained to study the changing nature of human reality, he wrote with a broad pen documenting the intersection of ecological, spiritual, and cultural issues. An anecdote reveals his relationship with traditional labels. Gazing down on the Nile River valley from thirty thousand feet, he had a realization. As a being who'd emerged out of eons of geological and biological evolution, a being that now reflected on its own story, he was not merely a theologian, a student of a divinity and servant of the Church. He was a geologian, a student of planetary process and a servant of the Earth. The new cosmology, Berry teaches, demands a playful and inventive relationship with language. New language makes creators of us all.

How I wish I'd had Thomas' panentheistic story and playful way with verbiage during my years of congregational ministry. Like the time I proposed a Blessing of the Animals to a worship committee. Believing the traditional story – the non-human world lacks the blessing of a soul or spirit – they directed me to offer thanks to God instead of a blessing to the beloved dogs, cats, rabbits, turtles, fish, and birds that comforted and enriched their lives. This anthropocentric worldview is still held by many.

If only I'd known there was another story. I'd have been able to tell them how everything has divine nature because the divine is in everything. Those beings we call our pets, being blessed with sacred life and living as blessing to the whole, are holy beings in their own right. I could have celebrated that just as animals are blessings to humans, humans are intended to be blessing to animals. I could have advocated, as Thomas did, for religious reform and environmental bio-diversity. Not from a standpoint of religious stewardship or social conservation, but out of a story that recognizes the intrinsic value of each thing.

But at the time, I didn't have a good story to inspire either an evolution of consciousness or an ethics of holistic compassion. I was unable to say then what I have since learned from Thomas – we are bio-spiritual planetary beings. Ours is a story of all creation as a vast communion and mode of celebration. This was the story I was missing as I presided over too many formal, mournful, and mechanistic Eucharist services.

The Lord's supper, Holy Communion, is the central ritual of Christianity. At best, it is a faithful reflection of a love story and a celebration of oneness. At its most dogmatic, it is an embodiment of a dualistic and divisive theology that tells us God gave Jesus, his only child, to die in exchange for our sins. In response, we offer a litany of our transgressions, prayers of repentance, and psalms of lamentation. At its end, the people are supposedly left refreshed, thankful, and recommitted to a moral life.

In one congregation, this ritual played out with extraordinary solemnity. Sombre-faced elders called deacons fanned up the steps of the chancel where it was my role to pass out silver trays of precisely cubed bread – the body of Christ broken for us. When every server had a tray, like a highly drilled platoon of soldiers, they turned as one. Descending the stairs, they moved through the congregation to their designated positions where, on the command of the head elder's nod, they passed the trays to the people. Likewise, thimble-size portions of grape juice – the blood of Christ shed for us – was distributed in a stern and penitential manner. The remembrance of Jesus' last supper felt like a state funeral.

At odds with this so-called high Christology, I was longing for Berry's good story. What a difference it would have made to believe all things in Earth and Cosmos, all birthing and dying are part of a vast communion and a mode of celebration.

When, a decade later, I began wondering if my work was in or outside the congregation Thomas's writing expanded my thinking again. A cultural historian, he believed the work of society was to understand,"the community of all living species includes the human and is of the greater reality and greater value."[vi] This idea helped me recognize the story I knew never considered Earth as a community of species, nor did it value the whole more than humanity. Church and society had schooled me to believe in the primacy of the human. I began to recognize Christianity's story was deeply humancentric.

As I continued to raise the 'E' word (environment) in the congregation, the more I became a misfit. The more passionate I became about life beyond my religious culture, the less I felt fitted for its ministry. I left believing it was the only way to live with integrity. On the occasions I returned from the woods, it was to serve in a new way. Not by preserving the doctrine and rituals, but by telling a good story, one that was comprehensive and still-evolving.

Retired now, I see in the rear-view mirror how hard I'd worked at being a loyal Christian. I see how ministers are over-worked, and over-work themselves. I see how many hours I lost with my human and non-human family. Clearly, I was indoctrinated with the Protestant work-ethic and Methodist philosophy: work as hard as you can to make as much as you can to give as much as you can. I was raised on the writings of Paul – faith, apart from good works, is dead. (James 2:14–26) The result was that I became part of a culture that worshipped, worked, produced, and consumed like our eternity depended on it.

Deep in my psyche, I equated the work I did to make a living with worthiness. So deeply was this true, that when a teacher of Hawaiian spirituality declared life's purpose to be "joy," I was angry. Feeling betrayed by my tradition, I cried angry tears.

Yes, I'd like to have grown up according to Thomas's story – taking joy in my life as a work of the Universe, and finding joy in my occupation because it played a role in the circle of life. Refired by Berry's new cosmology, refocused by the planet's distress, today I speak not of life and work as two separate things, but valuing all my existence as my lifework.

You may wonder at the familiar and familial tone with which I speak of the iconic Father Berry. Do we not speak of Abraham, Mother Theresa, Buddha, Jesus and all our forefathers and mothers? Yes, in Thomas we have known one of the world's spiritual masters. His legacy is nothing short of a totally new narrative that tells how we are, as emergent beings, not only manifestations of rock and rain, sun and soil, space and time, but also mirror images of the planet. We are "Universe in a special mode of conscious self-awareness."[vii] We are the story become storytellers.

Thanks to my dance with the spirit of Thomas, one of the most important evolutionary elders of the last century, I recovered an identity I didn't know I'd lost. I am a storyteller who knows herself as Grandmother Universe. I regained sight I didn't realize was compromised. And gratefully, I embraced myself as the cosmic dance of unabashed celebration I was created to be.

Evolutionary Wisdom

- The environmental crisis is a spiritual crisis.
- The Cosmos is becoming conscious in you and me.
- We must do our inner work – remembering our cosmic origins – to reinvent our outer work, to be part of the Great Work.

The Shell Dance – Miriam MacGillis

Life and spirit are nurtured within the boundaries given by our cultures, but our spirit must ever break through those shells or die imprisoned in its own narrowness and fear.[viii]
Miriam MacGillis OP

It all started with a ball of yarn. Miriam MacGillis, a student of Thomas Berry's Universe Story, was trying to imagine when everything – galaxies, planets, mountains, birds, bees – happened. The former high school art teacher knew about making the intangible visible. Perhaps her biggest accomplishment will be designing and teaching the Cosmic Walk, an exercise that makes conceivable the inconceivable immensity of the newest creation story.

If you've never experienced the Cosmic Walk, visualize a 140-foot rope laid down in a large spiral. Every ten feet represents a billion years. At the centre, the first candle represents the Big Bang 13.8 billion years ago. All along the cosmic timeline, candles mark significant events: the emergence of galaxies, primal stars, our solar system, Earth, Moon, life – biological, animal, human – religion, agriculture, space travel, and more.

The Walk is not just another educational tool. In designing the exercise, Miriam brought science and spirituality together thereby creating an evolutionary ritual. What makes it evolutionary is in teaching a new worldview, it contributes to the evolution of human consciousness.

Most brilliantly, the exercise helps us understand evolution more fully. Usually assumed to be that process by which animal became human, the cosmic walk shows it to be a cosmic pattern. Rejected in some Christian corners as a theory that denies the existence of God, the Cosmic Walk portrays evolution using the universal archetype of the sacred pilgrimage.

The pilgrimage is enacted as the Universe story is told to the strains of Rowland's Fairy Ring. The pilgrim begins moving from the centre of the spiral toward its outer edge. As a narrator relates the events of the cosmic drama, the pilgrim glides along lighting the candles. It ends with the pilgrim lighting the last candle – humanity at this moment in time. Standing with one foot poised to take the next step, watchers are reminded all the cosmos waits to see if the human pilgrimage will lead to evolution or devolution.

The end of the walk for me was the beginning of a new cosmology. Since then, the oxygen I breathe is the oxygen created at the Big Bang. The minerals in my body – selenium, carbon, sodium, and calcium – originated in the stars. My backbone is but a later model of the first fish's skeletal framework. My eyes are but sophisticated versions of the first photo-receptor proteins in microscopic unicellular organism. Like the infant in her mother's arms who looks into a mirror and sees not two but one being, the cosmic walk revealed the ineffable oneness of the Universe. And like that child in arms, cradled and emergent, I was enthralled.

In her seventh decade when I met her, this Dominican sister was not planning her retirement. Protecting and preparing for the next era, teaching the Universe story and Earth literacy – that was her priority. In her blue jeans, cotton shirt, and sneakers, she was five feet of pure dedication. With the support of her religious community, she co-founded the Earth-literacy centre and its community-shared agricultural program. Hers has been a life dedicated to teaching the scientific account of the Universe as a new sacred creation story and preparing the way for an Ecozoic age.

Like a great teacher shows a child what she will become when she grows up, she showed me there was another way of being in ministry. So intensely committed to the story, she was a new kind of elder, the kind I wanted to be.

What made her different? I think it was because, like a hospice nurse, she lived aware of each day as precious. With little energy for frivolous small talk, she moved in and out of our gatherings. We are living at the end of the Cenozoic era, she explained. Earth's era of extravagant fluorescence that has lasted for some 65 million years – the period when today's continents took form, the diversity of plants and mammals exploded, grasses appeared, ice ages came and went, and humans first appeared – is over.

Unaccustomed to thinking in geologic time, the news was hard to grasp. I recalled when my childhood home was sold, remodelled into something smaller. I could only understand the loss ahead to be, on some level of immeasurable magnitude, a time when what we have known as home will be a lesser version of itself. Miriam was the first person I'd met who believed there was no turning back. The ship called global warming had sailed.

We are living through an exodus of cosmic proportions. Her teaching called up the biblical account of Moses leading the Hebrews out of slavery after having spent centuries in a foreign land. For those who never saw the movie or read the book, there's a twist in the plot. After so many generations, the tribe was reluctant to leave; Egypt had become a comfortable prison. A long and arduous journey of an unknown length in the desert wilderness, would not have been their vote. Thought by some to be more likely a teaching myth than a historical account, it resonates with those resistant to move out of environmentally destructive economic and social lifestyles.

But Miriam understood the exodus as more than a spiritual parable – it is a Universal pattern. We are always leaving one age, entering the wilderness of chaos in order to enter the next age. It is the story of these times. Exiting the age of industrialization which has triggered the massive extinction of so many lifeforms, we are leaving the Cenozoic era. Thomas's hope, she explained, was that we are entering the Ecozoic, a period of integral community inclusive of the human and non-human.

Again, the Green Nun put the story into ritual. She led the group in a prayer of lamentation for the 41% of amphibians, 26% of mammal species, and 13% of birds that are endangered by the Sixth Mass Extinction.[ix] In this traditional way, MacGillis led me out of a Christianity that was anthropocentric and into one of deep integration.

In the mirror of the Green Nun's lifework at the Earth-literacy centre, I saw my future. My exodus from the institutional church became imminent. I would not retire but reinvent my lifework on behalf of the future we will not see. I would create evolutionary rituals – sacred acts set within the context of *The Universe Story,* spiritual practices grounded in the cosmic patterns of exodus and becoming.

A new kind of religious, Miriam was named one of the planet's top 15 green religious leaders by Grist magazine in 2007. Less about theology than eco-education, more about ecojustice than the salvation of souls, her post-modern ministry was a mirror for what mine could become.

It was Thursday of Holy Week, the day before Good Friday at Genesis Farm. Miriam had gathered us in an extraordinary fashion. Not as the church would have – in a carpeted sanctuary round a table laid with fine linen and lit by tall tapers to remember Jesus' last supper with his disciples. In a giant teepee in the middle of a dark field with our feet on damp ground and a single candle, we participated in a retelling of the Jewish Passover Seder, a ritual that remembers the exodus.

As part of her Earth-literacy program, she had contextualized the symbols of the ancient ritual. The teaching of the hard-boiled egg, historically a sign of Israel's sacrifice, not coincidentally fell to me to read aloud:

"Life and spirit are nurtured within the boundaries given by our cultures, but our spirit must ever break through those shells or die imprisoned in its own narrowness and fear."

In the days and nights that followed, this wisdom became the ear-worm that would not cease.

The liturgy was unique. Some would denounce it as unchristian. Some would say using it to explain a cosmic pattern wasn't Jewish. A recitation of Earth's leaving behind the Cenozoic era, it was an ecological, educational, and evolutionary ritual. There was no word of God saving his people. Instead there was a story portraying humanity as the co-creators of the planetary future. It was, for me and all those dancing out, in, and on the fringe of the Church for the sake of Mother Earth, a rite of passage signalling our becoming a new kind of human.

Saturday was a day of silence, art, and meditation. Miriam instructed us in the Ukrainian art of Easter egg painting called Pysanky, which means to scribe. The goal was to portray the symbols of all the world religions on a raw egg without breaking the shell. It was no subtle metaphor. The test of our times is to draw out our lives on a fragile planet but do no harm.

Through the day, the words I'd read the night before were working their way deeper into my psyche. "Our spirit must ever break through those shells or die." I remembered the many shells within which I lived my life. Christianity, colonialism, individualism, nationalism, and more – so many ideologies and philosophies shaped my life to think, believe, hope, and act in certain ways. By day's end, I fully expected there to be only one conclusion to this artistic exercise – break the egg. But the day ended with no such direction. The impulse to break out of vocational ministry – a life I'd worked so intentionally to create – was only mine.

At the next sunrise, Easter Sunday, we celebrated. No one mentioned the bodily resurrection of Jesus or the salvation of anyone's soul. We gathered at the foot of a Black Walnut tree, named by a neighbourhood Shaman as the grandfather tree of those farmlands. Ringed with yellow forsythia, and tulips – orange, lavender, and pink – it was more breathtaking than the most ornate alter. The strains of a flute called forth our dance. We danced to welcome the rising up of an Ecozoic age and our own emergence as Gaia-centred humans. When the festivities reached their natural conclusion and the exuberant group made their way to the kitchen, I stayed behind. It was this moment, I realized, for which I'd driven ten hours, crossing international and religious borders.

Taking the raw egg, I'd so painstakingly decorated the day before, I cracked its shell against the root of the great tree letting the fluid body, and my lifework with it, return to Earth. My own sacred ritual, it signalled my exodus from ordered ministry was certain. It declared my "yes" to some Evolutionary Impulse calling me to serve Gaia, the Holy Mother.

As I joined the group for breakfast, I felt elated at having taken the next step in my pilgrimage. I would carry on Earth's work, as Miriam MacGillis and so many others had done before me. It would be two years before the Gaia Centre for Eco-Spirituality and Sustainable Work opened. Then, the guiding principles of the non-profit, educational organization were based not in theology but cosmology. The intention was to share a new cosmology, inspire higher ecological consciousness, and deeper commitment to working with respect in the Earth community. My ministry was crafting retreats, workshops, conferences, and evolutionary rituals that were grounded in the story of the Cosmic Walk.

The significance of the iconic spiral lies in its ability to awaken us to who we are. We are Universe in human form. The power of the sacred ritual is its capacity to teach us Universe is not a fixed place or finished entity, but a process of continual regeneration that is not separate from, but happening in and through us. The genius of Miriam's Cosmic Walk is its invitation to see, as one sees in a mirror, the body is part of an immensely bigger reality.

Many versions of the Cosmic Walk exist around the globe. In the form of a 300 meters-long, lantern-lit, woodland path spiralling through the woods, it became the heart and soul of the Gaia Centre. At the end of the ritual telling of the story, each walker was asked to stand with one foot poised as though to step into the future. In this position, they were asked to consider that, for the first time in human history, it will be the human species to decide Earth's future. There are other ways of telling the Universe story, but this experiential version challenges us to embody what is both the core of humanity's dilemma and potential at this planetary moment.

Whenever I lead a group through the Cosmic Walk, MacGillis, in her blue jeans and rubber boots, goes before me. Mentor and mirror, spiritual elder and Evolutionary, she has led me to understand myself as Universe, as star-stuff become human, a partner in an ever-expanding cosmic event. Following Miriam's steps, I found, as a storyteller and evolutionary ritualist, my own unique way to become what these times need me to be.

I'll be ever grateful for that first time I heard the scientific story in the form of a sacred and evolutionary ritual. When the storyteller was quiet, and the music faded, it was the end of one time and the beginning of another. And what time was it? It was time to move beyond building the church to re-building the sacred human-Earth relationship. In that moment I was like the young girl who, receiving her first watch, intuitively understands she's old enough to take more responsibility in the family.

Evolutionary Wisdom

- Life and spirit are nurtured within the boundaries given by our cultures, but our spirit must ever break through those shells or die imprisoned in its own narrowness and fear.
- As a chick breaks through the shell at a particular time or loses the opportunity, it is our time to break into our next stage of potential.
- In most traditions, pilgrimage is a spiritual practice. Taking a journey to discover something about oneself and life is ancient and archetypal.

Dancing with the Powers – Brian Swimme

This is the greatest discovery of the scientific enterprise: You take hydrogen gas, and you leave it alone, and it turns into rosebushes, giraffes, and humans. Brian Swimme

The auditorium was humming, literally. The rumble of the Bloor Street subway directly beneath our venue, the Ontario Institute for Studies in Education, added no small amount of vibrational energy. I looked over the gathering audience. They were Toronto's spiritual and religious, educators and academics, teachers and students, the environmentalists and scientifically inclined. And they were all allured by one man and his story. It was opening night of Gaia Centre's annual conference, and cosmologist Brian Swimme was our featured teacher. The excitement was palpable.

How does one introduce the man who helped write and taught the most important story of his age? Certainly, the Universe story had been the most important story of my life. I'd even incorporated it into the woodland labyrinth at Gaia farmhouse, and told it to all our guests. Cooking, driving, sewing, I listened to Swimme's lectures on the powers that drove the story. I'd written and preached about those powers. The introduction needed to be big!

As the clock sped closer to the hour of commencement, my anxiety raced toward spontaneous combustion. Given his travel schedule, I hadn't been able to communicate personally with our key speaker before hand. Forty minutes to go and he hadn't yet arrived. I was feeling powerless. Then, suddenly, he was there. I knew it by the visceral ripple of recognition travelling through the crowd. Tall, affable, a boyish face with a beguiling smile and wandering white hair, his appearance generated my relief and the room's delight. As the energy crescendoed, I knew no words were needed to inspire excitement in this audience. It wasn't my recitation of awards and letters the crowd had come to hear. It was the passionate rendition of the new epic of evolution he would offer.

The way this scientist teaches the newest account of our origins, and the way he explains the development and characteristics of the Universe are not only motivating, inspired, and electric, they're personal. It's as though his very purpose for being is to tell this, his story.

Our guest hadn't always been a storyteller. Like many of us, he'd had a life-changing teacher. Swimme's mentor once challenged him to stop looking at the history of the cosmos in a quantitative way. Start seeing it as a stupendous story, a spiritual tradition in itself. Tell the story with a feel for its music was Thomas Berry's advice. Taking the wisdom to heart, Swimme's storyteller was born.

The power of his story and teaching for many has been cataclysmic. That's to say, it has broken through the literalism too often implied in the Church's teaching of how, in six days a great sky god created all that is. Based in twenty-first-century science, Swimme reminds us nothing is finished; everything is emerging. Accepting his revelation of reality as an emergent paradigm is to break away from our tradition's doctrine of a completed creation. Personally, I found the idea hopeful.

Likewise, Swimme's teaching on the Powers of the Universe are shattering. Hearing how the universal forces and creative energies that brought stars and galaxies into being – centration, allurement, emergence, homeostasis, cataclysm, synergy, transmutation, transformation, interrelatedness, and radiance – are also moving in and through us shatters the denigrating doctrine of humanity. No longer do we know ourselves as born sinful and in need of salvation. Now we look in the mirror and see we are cosmic beings with agency in these times of planetary breakdown.

Perhaps I'd start my introduction with the question he loved to ask his students. "What would be different if we paid attention to our cosmic powers?" On more than one chaotic occasion, I'd shifted from helpless victim trapped in a chaotic situation to cosmic consciousness by reflecting on those powers. "Ah, here comes cataclysm making way for the emergence of a more just and compassionate world," I'd say. Or, turning to face whatever was my current anxiety or conflict, I'd asked, "How can I use my radiance, today?" Acknowledging how Swimme's teaching on the powers had helped me navigate the valleys of the shadow, that would be a fitting, opening tribute.

Or perhaps I could read an excerpt from Grandmother's Power-full Treasures. I'd written the story following an unusual visit from a young neighbour depressed at the thought his sons might grow up in a wounded Earth. After talking of our cosmic powers as treasures we can use to dance with uncertainty, I watched him leave with more energy than he'd had when he'd arrived. Brian Swimme was absolutely right when he said, "when we understand the powers, we're well on our way to becoming co-creators of the future."

Compelling is Swimme's sense of awe. One place it's evident is in answering the one question that's asked at any speaking event: is there other life in the Universe? Swimme has a ready and enthusiastic answer. "If there is other intelligent life out there, then, Wow! And if there isn't, then, Wow!" The professor doesn't just teach cosmological science but the passion it can inspire in us.

The man's genuine awe broadcasts even through video and television. It was on one such interview, I heard him say: "I have a sense that something amazing is at work in this time ... we're entering into a period of transformation of the human species out of the modern period into this new era." Despite his not knowing "whether that's going to take 600 years or 6 days,"[x] any despair I was feeling was defeated by his radical amazement and confidence in the future.

In a time hungry for meaning and mystery, this mystic who finds poetry in science is able to convey the Universe as a radiant and numinous revelation. It is a remarkable contribution.

Yet, all and none of these ideas would do as my opening words to the conference. I asked myself, what's most transformative about Swimme's scientific contribution? The answer was immediate – unity.

If society were to embrace the message of cosmic communion as the norm, the destructive myth of dualism would more quickly shift into a philosophy of interdependence. With greater awareness of the evolutionary powers as human response-abilities, our species might just come of age. Preparing to introduce the professor, I realized community must be the theme of the conference. A word that in these times is evolving to include all animal, plant, and mineral existence, not to mention all cultures and creeds, one sacred communion sharing in one desire – to thrive in harmony – this was surely the heart of it all. And so in the end, all that was really needed to introduce the cosmic storyteller, was one word.

Inviting the gathering to stand and sway like so many birches bowing to the winds, I began to chant. Arms moving right, then left, beckoning the whole Earth to join us, we sang "Com(e), Com(e), Com(e)-unity." Over and over, "Com(e), Com(e), Com(e)-unity." Sing into the fullness of the word. Express the fullness of its vision, I directed them, and the esteemed audience did just that. As we chanted, the one word that carried the story's magnanimous promise and the gathering's most ambitious dream, the song swelled into a prayerful intention resonating out and beyond us. When it was done, we were ready to hear the storyteller's message.

Of course, someone did make a formal speech. Steven Scharper, co-author of the Green Bible, spoke of Brian Swimme's work at San Francisco's California Institute of Integral Studies, listed his academic degrees, and described his research in singularity theory. We heard how Swimme had taught at the Passionist Holy Cross Centre for Ecology and Spirituality in Port Burwell, Ontario through the '90s, and at Matthew Fox's innovative Institute in Culture and Creation Spirituality in Chicago. A winner of many awards, author, and filmmaker – there was much to be said about this alluring Evolutionary.

"Brilliant!" At the end of the evening, my son-in-law summed up the event. Appropriate praise I thought to capture the radiance of Brian Swimme.

But where were folks his age, my thirty-five-year old guest wanted to know. Other than a few university students, it had been a grey gathering. Was it because this generation's too busy raising children and making ends meet? Today I like to imagine it was because the Universe Story, even then, was already seeping into the consciousness of these new generations and changing the future. Time will tell.

But that night, the question I was left with was for the audience. What will we do with this story of awe, passion, and interconnectedness? The only answer I can report with assurance is my own. Become an evolutionary storyteller – even if the story is but one word long.

Evolutionary Wisdom

- There is a 21st-century creation story.
- From the Big Bang to Universe, Earth, cellular life, biological life, human life, to infinite potential – this is the new story of cosmogenesis.
- Earth and humanity are unfinished.
- The cosmic powers – centration, allurement, emergence, homeostasis, cataclysm, synergy, transmutation, transformation, interrelatedness, and radiance – are also our powers.

The Dance of Becoming the Medicine with Jeannette McCullough

For over 100,000 years, shamans around the world have perfected the art of travelling in consciousness to other levels of reality, gaining access to information that can seem quite extraordinary about how to treat and prevent disease, avoid negative situations, clear family issues, plan for our future, and more. Sandra Ingerman

Daring the cruel cold of March, eleven women lined the farmhouse porch to await their turn in the smudging ceremony. At the end of the line, I unceremoniously rushed toward Jeannette and her abalone shell of smouldering sage.

A Shamanic practitioner, presiding over the ancient indigenous ritual with grateful reverence, she was the opposite of rushed. Carefully, silently she guided the smoke above my head, down and around my body trusting the intent of the rite to be obvious – cleansing negative thought and energy. And it was. My fear of the cold, the week's anxiety of preparing to house and feed ten women washed away. When she placed the shell in my hands, surprise turned to blessing as I administered the sacrament for her. Then, refreshed and open to the unknown, ready to dance once again with the Evolutionary Impulse, we entered the farmhouse and joined the others.

The ritual, celebrated beneath the snowy robes of the priestly Pines, felt right. After all, these forests and lakes had been the traditional homelands and hunting grounds of the Ojibway, Mohawk, Wendat, Pottawatomi, and the Métis Nations. They'd been surrendered to the colonial government in the Indian Lands Act of 1860. Participating in this rite of purification on the land from which they'd sprung felt right, unlike my first smudging.

That experience, in a richly carpeted and stained-glass sanctuary, had been awkward, out of place. It was the early

'90s. To acknowledge the United Church's apology in 1986 for its role in the residential schools, we'd included a smudging in a Sunday worship. But that day I'd felt less remorse than embarrassment at choking on the smoke. I'd been uneasy with the unfamiliar, i.e. non-Christian ritual. I'd seen only the differences, felt only the deep, collective guilt for the sins of Canada's Founding Fathers visited, as the Bible promised, on the third and fourth generations. (Numbers 14:18) Though the intention of bringing the smudging into the sanctuary was for the good, the experience was riddled with mixed emotions, and of course, with good reason.

The cultural genocide of the first peoples haunts our history. It had been the Anglican, Roman Catholic, and Protestant Churches who'd administered the government-funded boarding schools. It had been a Christian culture that carried out the mandate to remove Indigenous children from their homes to assimilate them into society. The last so-called school closed as recently as 1996. Some one hundred and fifty thousand children had suffered this system. The reports of sexual abuse are just now surfacing. The actual percentages of those who died while incarcerated is estimated to be higher than 50%.

Emotions were mixed the day we lit the smudge pot and passed it through the polished pews. Guilt, anxiety, even the resentment residing in the Canadian psyche, they were all stirred. Some hopefully were released. In the rear-view mirror, it seems evident bringing rituals that tell another story into our sacred places is important. Discomforting as they may be, they are necessary for reconciliation. Perhaps even more importantly, such rituals can serve as vessels of conscious evolution.

But a dozen years later, outside the Church, here on the land, I was ready and able to recognize the similarities. The fire in the embers of the smudge pot was the same fire in the flame of the Christ candle. Smudging, like baptism, is a sacrament of purification. I had moved not just physically but spiritually.

Not a Shaman but a trained Shamanic practitioner, Jeannette explained the intent of the weekend was to learn practices to enable our becoming the medicine. To each ceremony we could bring questions and invite answers from the ancestors. We could discover how to change limiting attitudes, beliefs, and thoughts often from early traumatic experiences. The Shamanic journey was for those in search of health, spiritual healing, wisdom, or information about the future. These would be healing journeys. Healing into wholeness.

Jeannette had experienced the promise and power of these practices personally. A highly trained health practitioner, she'd been a mover and a shaker in a wide range of community ventures. A nurse, she'd worked in the areas of cardiology, orthopaedics, and addictions. She'd been an educator in life skills, hospice, pharmacology, human growth and behaviour, and psychology. But she'd come to what she called her whole self as a healer in Shamanic practice.

At home in her new guise, she stood before us relaxed. Her long white, wavy hair hung like a shawl against her red and black plaid shirt. Precise, professional, confident, she created a safe and relaxed circle of seekers. Like coming back to one's favourite armchair after wrestling with demon- traffic, we sank into the comfortable embrace of her leadership. I recognized the vital, 60-something woman as a sister-Evolutionary in her opening words, "We are all part of a cosmic story."

The weekend was devoted to healing which she defined in a new way. It was not the end goal but a power that extends beyond any human profession. Our health and that of the planet are one. It is the nature of the planetary body and our own body to heal. With practice, she taught, we can become the medicine. "As within so without," she loved to say.

Becoming the medicine – at first the concept stretched my imagination. When I recognized the idea resonated with my own tradition's teaching of incarnation – embodiment of the divine – my own healing began. Today I can say, medicine is not only what modern science prescribes. It is the pre-scripted power within all Earth and its Earthlings.

Over the weekend, the skilled guide led the group on three unique healing journeys. The first was to strengthen the inner self. The next was to become a healing presence to others. The last was to gather the medicine/wisdom of the ancestors. In the end, my religious and cultural biases were further healed. I realized the work of becoming our own healers and most powerful divine selves as a universal trajectory.

Jeannette and I were compatible co-leaders. While her role was to guide our journey in the spiritual realm, mine was to lead us through the Universe story. Referring to the writings of Dr. Larry Dossey, pioneering physician on the healing power of prayer, she taught we are all connected to a larger order of things. Based on the work of Berry and Swimme, I demonstrated our cosmic communion in the woodland labyrinth. These new times of modern medicine, Jeannette called The Age of Spiritual or Trans-Human Medicine. Placing these times within the 13.8 billion-year epic of oneness, I named it an evolutionary moment. The opportunity of our times, she said, was rediscovering our part in the Universe. I was more pointed. The imperative of the environmental crisis was the reinvention of life and work that contributed to a new era of sustainability. Together the aim of Shamanic medicine – healing the brokenness – resonated with the intent of eco-spirituality – a consciousness of oneness. It was a good partnership.

The Shamanic leader's means of healing, however, was yet another encounter with *the strange.* Jeannette used drums and rattles made of animal skulls and skins. Holding the ceremonial drum as reverently as she would an expensive piece of medical technology, she struck it firmly, slowly, and steadily. The sound filled the room, reaching deep, deeper, and deeper until drum and heart beat as one. My skeptic, along with the group, settled into an altered reality. In that trance-like state, we experienced vivid images, wandered through strange and familiar landscapes, met unsettling and comforting beings, heard threatening and friendly voices. A powerful sedative, the drumming had opened a threshold into the unconscious and invisible dimension of a holographic and conscious Universe.

Afterwards, Mary Ann was unsettled. In her dream she'd met a tribe that disassembled her body. Jeannette explained the participant had experienced what's called a dismemberment journey. In the language of Creation Spirituality, I understood that she'd entered the Via Negativa, the path of emptying, letting go, what Christianity calls the Way of the Cross. These interpretations resonated with the dreamer who was approaching retirement, anticipating the loss of professional identity, and soon relocating away from friends and colleagues. Today, deeply engaged in her new life, Mary Ann would say her Shamanic journey helped her acknowledge the endings and accept responsibility for the reconciliation of her life's ages and stages.

On the next journey, Jeannette instructed us to ask for images of the divine. On occasions of heartbreak, when our spiritual energy is disrupted, or the immune system is weak, a symbol helps us reconnect with source, she explained. The images received were varied – an Indigenous Wise Man, an ancient woman, a wolf, a mountain, and others. I was reminded of Christianity's many messengers – saints and angels, Mother Mary, the Good Shepherd, and burning bush. The gift of all traditions, I learned, is to help us find that connection to the invisible realm that helps us live wholly in the world.

On the third journey, our Shamanic practice included rattles. Their noise called in the spirits to aid the restoration of inner strength at the cellular level, and our search for reunion with Source, Creator, God, The Great Spirit, Wisdom, the Goddess – call it what you will. Like the rain-stick of Hawaii, the drums of Africa, or the organs of the greatest Christian cathedrals, sound is an ancient tool that transports us into a state where we can access a higher consciousness.

As the weekend came to a close, I had acquired a higher and deeper appreciation for the Shamanic spiritual practices. Journey-work is becoming more widely recognized as part of holistic health care systems and Integrative Medicine. McCullough, a part of the steering committee of Toronto's Spirituality in Health Care Network since 2000, helped this happen. She helped found the Complementary Therapies Nurses' Interest Group, which has received special interest group status from the Registered Nursing Association of Ontario. Sitting at the Integrative Health Care Round Table, an affiliation of conventional and complementary organizations, Jeannette helped Shamanic practice take its place in Canadian health care. Her lifework helped legitimize Complementary Medicine.

Indigenous teachings, by reminding us of our relationship with both Mother Earth and Father Universe, reveal unity-consciousness. Many like Jeannette believe this is what's necessary if we're to navigate the unstable and unjust landscape in which we find ourselves. Jeannette reemphasized this oneness when the group tried to express their gratitude for her leadership. The power to heal, be it physical or emotional, she said, deflecting the praise, comes from the compassionate helping spirits accompanying us on our journeys. It's in our interest to gratefully attend to what they've shown to be within us so healing can occur and our energy field expand. Direct gratitude toward the whole and embrace your potential, she counselled. It was a powerful message.

Dancing with Jeannette, I found more similarities than differences between Christian and Shamanic teachings. Both cultural gatherings intend for participants to leave refreshed, recommitted and reassured of their sacred purpose. Seeking the wisdom of the ancestor spirits, I realized, was not unlike my Roman Catholic Dad praying to the Saints. Drums and rattles paralleled the role of religious music. Both serve to transport us into an altered state of consciousness. Symbols, rituals, including the dream journey, are common across traditions. All are important as humanity strives to evolve and become our best and future selves.

Shamanism, an ancient form of divination, has something to offer seekers in these contemporary times. Journeying can open to us a world of sacred guides and help us rediscover two essential aspects of life. Firstly, we are cosmic beings of light with work to do at this time and place in the unfolding of the Universe. And secondly, as we say in the United Church of Canada creed, "we are not alone." Those discoveries are vital because they enable us to become who we can be, and who we become can heal the world.

When we gather with Evolutionaries who understand and offer sacred ritual like the Shamanic Practitioner, Jeannette McCullough, we see the possibility in ourselves. We discover we are partners in the dance of intimacy becoming the humans Universe need us to be.

Dedicated to Jeannette who joined the ancestors August 28, 2016.

Evolutionary Wisdom

- As above, so below.
- Each is an expression of the creative energy moving in the Universe.
- Embrace guidance of the Spirit-helpers.
- Direct gratitude toward your own potential.

Dance to Raise your Vibrations with Abbess Khenmo Drolma, author Dawn James, and mystic Joseph Rael

We are vibrational beings designed to be healthy and happy. It's time to reclaim your birthright. Dawn James

The Compassion of Sound

The chime echoed around the farmhouse living room stretching space and time. The chatter stopped, eyes closed, and breathing deepened. To-do lists disappeared, anxieties for our kids and aging parents fell away, deadlines were left for another day. A sweet calm rose on the burning incense and blanketed the room. Energies slowed. Minds quieted. Faces softened. Shoulders dropped. Clenched hands opened. We'd become the beings we longed to be, peaceful within and without, loving the lovable and unlovable, confident we could affect the future we wanted. The chime faded like fog in the sunlight. For the twenty women who'd come allured by a life of greater compassion, all was changed.

Compassion is compelling. It's that involuntary rush in one infant to cry when another is crying. It's that intuition in my cat to stay close when I'm sick. It's the sap in the Maple tree delivering carbohydrates made last summer, and frozen in winter, thawing to grow new leaves in the Spring. It's what's happening when one drop dings in the bottom of the sap bucket in the silent spring woods. Compassion is the way of nature.

Believing greater human compassion towards the Earth community is necessary if we're to co-create an Ecozoic age, Gaia Centre had invited Khenmo Drolma to teach. Though the former professor of art history had grown up in Christian America, she was now, by all appearances – shaved head, beet-dyed toga – an Eastern Buddhist nun. She'd spent years in India, the United States, and Canada studying her path. At first, her strange appearance and her disciples' deference was intimidating. But over the half-dozen years she'd been our guest teacher, I'd come to regard her as a friend. Her meditation workshop, *Living with Compassion in a Hurting World,* drew more registrations than we imagined. She taught me compassion was a wide-spread hunger.

After some time (for it had been time too deep to measure in minutes), the Abbess struck the bowl calling us back to the work at hand. At the time, I didn't understand the singing bowl's song to be anything different than a hockey coach's whistle, a signal, a call for my attention. But a few months later, when Dawn James, my writing coach, invited me to listen to her YouTube video, I came to understand sound to be so much more than I ever knew. Sound, as I'd experienced in that Buddhist meditation practice, can carry the vibrations of compassion.

The Cosmic Power of Sound

James' video, *Raise Your Vibration, Transform Your Life,*[xi] begins when she strikes her crystal singing bowl. The bowl's melody vibrated across time and cyberspace. Even via technology, it was powerful. My thoughts softened, my breathing slowed and deepened. What is this power of sound?

Dawn's brief introduction captured my imagination.

> "Before we were physical forms, we were formed energy. Before that, we were pure energy. We are bio-electric beings."

This was also the cosmic story. She had my attention. The science of quantum physics, the study of how things work at the smallest of levels, explains it this way: from quarks to molecules, to atoms to the cells that make up tissues and organs, we are not inert matter but vibrating packets of energy. Involuntarily, and unconsciously, electric currents are ceaselessly flowing through our cells, nerves, muscles, and entire biological systems.

Here was yet another paradigm of reality unacknowledged by mainline theology. It is thanks to Oprah and a profusion of spiritual teachers like Deepak Chopra that the populace is learning about how the energetic state of environment, food, and relationships can impact our health. The body, declares the new news, is held together by sound. Sound healing, restoring healthy vibration to the body, is part of this new age.

The science of sound is this: organs, bones, and emotions all have specific frequencies. Sound frequency impacts our sympathetic nervous system. When the body hears a frequency that it's not in tune with, the disharmony causes a state of disease. The new news, however, is that we can retune our systems like my life-partner Paul can retune his violin. This is the essence of sound healing.

The power of sound healing is exciting. "We can learn to raise our vibrations, and when we do, it can transform our lives." Dawn James' message is all about transformation. It's about achieving one's highest potential. "Learning to raise our vibrations we learn to manage our anatomic energy field."

James is an example of someone who's taken the power of sound personally. Once a corporate executive and business consultant, she evolved into a best-selling author, publisher, international speaker, and retreat leader. She spoke with the conviction of a woman who, following a spiritual awakening and introduction to cosmic consciousness, had come to know her truest self as a dance of vibrations.

Her claims stretched my sacred imagination. I'd grown up calling on God for strength and power. The science of sound and idea of myself as dancing energy sent me on a quest: discover the connections between the spiritual, scientific, and this thing called compassion.

This compassion that Khenmo teaches us how to access, Dawn suggests, is what one achieves at the highest level of vibrations. The Jewish Bible teaches compassion to be the nature of the divine source. The Christian wisdom is that we can come back into attunement with this divine cosmic vibration, "Ask and you shall receive." (Matthew 7:7,8. NIV) Compassion is not only an emotion we feel within us. Nor is it the power of a distant deity. An energy and energetic way of being, it is the way we can co-create more life, deeper connectivity, healing and wholeness. Compassion is a sacred power that when cultivated, expands one's lifework immeasurably. It's a wondrous and timely discovery.

Moving back and forth from one circle of thought to another, I came to a delightful conclusion. If by raising one's vibrations to the level of compassion we align ourselves with what's been called God, that divine intelligence dancing at the heart of the evolutionary process, I can also name that entity Evolutionary Dancer.

One way of reaching the vibrational level of compassion, said the Abbess, is chanting "Om." The supreme and most sacred syllable in Sanskrit, it contains the three sounds (a), (u), and (m). These represent various fundamental triads believed to be the spoken essence of the Universe. It has been called the sound of perfection or wholeness. Chanting it, we raise our vibrations to a state identified as compassion. Intoning the sound was a way to empty out all that's not of the present moment and relax into a state of pure being, and that being a state of oneness with a compassionate Universe.

Coming into an accepting and compassionate relationship with oneself, you might agree, is not a simple thing. But after a time, when nothing but Om could be heard and felt, the energy in the crowded room was surprisingly and deeply peaceful. I'm here to tell you, that once, given my religious mythology of difference, chanting in the Buddhist way would have made me anxious. This new way of meditation to activate compassion using sound, however, brought only peace.

The Biology of Sound

There is, according to James, a biology of sound healing. The respiratory system, the brain, and heart rate, all of which accelerate in response to worry and suffering, are slowed as certain sounds' harmonic vibrations engage the relaxation reflex. Shalom, in Judaism and Wa Alaikum Salaam in Islam, words that express one's desire for peace with another, end in the sound of compassion. Language, she taught me, both in meaning and vibration, can be powerful.

Specific techniques, according to the Buddhist teacher, help us reacquaint ourselves with what innate compassion feels like. Visualizing hurt pets, crying babies, lonely grandparents, refugees in camps ... we sat in silence as students of compassion. Remember this feeling, memorize this feeling, make it as familiar as taking a breath. This is what is ours to send to the world. Visualize it skipping like a ripple on a lake across the vibratory field of the whole Earth community, she instructed. Hopeful and inspiring, these were practices, she said, for in and out of the Ashram.

Outside Protestantism, my life was one of discovery. Compassion was less a spiritual quality we can aspire to than a mindful power we can practise.

Did our spiritual practices as opposed to God's intervention actually affect change on the object of our compassion? I wondered. The answer came from James and quantum science: the nature of existence is sacred connectedness. There's no such thing as empty space. You, me, tree, and tree toad exist not in isolation but within a web of oneness. It was not only a new cosmology but an instructional gift of how to use much unacknowledged potential.

This web of communication, otherwise known as magnetic energy, has been called many things: the Akashic field, Logos, the Higgs field, even the music of the spheres. I like to call it nature's internet because it's within our power to send compassion to another over that pre-existing network. Experiments have shown one's compassionate concentration for another can be felt not only in the next room, but miles away. Like a twenty-first century book of Revelation, the new science made the stuff of faith into the nature of existence.

Compassion – it's where faith and the new science come together. While I'd always thought of it as a way of being to which I could only aspire, or the gaze with which God looked down upon me, now it was an energy in and around me, an electromagnetic field I could create. Prayer became the intentional direction of compassionate energy.

Today I believe it was not only the individual or societal hunger to live in greater harmony in distressing times that caused those women to crowd round the Abbess; it was the allurement of the Evolutionary Dancer who is original compassion.

The lesson was huge. Don't make your practice of compassion too small. Let it be the heart and source of the life you desire. For it isn't an inert emotion but a vibration dancing in and through and around us pulling us into the fullness of our potential.

I dare to write such claims, based not on any authorized teachings, but on random and wonder-ful experiences. Such was the case in a chance meeting with an Amer-Indian shaman.

Sound is Shattered Light

We were high in the red deserts of New Mexico. It is a mystical place where any walk in the mesas can lead to dinosaur fossils and every sunset is a Georgia O'Keeffe painting. We'd booked weekend accommodation at Ghost Ranch, a Presbyterian retreat centre. Unaware of what else was happening or who else would be there, we were awed to find ourselves in the midst of an ecojustice conference and indigenous water ceremony.

After a decade of drought, Joseph Rael, the Tiwa elder from Picuris Pueblo had been invited to conduct a sacred ritual. Surrounded by faithful followers who'd come from every point on the compass, Rael spoke of life as the vibration coming from shattered light. It is a vibration deserving of our trust, he explained, because the essential nature of light and vibration is goodness. Though his manner of speaking was unfamiliar at the time, it resonated with those Biblical texts that call us to know God as light and trust in God.

Beside the barren riverbed, Joseph unwrapped the Grandfather – a rock. He'd brought it from Picuris, from a ceremony circle there, and laid it at the river's edge. Beside it he placed a bag of ground white maize. He invited us to take some and to put our prayers along with the sacred grains on the Grandfather. The winds would then carry them to the Creator. He knew we would all want to do this, he intoned in a voice soft as the breeze, because we'd all chosen to be born into this time and be at this place for this purpose. His cosmology, at once strange and compelling, painted both an intelligent Universe and my presence as part of some cosmic dance of compassion.

The way Rael prayed, in deep and searching song-tones, was also different. But not that different to a Jewish cantor, I reminded myself. Sound, he told us, returns us to the creative emptiness from which it came. In that void, he explained, both the need and something to satisfy that need is created. Vibration creates inner meaning, then materializes it. Nothing is separate. In this way, he taught, everything is taking care of itself. All existence he understood as sound and dancing energy. His words sounded like quantum science, echoed the wisdom of Buddhism, and united us all with Source, my Evolutionary Dancer.

Back at the ranch – I've never had the opportunity to say that before and mean it – we gathered round Joseph for more teaching. The shaman spoke softly. I kept shifting my place in the room to hear better. In the front row, only half-a-dozen feet away, I was still unable to understand what he was saying. I could do nothing but surrender my need to hear to fully comprehend my experience. I let go of my Protestant attachment to reason and the intellectual path to meaning. I allowed myself to feel his message: life is listening to the message in the vibration. The vibration of sound, I learned in the wilderness, is a pre-religious language.

Today, this is my truth. When we take great care of the sound we make, and listen from a place deeper than words, we can become like the singing bowl – we can be vessels of creative and compassionate vibration. When we accept that what we say and how we say it actually creates the tone of life – past, present, and future – we can live consciously, carefully, and responsibly for the power of our voice.

Driving away from that not-by-chance encounter by the dry red river bed below Chimney Rock, Paul and I were unusually silent. When we spoke it was to ponder our evolutionary encounter with a spirituality born of science and ancient spirituality. What had really happened with Joseph Rael, we wondered. The only answer we could find was this. In a time of personal and planetary drought, we had participated in an evolutionary ritual.

Sound as a spiritual practice

It's two in the afternoon, and my husband's laid low with a migraine. I reach for the singing bowl. I strike it once, twice, three times. The Tibetan tradition claims that when we sound the bowl, we call the angels. As its song fills the room, my partner's face softens, his upper body relaxes. His silent screams of pain fade as the outer and inner vibrations harmonize.

Now, it's two in the morning. A pending decision torments me. To make a choice, one way or the other, means trusting the unknown. I open my ever-expanding bag of spiritual practices. I reach for the singing bowl, sound it, and tune to its song, "Om." 10th-century Tibetan Buddhism dances with 21st-century quantum science. I do so believing I can live with greater trust in the unknown by raising my vibrations. A restfulness that starts at my heart, ripples throughout my body, brings me not to any decision, but into resonance with that infinite vibration that is pure goodness. And I relax into restorative sleep.

The new science, in unpacking ancient spiritual wisdom, is returning to us our birthright – the power of healing. For too long, we've abdicated this to the medical profession and absentee gods. Now we understand the measure of bio-electricity in our body determines one's health. When the vibrational frequency in our bodies is low, we lose vital energy. Our cells can't regenerate at the same rate or maintain an optimal state. They mutate, and dis-ease can occur. But now, aware of our bodies as collections of dancing vibrations, we're able to change the rate of the electrical flow. We can calm anxious energies without caffeine, nicotine, alcohol, hallucinogens, or pharmaceuticals. In these times of agonizing social and climate dis-ease, we are re-awakening to our healing powers of compassion.

Ancient monastic practices, indigenous spirituality, 21st-century science – together they have danced me to a very new view of reality.

Universe is no longer some flat and empty black canvas splattered with drops of light but an inter-connected dance of vibrations.

Source – what we have called the Cosmic Christ, Buddha nature, or Great Spirit – is the intelligence, the godhead from which flows forth compassion, creativity, and the infinite potential at the heart of all that is.

The human is not the centre and purpose of the Universe, but a vibrational, energetic being, a species like other species, emerging from and returning to the cosmic whole. As a species, we can learn to direct compassion creatively toward suffering and injustice in emotion, thought, and sound.

Visualization, music, prayer – silent or spoken – all are means of restoring harmony and affecting the healing of the cosmic whole.

Ineffably within this dynamic oneness, the personal is cosmic, and the cosmic is personal; the scientific is spiritual, and the spiritual is all there is. My whole being is an expression of the evolutionary dance. This is my new worldview and I call it Evolutionary Spirituality.

It's 2018. Singing bowls and sound healing have come out of the monasteries and down from the mesas. More and more employers use recorded sound to create environments with a healthy flow of bio-electricity. And more employees enjoy increased memory, clarity, vitality, and the ability to take action. We're learning to turn off the chaos of a competitive culture and tune into the body-mind-spirit dance of a compassionate Universe.

As everyday friends and total strangers, in person and on the internet, we meet the Evolutionaries. They are Buddhist nuns, Sound Healers, webinar teachers, and Indigenous elders. We're unaware of just what in the human species is happening when we meet them, but in them we see a reflection of our own potential to become partners dancing into an evolution of consciousness, becoming what Earth needs us to be.

Evolutionary Wisdom

- We are energetic beings. We can raise our vibrations.
- Visualization, music, prayer, silent or spoken, raises and restores harmony.
- Conscious and care-full of our energy, we cooperate with our own evolution.
- The personal is cosmic, and the cosmic is personal.
- The scientific is spiritual, and the spiritual is all there is.
- My whole being is an expression of the evolutionary dance.
- What I once called God, I can also name Compassion or Evolutionary Dancer.

Dancing into Joy with Celeste Shirley and Barbara Marx Hubbard

> *Synergy is that power working in all the cosmos bringing seemingly separate parts to form a new whole that is greater than and unpredictable from the sum of its parts.* Barbara Marx Hubbard

It was almost midnight and I was carrying some hefty eleventh-hour doubts. How had I come to be at the door of a complete stranger? There I was, delivering Gaia Centre's prestigious guest teacher, Barbara Marx Hubbard from the Foundation for Conscious Evolution, to the Yoga House, the home of Celeste Shirley, a woman I'd never met. Then Celeste opened the door and I was enfolded in a welcoming energy field. Any fears I'd had that this trinity wasn't the result of something more than chance evaporated like dew in the noonday sun.

The evolutionary wisdom of our California guest is that "chance is exactly what the self-transcending drive of the Cosmos overcomes."[xii] There could be no doubt, we three women stood together at the threshold of that weekend because of the universal force of synergy. Barbara explains it's what "brings seemingly separate parts to form a new whole greater than and unpredictable from its sum of the parts." But, I'm ahead of my story.

Let me take you back several months to a meeting of the Gaia Centre board. In response to my proposal to bring Hubbard, the revered futurist to Toronto, their rational reply was negative. They had sound reasons. Her book, *Conscious Evolution and Its Social Potential,* wasn't on any best seller list. From California, she was an unknown in Ontario. Her subject, conscious evolution, wasn't really understood. Her travel, accommodation, and fees – on top of hall rental, food, and marketing – made the costs prohibitive. On paper, nothing added up to this being a viable choice.

But something in my heart of hearts wasn't rational. I felt powerfully attracted to the topic, convinced even that a conscious evolution was the key to a sustainable future. I asked the board to vigil for the weekend and reflect further on the decision. They agreed. We informed Ms. Hubbard's office a decision was pending, lit candles, and the listening for a clear way forward began. Few would agree this was a smart way to do business.

In the shadows of Saturday evening, a phone call from the California headquarters interrupted our vigil. An email had come from a Celeste Shirley in Toronto and with it an open invitation. Barbara was welcome to be guest of the Yoga House anytime she might be in the city. It felt like a sign.

The call told the Board there were, in fact, others in our area who knew of Barbara's work. We wouldn't have to be responsible for the costs of accommodation. Feeling like Universe had joined the conversation and was telling us to trust, the decision was revised. Barbara Marx Hubbard, co-founder of the Association for Global New Thought and the World Future Society, would be our next teacher.

The cosmic gifts kept on coming. A board member's son-in-law donated space for the event – in an award-winning sustainable building no less. Celeste, Jeannette McCollough, and Elder Diane Longboat offered to circulate our marketing throughout their networks. In the end, 150 folks registered.

How had it happened we'd gone from the impossible to the probable? What could explain how seemingly unconnected entities thousands of miles apart had come together? The answer came some months later during Barbara's address.

There is an increase in synchronicity in these times of social and planetary breakdown. Heads nodded. The media focuses on entropy – disorder. No one disagreed. The new news is that concurrently, we are seeing a rush of positive social innovations. The tension of the looming catastrophe, that being the collapse of a sustainable environment, is driving a convergence of social innovators to restructure a new order. Hands applauded. But what's hopeful is this. These innovators, in letting go ego, rejecting the patterns of competition, and joining genius to genius are not struggling for survival. They are struggling to evolve; they are becoming a new kind of human, co-creators. As a result, they find greater stability, enhanced creativity, and synergy. The registrants leaned into her teaching.

Synergy, a recurring pattern in the evolutionary process, is the way the intelligent Universe brings seemingly separate parts together into a new, unpredictable, and larger reality. And there it was, the explanation of how Gaia Centre, the Yoga House, the Foundation for Conscious Evolution, and an ever-widening number of partners had come together to create this conference on the evolution of consciousness. Synergy, according to the new science, is that tendency observed in the Universe toward ever-deeper cooperation and higher consciousness. As parts more deeply participate with one another, an evolution of consciousness occurs.

Nothing I'd studied in theology, synergy seemed to explain what the Church called communion, all being a part of the body of Christ. Our conference – post-religious, inter-disciplinary, and inter-spiritual – seemed an evolution of that two thousand year old institution. What we were able to present *together* was more than the practice of yoga, more than the principles of eco-spirituality, and more than the tenets of conscious evolution. It was something new. Bearing witness to how body, earth, and cosmos are one in a synergistic Universe, it was an experiment in social synergy.

Synergy, communion, co-creation – these were the words of the day. They made separateness, individualism, and competition ideas of the past. The myth of separateness, Barbara suggested, is the sin behind the sin of environmental pollution. The climate crisis could be traced to society's refusal to accept the nature of our reality. We live within a unified, synergistic Universe in which everything is inter-dependent one thing with another.

Everything is part of the Implicate Order. The futurist went on to share the discoveries of theoretical physicist, David

Baum. There is an underlying and invisible reality out of which comes everything that is manifested in the visible and explicate order of the Universe. While the words were strange the truth resonated, I'd been raised, after all, in a world of Heaven and Earth, the invisible and visible.

Reality, she described as a limitless and ever evolving whole continually enfolding and unfolding. I imagined each person at the conference like individual currents in a dough being raised up by the yeasty power of Consciousness, a.k.a. God. The science of synergy resonated with the old parable: "The kingdom of heaven is like yeast that a woman took and mixed into about sixty pounds of flour until it worked all through the dough." (Matthew 13:33. NIV) My world made more sense. I came to see how the deep-seated worldview of separateness had led the board to vote against the conference. But synergy, stronger than either belief or disbelief, had brought out of the impossible something greater and wholly possible. In waiting and watching, we'd been shown we were partners in some greater dance.

That weekend with the Mother of Conscious Evolution was life changing. It's allowed me to face into confusion wondering not, "how I will solve it?" but, "what synergy is at work?" It was in those few days, I began to gain what she called *evolutionary eyes,* the inclination to view life within the larger context of the evolutionary story.

We come to this holistic perspective in different ways. For Barbara, it had been through journaling and meditation, asking questions, and receiving answers from what the futurist called the Universal Self. I, on the other hand, shifted into greater alignment with the one story by teaching it.

It's the difference of living with a holistic worldview, however, that's important. Take one's thoughts. Once I only ever imagined them to be my own, to matter only to me. The evolutionary perspective tells us otherwise. Positive or negative, thoughts weave the fabric of the future. That being the case, we must take responsibility not only for our actions in life, but also for the thoughts we choose to entertain. What we think about Mother Earth creates that reality. To make a mistake about nature is to make a mistake about life. The proof is in the environmental crisis.

The power of thoughts, of course. is not anything new. Thomas Aquinas, the foremost medieval scholar had taught we can't do theology without science. An error in our judgment of nature, he'd said, leads to an error about God. In other words, thoughts have consequences in an interconnected reality.

Incorporating synergy – the evolutionary process by which all things are interconnected – into my worldview topped up my cup of faith. In Sunday School, we'd learned, 'What a friend we have in Jesus.' In the pulpit I'd preached, "trust in God." The impact of the planetary crisis, however, had left that cup cracked and leaking. But then Barbara spoke of the Synergy Engine driving the ever-expanding Universe. It offered a hopeful cosmic explanation; at the edges of every crisis awaits creative connections to the future. As a result, she envisioned humanity to be on the threshold of a quantum leap. If we could integrate emerging scientific, social, and spiritual capacities, we could become a new kind of humanity equal to our vast new potential. Then we could move beyond our current global crises. This was a comforting idea. More than that, it was a belief that inspired my active cooperation with spreading this new-world thought.

An evolved and evolving cosmos, an interconnected and communicative web – these new ideas of a synergistic Universe help me understand Earth's crisis, my lifework, even past events in never-before ways. It was 2008. A tornado ripped through the ten kilometre-wide swath of land I called home. Broken White Pines blocked the lanes and roadways. Decades-old, some centuries-old, White Pines were torn from the Canadian Shield in seconds. Locals, cottagers, and reporters rushed, cameras in hand, to view the disaster and document the powerful face of nature. In conversations, news headlines, on TV and radio – everywhere folks expressed gratitude that no human life was lost. To make the best of the ensuing power outage, neighbours held freezer parties. The convivial exuberance escaped me. I was, literally, grief-stricken. When hydro workers arrived to clear more trees to restore the power lines, I forbid them to cut one more branch on our property. Paul feared I was having a breakdown. But this was no breakdown. It was a breakthrough.

The Pines to me were the beloved elders of the land. The memory keepers, they remembered a story from some seventy years ago. The one hundred Pines Mrs. Charles Barry had ordered from the Sears catalogue had arrived at the West Guilford Post Office. Nothing would do but for Charles to hook the logging sleigh to the horses and travel the seven kilometres to the general store and pull the young trees home. That all seventy seedlings fit in a single shoebox still brings a smile to the descendants of this land. Full-grown now, the Pines were both the sturdy windbreak that lined the lane and harbingers of home. I felt their loss like they'd been beloved relations.

At some point in living on this land, I'd broken free of the anthropocentric illusion – humans are separate from and superior to White Pine, Porcupine, Pine Siskin and all creation. Somehow I'd begun to live my life in conversation with the whole. The lamentations of a planet suffering from the extremes of wind and fire, drought and storms had become my own.

At the time, I had no words to explain my seemingly excessive grief. Only after Barbara had schooled us in the subject of the evolution of consciousness as driven by the environmental devastation, did I come to realize I hadn't had a breakdown. I'd experienced a breakthrough into one-Universe-consciousness.

Conscious Evolution, Now! This was the title of that first event with Ms. Hubbard. I came to understand something wholly amazing, hopeful and frightening. In our era, our species' future depends on the evolution of consciousness. The time for humanity to recognize we are co-creators of both the present devastation and future hope is now.

This evolution of consciousness completed my shift from one story to another. My frame of reference, once the Christ story, became the epic of evolution. My vocation, once growing the Church, became aiding the evolution of consciousness – in myself, my society, and my religious tradition. God I came to understand as the Evolutionary Impulse. My biases, once those of a western, middle-class woman, I now strive to align with those of the Cosmos – higher consciousness, greater complexity, and deeper inter-dependence. My wisdom sources, once the Gospels, broadened to include *Gateways to Conscious Evolution*, and *52 Codes for Conscious Evolution*. Once a follower of Jesus and teacher of Christianity, I identified Jesus as an Evolutionary, a vessel of conscious evolution. The shift-work continues.

Like cataract surgery, the teachings of Conscious Evolution made for new clarity. While I'd gained a new cosmology from Thomas, Brian, and Miriam, and an ancient spirituality of creation and work from Matthew, Barbara's teachings were like the line under a column of numbers. Everything that had gone before added up. I saw what I'd never been able to see before; an evolution of consciousness was happening in my lifetime. And I was part of it.

Evolutionary Spirituality – that view of Universe as conscious and synergistic – became my worldview. With this understanding, the unusual became the usual. Crisis allowed for opportunities. The unexpected was to be expected. The synergistic not the rational rules; more than a philosophy, this became our experience. Like the weekend Paul and I said "yes."

Within hours of committing to the less than sensible idea of retiring early to open an eco-spirituality retreat, things fell in place. We came across a perfect property. In ten days, we'd purchased it. While still painting the house, even before we'd hung out our shingle, Gaia-friendly teachers showed up – at the door, on the deck, and in our inbox. On opening our lives to the possibility of the improbable, we discovered we had what we needed to make it a reality. We were shown we weren't in this alone. The Universe said, "yes" back.

How can I explain it? We'd said yes to the evolutionary forces unleashed by the environmental crisis. Not only yes to cooperating, but to cocreating with these forces. As a result, according to Brian and Barbara, we'd opened ourselves to something larger than our personal, social, religious, or political identity. That's one way of explaining how it felt. Living out of this cosmic story, we experienced, perhaps as never before, ever greater consciousness, complexity, and interdependence – the three biases of Evolutionary Spirituality.

Something one might not expect to gain on saying yes to a life of ecojustice and climate activism was joy. But Barbara had it in spades. She found it in journaling – asking questions and receiving answers from her Evolutionary Self. She found it in teaching the evolution of consciousness. "We now have the powers we once ascribed to the gods," she liked to say; or " I'm not getting older, I'm getting newer." Then she'd throw back her head and laugh. Her delight seemed to come from knowing the preposterous was becoming possible.

The yogi, Celeste, also embodied joy and laughed often. Hers originated in her spiritual practice of dancing out of time and back into oneness. But what of genuine anguish? Didn't she despair at the demise of Mother Earth? She assured me that she'd had her share of discouragement, everything from dishonest home renovators, to a complaining neighbour, and a rezoning battle with the city. She hadn't given up because she believed in her work. Believing in the impossible helped her live with less fear than joy.

Permission to feel joy in the face of mass extinction – this has been one of the gifts from my dance with these two Evolutionaries. In the drudgery of writing and editing, editing and writing, remembering and believing this is the work that's mine to do in the evolutionary scheme of things gives me joy.

It was midnight. I stood with the wise woman from the west, in the doorway of the Yoga House in East Toronto. It was a joyful moment hatched from synergy. Together, we enabled one another to reach otherwise unattainable peaks. In the mirror of that memory, I don't see three single women. I see the continuation of a dance that is ever-spiralling outward, ever-embracing more co-creators, ever-transforming humanity into a species living more respectfully and carefully in the Earth. To know synergy and feel the communion, that was joyous.

Evolutionary Wisdom

- In a conscious Universe, there are no random events or coincidences.
- Synergy, the deep cooperation for expansion, is the nature of the Universe.
- Expect the unexpected. Honour your instincts. Follow the energy.
- Enjoy the joy of cosmic communion.

Dancing with Technology with Alice Miller

The coming of a spiritual age must be preceded by the appearance of individuals no longer satisfied with the normal existence (of humanity) but perceive a greater evolution is the real goal, attempt to affect it in themselves, lead others to it, and make it the goal of the race. Sri Aurobindo

When an unexpected knock came at the door, I shouldn't have been surprised. Ever since saying yes to our Gaia-centred work, all sorts of strangers had been showing up as could-be partners. Each one seemed evidence of a conscious and intelligent Universe affirming and assisting our choice.

This time it was Alice. Like a warm spring wind, the tall, vibrant woman with blue-green eyes and brown-black hair swept into our house and lifework. A unique weave of ancient tradition and post-modern technology, she was passionate about climate change and the spiritual awakening – her own and society's. How did we explain the arrival of this Gaia-centred dance partner, our adult children observing this meeting wanted to know. While I didn't have the language then, today I would say, it was the cosmic power of synergy creating a new whole that is different and unpredictable.

Of Ojibway-Scottish descent, Alice had come looking for a venue to host her spiritual teacher. Eskimo-Kalaallit Elder, Angaangaq Angakkorsuaq of Greenland. Uncle, as she called him, was a shaman and a healer with a mission – to melt the ice in the hearts of man. And with good cause. Greenhouse gases created by our industrial economy were destroying the way of life in the North. Alice, Uncle's student and emissary, was to be my link to yet another part of the global family's environmental tragedy.

Professionally, Alice was an Information Technologist. Her work was managing computer programming for a successful Canadian business. Part of that organization's Green Team, she headed a village-wide project: transportation-sharing to reduce the use of fossil fuels. The initiative won an international environmental award. Alice taught me the potential of technology to improve social communication for the advancement of the sustainability movement. She demonstrated what is key to the future – an Evolutionary never works alone but by social synergy.

Attracted to the future, Alice's life was an adventure. When Uncle invited her to be the coordinator of an upcoming international gathering on the environment, she said yes. When a friend promised Alpha One Brain Wave Training would change her life, she entered a seven-day neuro-feedback program. Invited to become a trainer by the founder of the Biocybernaut Institute, she resigned her IT position. When offered a position assisting with the research, managing the schedule and that cutting-edge company's scholarships, she said yes, sold her Ontario home, left family and friends, and relocated to the West Coast. Asked to present the futuristic technology to the United Nations, she went. A decade later, as one of the Institute's European trainers, she continues to live on a trajectory of adventure, open to and laying the foundation for what is coming.

Evolutionaries, I observed in watching Alice, are telerotic: passionately attracted to the fulfillment of their telos, one's highest purpose and potential. They are always ready to jump into the stream of Cosmic Consciousness whenever it promises another opportunity to co-create a future that works for all.

As a result of meeting Alice, I opened to the positive uses and potential of technology. Once, I would have tuned out her passionate description of how electro-encephalogram (EEG) machines enable clients to explore their biological control systems. I would have remembered a thousand critical chores demanding my attention. But not anymore. Now, I believe innovative technology an essential tool for anyone wanting to maximize their impact for good in this climate crisis.

Technology is proof of humanity's rapidly evolving consciousness. This was Barbara Marx Hubbard's message. She was eighty-one when, speaking to our conference in Toronto, she issued the challenge – take technology seriously. It is not only a means of connecting and communicating with unimaginable speed and precision, she said. The internet could be a tool to enable the healing of our broken species and stabilize our connection with Universal Consciousness. Technology offers us the power to expand our creativity. Her challenge shifted my thinking. I began to consider technology as something beyond a marketing tool, as an extension of myself by which to extend my lifework. Alice, however, would show me just how far technology, in the form of biocybernautics, can expand the good we do.

Biocybernautics, a form of biomedical engineering, analyses the physiological processes in living organisms and develops methods of therapy. At the Institute of Biocybernatics, Alice uses eight-channel, state-of-the-art EEG technology to evaluate the electrical activity in the brain by tracking and recording brain wave patterns. Adapted, they allow Alice's trainees to hear their own alpha brain wave rhythms in changing musical tones. The feedback teaches how to change a negative brainwave to a positive one. Her clients can actually learn to replace fear, despair, and hate with love, joy, or happiness. What takes a monk a lifetime can now take a single week.

Here is the power of the modern *Homo sapiens* used for good. Technology enables us to add to the brain's spiritual skill set. It can enable us to live with more love, forgiveness, joy, creativity, and connection. Given such power, maybe churches need to replace prayers of confession and confessional booths with EEG carrels where we can plug in for a weekly tune-up.

How does Alpha Brain Wave Training work? It enables a person to revisit their memories in two-minute segments called epochs. Literally, participants go out of time to change the brain waves associated with a life event that has been retarding their potential. Compared to the time-intense work of psychology and psychiatry, technology offers a new approach to mental health.

Who is this advanced training for? Individuals trapped in addictions, depression, anxiety, jealousies, betrayals, divorce, and separation. Also victims of rape, incest, murder, torture, and those suffering post-traumatic stress. The treatment, I learned, could also overcome effects of the brain's aging, including memory loss.

Technology, I've come to believe, adds to the brain's skill set. This insight thrilled and challenged me to stop feeling intimidated by the power tools of artificial intelligence creeping into every corner of my everyday. It wasn't something to avoid but a way to cooperate with a conscious evolution in response to the growing climate crisis. That recognized, I wanted figures.

After neurofeedback, results show a client's creativity increases by 50%. Intelligence scores have been boosted by nearly twelve points. Within seven days, a trainee can change their brainwaves to the same degree as an advanced Zen master. Studies demonstrate, not only how recipients experienced noticeable, positive changes in their own lives, but how friends, family, and co-workers also change. Miller herself was an example. Watching the fears and terrors of clients dissolve through the training, witnessing them change themselves at an identity level, she told me, "I feel I'm the one in training. I'm always changing." But this innovative experiment with technology is changing more than individual lives. It's contributing to the future field of mental health.

The more I understood, the more hopeful I became that Alice's work is a sign of a healthier paradigm still-emerging. For myself, and anyone longing to cooperate with their own evolution, I wanted to know if the technology was widely available. In its early days, unfortunately only CEOs, scientists, police, military personnel, athletes, and artists who could independently afford it were taking the program. Miller envisions the day when this technology is accessible to the masses. A day, she hoped to make happen. Clearly this vibrant woman's dance with life-purpose wasn't over.

Living life as though it has meaning in the future, this is the essence of an Evolutionary Spirituality. Technology and spirituality, some might think them strange dance partners. And yet, for Miller, like a Cabernet Sauvignon and aged Gouda, they're the ultimate pairing.

When Alice first knocked at the door, I faced the stranger called technology. A biocybernautics trainer, she taught me how, through technological advances, humanity's learned to mirror nature's evolutionary process of syntropy. Another new word for my growing vocabulary, this is the tendency in the cosmos to bring out of separate parts whole systems of greater complexity, consciousness, and freedom. From molecules to planets, to galaxies, to societies, Universe is ever seeking more advantageous and orderly patterns. Now, Alice was informing me, we were discovering how to apply this cosmic concept to develop human potential.

Alice is for me an example of a technically competent species. She's shown me how in gaining an understanding of matter, we're developing our potential to change the nature of evolution itself. Using this applied cosmological process, we're actually learning how to shift our responses to crisis away from reactive panic to conscious creativity. The outcome is nothing less than the conscious reinvention of ourselves and our world. It's hopeful.

Before the Conscious Evolution Now! conference with Barbara Marx Hubbard, I didn't pay attention to technology beyond its benefits to the Gaia Centre. But this elder's passionate belief that technology is an opportunity to evolve and co-create a Universal Humanity has broadened my thinking. Today I see Alice for who she is – a pioneer in the Conscious Evolution movement. And I look to our emerging capabilities – nano-technology, bio-technology, quantum computing, the internet – and recognize it's evolutionaries like Alice who are aiding the rise in planetary consciousness.

I also see we must cradle technology carefully. We cannot afford to overlook how these new powers can also be used for destruction. If it is to midwife a species of humanity with love for, and protective of their Mother Earth's unborn future, it must be embraced, nurtured, and treated with ultimate respect. The conversation for integrity in technology is essential. Going forward, we must ask of each innovation the question, "is this in cooperation with the Evolutionary Impulse?"

Be it at Gaia Farmhouse in the woods of Ontario, or the Institute for Biocybernautics in British Columbia, technology is enabling our awakening. Everywhere, Evolutionaries no longer satisfied with a stunted existence or the devolution of the planet are finding a never-before means of communicating, healing, and evolving in consciousness.

Evolutionary Wisdom

- Say yes to the evolutionary dance.
- Live on a future-oriented trajectory.
- Embrace technology as an evolutionary tool.

Dancing into Evolutionary Spirituality

Two decades ago, in that circle of dancers for universal peace, all was strange and unusual. My small self would have had me return to the pleasures of the predictable. Resistance to change, be it in belief or lifestyle, can be the enemy of both our personal potential and our species' evolution. On the largest scale, metathesiophobia, the aversion to the unknown, is no small factor in climate change denial. In my case, I can only say the Evolutionary Dancer helped extricate me from the strictures of the structures and put Evolutionaries in my path.

In this chapter and those ahead are stories of futuristic folk that would suggest there is some nobler pragmatism – impartial and inclusive – guiding the whole. They point to a worldview of interconnectedness as the only belief system that makes sustainable sense.

To enter this new paradigm, I've had to relearn the hardest of spiritual lessons. Relinquishment – it's the letting go of who and what one has been. It's been at times frightening but always freeing. Only by stepping down from a pulpit held aloft by the polished pillars of redemption and salvation was I free to embrace the original blessings of existence itself. Only outside the stalwart walls of Christian conviction could I view the expansiveness of the spiritual and philosophical horizon. Only by following the way of the cross – shedding the position and privilege that comes with being clergy and relinquishing what had defined me – was I able to find my way to the evolutionary path of becoming. Now, not as a Canadian or a Christian first, but as an Evolutionary, I see more than I once knew to look for.

What I've seen may be surprising. First, I haven't seen the breakdown of the mainline church as a failure. Rather, I've witnessed Cosmic Consciousness, call it Universal Intelligence or God, breaking in. I don't see Christianity breaking apart; I see Evolutionary Spirituality emerging from the manger. Because this system of belief is still unfolding, I can only attempt a description.

Evolutionary Spirituality is not a religion. It doesn't claim a supreme being that's omnipotent and unchanging. Neither does it have dogmatic doctrine. Rather it is an experience of connectivity and a practice of being and becoming. Becoming what? Ever-more compassionate and consciously relational. Not a hierarchical system but a round dance, it celebrates the interdependence of the familiar and strange, the reunion of spirituality and science, the play between detachment and infinite discovery. It holds the synergistic story of the Universe as the sacred story for this evolutionary moment.

Once I believed in a Wizard of Oz god, hidden behind the curtain of Heaven. Today, I imagine a Universal Intelligence that is folded in all that is, out of which all is unfolding.

Once I believed God created everything to serve the human. Now I recognize both the human and non-human as integral vibrational beings in the ever-surprising drama.

Once I had no concept of the evolutionary nature of life, let alone the possibility of a future human species. Now I acknowledge such conscious beings are among us. They can change their vibrational frequency for healing self and others. They use the tools and language of technology. They live out of and tell a bigger story of the Universe. They are teachers and mystics and futurists. They are challenging and changing Christianity. They are spiritual, but not religious, and they are cocreating ecological consciousness. Now I see, I too am an evolutionary dancer. We are all evolutionary dancers.

Evolutionary Wisdom

- Step beyond any illusion of separation.
- Turn and face what is strange.
- Empty attachments to the familiar.
- Embrace guidance from the helping spirits.
- Sink into deep time.
- Incarnate Universal Intelligence.
- Stand for a sustainable democracy.

When Paul and I sold our patch of the suburb, bought the fixer-up farmhouse, and set out to create the not-for-profit Gaia Centre, we weren't choosing to be courageous. It was an involuntary response to the allurement of a vision that's time had come.

CHAPTER 2

Dance Like You Don't Need The Money

The most vital issue of the age is whether the future progress of humanity is to be governed by the modern economic and materialistic mind of the West, or by a nobler pragmatism guided, uplifted, and enlightened by spiritual culture and knowledge. Aurobindo Ghose

What the Heart Wants – A New Spirituality of Work

Some folks believe we can have what the heart wants. Many don't. Those looking for a new spirituality of work tend to be the former. Some confuse material wealth, security, and power – those things capitalistic consumerism tells us we want – with desires of the heart. Desires of the heart includes work that feels like the work we were born to do. Some might remind me, simply having desires of the heart is a middle-class privilege.

There are those who say their work is spiritually fulfilling. As well as earning them a life-sustaining income, their occupations contribute to the good of society. Work that provides a sense of personal meaning and benefits society is purposeful. This has been the definition of good work. The environmental crisis, however, changes this definition.

Bob Willard, author of *The Sustainability Advantage,* was one of Gaia Centre's first teachers. He came to Haliburton directly from speaking engagements in corporate China. Business must revise it's accounting framework, was his message. Like a three-legged stool, there must be balance between profits, people, and planet. More than just his environmental bias, Bob is a Certified Sustainability Professional and has a PhD in sustainability from the University of Toronto. His magic lies in being able to prove the business value of sustainability strategies. He's given over a thousand presentations, has authored six books, and provides extensive resources for incorporating principles and practices of sustainability into business. Bob's good work is in challenging the corporate world to provide jobs that satisfy what the heart wants: to live lives that are socially beneficial, ecologically sustainable, and have spiritual integrity.

Pat was one of those who follow their heart. A person of integrity. A business writer dependent on contracts, when the economy slumped and her income dropped off, she found her way to her minister's office. Privileged to be minister at the time, I was ill-equipped. Though the Bible suggested we sell everything and give it to the poor, with glad and sincere hearts no less, (Acts 2:45-46, 4:34) that hardly seemed appropriate for the 20th century single mother.

But Pat didn't want to talk about having enough money. She wanted to talk about how much she worried about it. She wanted to learn how we free ourselves from its emotional dominance over our lives. She was struggling with what is the message behind this familiar text: "Blessed are the poor for they shall inherit the kingdom of God." (Luke 6:20) The call to know true wealth lies not in money but in one's trust in their own divine power, creativity. Like Marmee in Little Women, she knew money wasn't the first or only prize to strive for. She wanted to live the truth of the country song, Work like you don't need the money.

That conversation, as it turned out, was pivotal – for me. The spirituality of work would become the topic of my doctoral thesis. My sources were the mystics, philosophers, and social reformers of the long-lost lineage of Creation Spirituality. My principle teacher was no scholar of economics but the modern mystic, priest, and Evolutionary, Matthew Fox.

In his book, *Reinvention of Work*, Rev. Fox says our occupations can be sacramental, revealing the divine in us and strengthening others. Quoting Hildegard Von Bingen, good work, he taught, is that which contributes to the wheel of life. A seminal read, I came away with my own definition. Good work satisfies the heart's longing – to live with a sense of what is enough, in touch with one's creativity, and contributing to an environmentally sustainable society.

To test this theory, I surveyed ten folks who had reinvented good work. Each one's story illustrated how they had followed the four ancient precepts of creation to realign their means to a life-giving livlihood: awe for life, detachment, creativity, and compassion. The result was my thesis: *Work Like You Don't Need the Money*, a curriculum for those looking for a new spirituality of work.

I piloted the program in downtown Toronto. The fourteen seekers who showed up had two things in common. They were no longer willing to be treated as commodities, and each yearned for more freedom, integrity, and meaning in their employment. A few wanted their livelihood to be without cost to the planet, an idea not yet a priority in business, medicine, education, manufacturing, law, or the service industry. As these counsellors, consultants, administrators, social workers and others shared their stories, it was clear. They were there because of the disconnect between the human spirit and the workplace. Some felt under-worked, others over-worked, others felt simply worked like parts of a machine. A recent retiree, was struggling with lack of purpose when not socially defined as part of the workforce. Others struggled with emotional and physical exhaustion. They were living examples of what Thomas Aquinas had declared in the thirteenth century: when there is no joy in our work, there is no joy in living.

Dance of the Heart

I bow to what's your work to do.
I bow to what's your part to play.
I bow to the work of stars.
I bow to the work you are.

Work is a dance. It is the dynamic relationship between our life purpose and Earth's future, between the personal and the cosmic. These were the words with which I'd greet any new group of folks in the *Work Like You Don't Need the Money* program. Then, I'd invite them to stand, echo my words, and mirror my movements. Join me in a dance of the heart, was the invitation.

Lynda said it was courageous to begin with a dance. One of the participants in the first group to meet in the living room of the Gaia Farmhouse, she was right. Courage, from *cor* – the Latin word for heart, was something the folks in these groups had in spades. They'd signed up because they were following their hearts' longing to work less as a way to earn a living and more as a way to live within the planet's means. And in a consumer culture, that took courage.

Life had taught me a funny thing about courage: it's not a conscious choice. When Paul and I sold our patch of the suburb, bought the fixer-up farmhouse, and set out to create the not-for-profit Gaia Centre, we weren't choosing to be courageous. It was an involuntary response to the allurement of a vision that's time had come. Courage, for us, was the response-ability to cooperate with the Evolutionary Impulse.

There are four spiritual steps in this dance of courage – awe, detachment, creativity, and compassion, also called transformation. Where does one learn these steps? Not in any business school. These are the ways of creation! A star, a sphere of burning gas explodes. It moves into seeming nothingness; this is detachment. The scattered stardust seeds new stars and planets: this is creativity. A new planet changes the gravitational curve of the Universe: this is transformation. You or I see the light and experience awe. Awe, detachment, creativity, compassion / transformation – these are steps in the cosmic dance.

The dance of the heart mirrors the ways of the Cosmos. If life came from these four steps, certainly they must be the basis for the reinvention of our life work. And, so the program began with a dance.

The fifteen-week program was to be taken over the course of a year. After all, if it takes nine months to create a life, shouldn't it take equally as long to reinvent one. Mirroring nature's interdependence, we met as a cocreative community, supporting each other's transformation. The three teachings that impacted the reinvention of my own lifework were the basis of the program – Berry's 13.8 billion-year story of the Cosmos, Swimme's ten ways of the Universe, and Fox's four paths of Creation.

The Dancers

Lynda, Doug, Kate, and Lisa were some of the more than thirty re-inventors who would take the program. Each one came was following a different path toward their heart's deep desire.

Lynda's Path of Creativity

A natural creator, Lynda had already birthed a yoga business. That was in the mid-nineties, a time when anything not-Christian in a small Ontario village would have been pejoratively deemed New Age. It would have been a daunting venture. But Lynda's courageous creativity was positive energy and therefore a powerful attractor. She'd both built a successful business and broadened her community's consciousness. She'd come to the reinvention of work program, after sharing a space with a vibrant dance studio for a decade, ready for a space of her own. But what we think we want and what nature reminds us we need, is not always the same.

Following the program, the community-minded yoga instructor joined in a dedicated collaboration with an entrepreneurial chiropractor. The result was the Blue Sky Yoga Studio – a multi-purpose, Gaia-centred space. Bamboo flooring, non-toxic paint, energy-saving lighting, a gas-burning fireplace, it was a sustainable building. Even the size of the studio was determined so as not to disturb a beloved Maple tree. The venture was a beautiful example of creatively working like Earth mattered. Operated on a conscious business model, other health practitioners and groups were able to use the space, thereby growing the employment opportunities in the village. On special occasions like Earth Day or New Year's Eve, fees from classes went to social projects like Food for Kids.

Lynda's reinvention of work on the path of creativity brought benefit to her bioregion and established her as a leader in Gaia-consciousness.

Doug's Path of Awe

He'd had many jobs, but none satisfied his soul. Even though they'd all been in nature – outdoor education, camp maintenance, water testing – they'd been container jobs, positions he'd filled. Doug wanted work that fulfilled him. He'd come to the program yearning for outer work that resonated with his inner hunger for awe.

Awe and soul – these are values in a reinvented spirituality of work. When reclaimed from religion, soul is no longer what needs to be saved. Soul is the Evolutionary Impulse for more life. It is what drives the spiritual journey and hungers for more. It's what calls Ontario's Crabapple to waken and Mexico's Hummingbird to feed from its blossoms. The soul feeds on awe, knows wonder, and when it does, fills with gratitude.

What Doug brought to the group was the conviction that soul-fulfilling work – like food, water, and shelter – was a human right. For him the program proved a stepping stone to a three-year course in Eco-psychology called *Soul Crafting*. The Vision Quest, an ancient, indigenous tool of discernment through immersion in nature, affirmed his deepest beliefs. The human and non-human are interdependent. The winged, crawling, swimming, and four-legged ones are intelligent, compassionate, and willing to lend us their wisdom.

Following his intuition, Doug's lifework evolved. But not as he'd expected. One might assume the outcome in a reinvention of work program to be a new occupation. It's not always the case. For many, including Doug, it's finding a way to do one's inner work. Today, in addition to making a livelihood as a carpenter, Doug guides others on the Vision Quest, invites friends to campfires, and invokes the non-human relations to be present. But it's the day-to-day conversations with the four-legged-ones that trek along the ancient trails past his woodland home, and his annual canoe trips in the wild waters of Lake Superior that feed his soul's deep hunger for awe.

Doug teaches us what is the real work of the human at this time: carving out time and ways to nurture our awe, learning to listen to the non-human, recovering our lost connection to the whole, and reshaping our lives within the planetary community.

Lisa's Step of Detachment

With her long sandy dreadlocks and a brand-new arts education, Lisa brought deeply principled enthusiasm and environmental awareness to the group. Building her first business, living in a new place, she enrolled attracted by the promise of a co-creative community. She wanted someplace to put ego and individualism aside, to let go doubts, exchange wisdom, and receive support.

She knew exactly what she wanted. Build a home on land she'd inherited from her grandfather, support her aging parents, have a family of her own, grow her own food, work in her own pottery studio with a wood kiln, and trade pottery for goods and services she couldn't create.

Most importantly, she wasn't afraid to let go of her dreams while she earned the monies needed to make them a reality. Washing dishes at the ski hill in the winter, teaching at the local art school in summer, Lisa pursued her heart work by multi-jobbing.

Unusually free of society's expectations, this artist had a lot to teach us about detachment. Contrary to the idea, we can have what we want when we want it, she showed us the value of taking the time to learn the sustainable ways of the ancestors – woodworking, pottery, gardening, and cooking. With her husband, she converted her grandfather's woodworking shop into an apartment. Without plumbing, this was where they lived while they built their dream home. Furnishings came from the local thrift shop as much to save money as our growing landfills. Resilience was a value and a goal as they shaped a life detached from a consumer-culture lifestyle of acquisition.

Impermanence, relinquishing, letting go – Lisa had learned the spiritual arts from pottery. Giving one of her mugs to everyone in the group, she passed on the lesson. Clay, she explained, being first and foremost a gift from Earth, calls forth our generosity. Everything we do and have is from the Earth and for giving back. Letting go rather than hoarding, sharing as opposed to acquisition, she understood to be the ways of nature.

As a potter, Lisa's lifework would follow certain principles – functionality, sustainability, beauty, harmony, and detachment.

Lisa's vision is now a reality. Her pottery is fired in a wood kiln and sold out of Homestead Pottery Studio. She's the mother of two boys, an elected municipal councillor, teaches art in the local schools, and lives in the house she and her husband built board-by-board. Her spirituality of work teaches that to move into the future we want, we must walk the path of letting go. To make one's lifework an art, we must let go the pathway of a manufacturing economy and embrace our artist.

Kate's Step of Transformation

Kate was the trusted face of a respected and innovative community-based research centre. She'd done much to bring important educational resources to the county, but like a caterpillar headed into a cocoon, it was time for a change.

Kate's story demonstrates what it means to find one's sacred work on the path of transformation. A seed of wheat grow into its fullest potential, a human changes from a child into an adult, a star becomes part of a galaxy – when something changes for the good of the whole, this is transformation. The motivation or nature of this forward-energy has been called compassion. Compassion or the hunger for right relationship, also called justice, is what drives us to the path of transformation. It was on this trajectory – where self growth leads to more holistic community, higher consciousness, and the improved well-being of all – I met Kate.

The reinvention of work program for Kate was a step on her way to a Masters program. She has since been involved in a variety of progressive community initiatives.

As an Active Transportation Planner, the title of her position, she promoted self-propelled modes of travel. This is a vital need in rural counties like ours. A higher-than-average seniors population means increasing numbers of non-drivers. 26% of families live in poverty with no access to a car. Work can be seasonal and public transportation is unavailable. Many must walk or bike to get to shops and medical services. In urban settings too, where density demands a limit on the number of private vehicles on the road, transportation-planning is an occupation of growing importance.

Paths and sidewalks are only part of a sustainable community. Safe communities must be increasingly fossil fuel-free if they're to be environmentally healthy. Given that the average car produces three times its weight, about six tons, in carbon dioxide emissions annually, infrastructures for auto-less transportation are essential. Transformation of social consciousness – is essential work.

Public Health Food Worker is another title on Kate's reinvented resume. Assisting community kitchens in planning and delivering food skills programs to youth, securing donations of lumber and soil for the community gardens, coordinating community food projects – her work has contributed to developing greater local resilience and social sustainability. In other words, this is transformative work.

Lynda, Doug, Lisa, and Kate – they are only four among the millions of individuals and businesses courageously reinventing work as though Earth depends on it. And it does.

We teach what we need to learn.

They say we teach what we need to learn. Teaching the program, I can say now, prepared me to redefine my own work outside the church. From Doug, I learned how to live on the land with deeper awe. Seeing how Oak and Birch afford one another space to grow, we pruned the forests felling only those trees that were diseased or limiting another tree's growth.

Lisa schooled us in detachment with joy. Like the Earth gives itself as clay with generosity, we learned to delight in making our programs affordable and available to everyone. The fees schedule invited those who could to contribute more to aid those with less discretionary income.

Creativity. It's the first force of life and the nature of the Evolutionary Impulse. It led Lynda to introduce the eastern spiritual exercise of yoga to her community, to be a co-creator of the Blue Sky Studio, and a member of the Gaïa Centre board. Creativity, this gregarious woman showed me, is what drives us to expand our sphere of influence and pursue ever-higher consciousness. She is one of those who inspire me to write of an Evolutionary Spirituality.

Community development is Kate's calling. Like the old apple tree feeds the Whitetail Deer that feeds the wolf, and wolf's scat nurtures the soil, lifework is good work when it feeds the hungers for more future. In hope that this book might become fodder for evolutionary consciousness conversations, I offer a section of study questions at the back.

The Evolutionaries I met in this reinvention of work program helped me practise what I taught. They demonstrate that the four paths are not predictable or progressive but interchangeable and often intermingled. At some point or other, however, all re-inventors dance on all four paths.

How does one know when to change paths? The answer, as I said earlier, is follow the energy. Excitement, passion, joy, exhaustion, resentment, anger – they inform us when and where to take a new path; they tell us what is our work to do and what is not. At Gaia Centre, energy was my teacher. When programs filled up quickly, it was clear there was energy for the topic in the leader, the Gaia Centre, and the participants. When registrations didn't happen, I learned to ask if it was because there was no interest or need for the content, or if there was insufficient energy for the program in myself or the leader. Often the answer pointed to dis-ease, illnesses, or fatigue to which one of us needed to attend. The experience taught me to stop trying to push the Universe up the hill. It was a lesson that made our own transitions at Gaia Centre more naturally a part of a vibrational, conscious, and communicative Universe. It was all part of learning how to work for reasons more or equally important as the money.

The reinvention of one's lifework is an essential part of these times. Called axial times, or the Great Turning, The Shift, an Evolutionary Moment, the Extinction Rebellion, even the post-doom awakening, this moment is a unique blip in human and planetary history. Our work, in such a time, includes awakening to what time it really is and to our species' responsibility for the environmental crisis. More importantly, it involves awakening to our personal potential to cooperate with the necessary evolution of human consciousness and society.

The work of our generation is awakening to awe, letting go of old paradigms, creating one in which we relate to the Earth community with compassion and transform devolution to evolution. Our work is reinventing a personal and social spirituality of work within the context of the cosmic story by following the ways of creation.

With Lynda, Doug, Lisa, Kate and the rest, our species is poised to take the next step on the evolutionary staircase. In these early moments of the new century, the task is not to amass personal wealth. It is to follow the energy, step out in courage, enter the heart dance, and be a part of the transformation.

Evolutionary Wisdom

- Work in our time means relinquishing the norms of acquisition, immediacy, and individualism.
- Work like it's more than a job, occupation, or profession.
- Work like it's a lifework, our role, and our right in the cosmic drama.
- Work like Earth depends on it.
- Work at what brings you to awe.
- Work to manifest your creativity.
- Work to transform the world with compassion.
- Work like you don't need the money as much as your Earth family needs resilience.

Stories are like window frames. They orient one's point of view and limit our perspective. Each frame in the Window Walk held a Gaia-centered story to re-frame the world we think we live in. Their purpose – to correct what has been a dangerous case of environmental myopia.

CHAPTER 3

I Spy with my Evolutionary Eye

One could say that the whole of life lies in seeing... history can be reduced to the elaboration of ever-more-perfect eyes. See or perish. It's part of the mysterious gift of all existence. Pierre Teilhard de Chardin

"I spy with my little eye ..." It wouldn't be long into any family road trip before these words came tumbling over the backseat. Soon the whole family was scanning the horizons for all things awesome and all things awful. "Black horse and colt!" "Rusting derelict tractor!"

In those days, we saw evidence of our throw-away society without seeing the consequences. Today, the children are not only calling us to pay attention to the reality of our ways, an example being the great Pacific garbage patch, they are also showing us how to clean-up our mess.

The Ocean Cleanup Array was designed by nineteen-year old Boyan Slat. The device collects plastic waste from the oceans, runs on solar and wave power with no harm to fish or plankton. Presented to TEDxDelft in 2013, this still controversial invention remains a good sign – environmental consciousness is growing.

The year I stepped out of the church to open Gaia Centre for Eco-spirituality and Sustainable Work was the International Year of Sustainability. A coincidence? I like to think of it as synchronicity – that phenomenon where one's psychological state of mind meaningfully coincides with an unknown and larger shift in human consciousness.

At the time, nothing appeared very sustainable. Industry had left such a trail of pollution behind that ahead, all existence was threatened. Population growth had accelerated to the tune of eighty-three million per year and was projected to reach eight billion by 2030. Between 1975 and 2011, while our numbers grew to seven billion, the number of pollinators responsible for three-quarters of the world's food dropped by 45%. Now it's 2020. One-quarter of the animal kingdom is endangered. Percentages are even higher for Elephants, Rhinoceroses, and Polar Bears. The loss of large predators means more rodents, parasites, and disease. Sustainability is seen by some as an unachievable goal.

When my focus shifted from the church to the planet, I began to see the stories I believed with fresh eyes. For example, I'd grown up believing that Canadians are loved around the world for being polite, our social welfare and health care systems, and environmentally progressive. And yet, we ranked seventeenth out of twenty for environmental sustainability, and dead last in the field of environmental prosperity based on a study of "the quality of the natural environment, environmental pressures, and preservation efforts."[xiii] In other words, I'd grown up in a time of climate change denial.

These are some stories that contribute to climate change denial. Technology will save the day. It's God will. It's part of a cycle. Climate change is a conspiracy. It's too expensive to fix. Developing countries are to blame. Global warming will help produce food.

There are dangers in blindly accepting our society's stories. Stories, like a window frames our view, both inform and limit our perception of life. Experts put it this way: we confuse "what exists objectively in the world with the image of the world supplied to us by our own distorted lenses."[xiv] Certainly, I had been seeing with lenses distorted and framed by my political, economic, religious, and cultural stories.

It was a shock when I finally began to spy with my little eye and see my nation objectively. It has more than its share of toxic landfills, fracking sites, and orphan oil wells. The shock became personal when I was diagnosed with asthma, a chronic lung disease that's more environmental than genetic. But the real awakening was recognizing that by living out of our myopic stories, the whole Earth-family is now endangered. Be warned: the stories we believe are the stories we live out.

With the coming of the new millennium, I began to look more closely at the stories I'd learned cradled in the lap of Mother Church. Take the Judaeo-Christian origin story.

When seen through the cultural lenses of impatience and immediate gratification, it might read something like this. "God created the Universe and everything in it in six days. And it was good! The seventh day, he declared a statutory holiday, a day of thanks." (Genesis 1 and 2) It's a good story – gratitude is always a good lesson.

But the lesson is missed when we don't take the time to put the biblical creation story into its proper context. Scholars attribute the story to Moses and associate it with the exodus. Imagine the tribe of Israel, after generations spent as slaves midst the opulence of Egypt, wandering for years in the desert. Imagine the hardships, discouragement, and discontent. Consider that some would have preferred to return to the security of a life they knew in servitude rather than continue to wander in the unknown. That's a very different framework in which to read the story.

> The first day, God created light to separate the darkness, day and night. *And it was good.*
> The second day, God made the sky separate from the waters. *And it was good.*
> A third day, God separated the waters with land rich with trees and plants. *It was good.*
> The fourth day, God put sun, moon, and stars in the sky to give light to the land, separated day and night, and ordered the days into seasons and years. *It was good.*
> The fifth day, Creator put all sorts of creatures in the sea and sky, blessed them to multiply and fill the world with life. *It was good.*
> Day six, God created all the animals, and in his likeness, a man and woman for companionship. *It was good.*
> On the seventh day, God rested. *It was good.*

This is the story of an oral culture that survived because of its teaching stories. The message is not in the facts; the truth is not in the historical account. The lesson is in the storytelling. A story of one step after another, perhaps it's intent was to teach patience and perseverance. A recitation of unbelievable achievements, surely it's purpose was to encourage faith in the impossible. After each stanza, there is a chorus, "it is good." If told in the oral fashion of call and response, we can imagine the story replaced words of discontent with words of gratitude for each and every single day of freedom.

When the story is told as a literal account of creation, we make mistakes. The first being that a creative sky god conjured up the Universe in a week with a statutory holiday at the end. The second being that science is the enemy of religion. Believing the story declares Earth to be a finished creation, we deny the discovery of evolution. When we interpret the story as directing all worship to a heaven-bound patriarch, we fail to appreciate and honour the sacred Mother Earth. The cost of this oversight to the Earth-communion has been disastrous.

In particular, the error of our ways can be traced to the story of the sixth day. God gave humanity ultimate authority over oceans and skies, and instructed the tribe to be fruitful, multiply, and subdue the Earth. (Genesis 1:26-28) And subdue it, we have.

Ignoring the text was written some 3,400 years ago to instill an attitude of survival, pride, and self-determination in a tribe that had been enslaved like animals, we became the oppressors. Misappropriation of scripture has served to justify colonialism and to issue captains of manufacturing tickets of entitlement, privilege, and power. It has justified our abuse to animal, plant, and mineral life. Interpreted for generations as a directive against birth control, it has contributed to overpopulation and the species inability to live within the planet's means. By failing to see this text for the liberation theology it is, we became captives ourselves to wrong beliefs about God, humanity, and nature.

Another powerful tale we grew up with is that of Adam and Eve. While it's been the source of much laughter about fig leaves, winks at women's wiles, and sneaky snakes, it's led us down a dangerous garden path. A summary in everyday vernacular might sound like this.

> Shame on you Adam for being tempted by Eve. Shame on you Eve for being tempted by the very fruit I'd forbidden you to eat.
> God was angry. Deeming them disobedient and unworthy of living in paradise, God punished them by banishing them from the garden. But that wasn't all. All men were cursed with hard labour and all women to suffer the pain of childbirth. (Genesis 2:4-3:24)

As a lesson in cause and effect, it was a good story. We can imagine it helped leaders maintain order in an unruly tribe. However, when Christianity turned the Jewish morality myth into a doctrine of fall and redemption, it set the stage for ecological and environmental disorder. Believing humanity and nature to be fallen from God's grace, seeing ourselves as born into original sin rather than original blessing, we've been blind to creation as sacred.

The result is that Christianity has been more concerned with securing the soul's entry into the next life than what's happening to Mother Earth in this one. Humanity is wandering in the wilderness of the sixth mass extinction and global warming. Climate scientists, sick seas, asphyxiating greenhouse gases, and spreading desertification bear witness to how stories have been used to justify an extraction economy for short-term gain. We are desperate for stories that inspire us to live seeing, loving, and gratefully protecting the Earth.

The world needs a new story. With this insight, Thomas Berry and Brian Swimme wrote the Universe Story. In it they declared the cosmos to be both the primary revelation of the divine, and a place of divine-human communication. The same processes that brought stars and planets out of the cosmos, brought plant and animal out of the ocean, and drove the evolution of all life forms. Reality, they declared, is essentially interdependent. The epic of evolution from cosmology, not theology, they said, was the new sacred story. But until it was widely accepted, Berry lamented, we are living in between stories.

When Gaia Centre opened, it was with a candlelit, ritual-telling of this new sacred story. Later, the cosmic narrative would be incorporated into a spiral labyrinth in the woods. Three hundred and twenty meters long, every twenty-two meters represented a billion years. The beginning of the story was located at the centre of the spiral and represented 13.8 billion years ago. The entrance of the labyrinth, which was also the end of the walk, we called the present moment. Along the time line, many more stations of the cosmos honoured significant events – the emergence of moon, the first insects, the appearance of the human, space travel. For all who had eyes to see and courage to face the mosquitoes, the woodland labyrinth was an initiation into the new story.

At another place on the land, Paul built a fire pit where we held Big Bang Bonfires. A forest path was called the Evolutionary Trail. Reclaiming a hill overgrown with wild raspberry canes, I created the Four-fold Wisdom Garden. This we dedicated to what Thomas had named the four wisdoms – modern science, classical religions, Indigenous spirituality, and the wisdom of women. These, he claimed, were what would guide humanity into a new era. The path through that garden we called the Ecozoic Pathway. Out of the church and on the land, I learned to see with new-story eyes.

The Window Walk

Stories are like window frames. They both orient one's point of view and limit our perspective. Like no one window can show us the whole world, no one story tells us all there is to know. And sometimes, like windows break and need repair, worldviews shatter and societies break down.

Earth is our natural resource. Capitalism is best! Christianity is the only way to God! These truths were the basis of the West's twentieth-century story. Being anthropocentric, the story assumed an extractive economy and ever-climbing gross national product were essential. As a result, government and industry, blind to the delicate ecological balance of the planet, have contributed to the climate crisis. Just as there comes a point when window frames in a house need replacing, humanity has come to that time when we must repair the stories that shape our perceptions.

Through an environmental framework, what we see is that climate has determined almost everything about how Canadians live, work, and play. Agriculture and industry have been dependent on fairly predictable temperatures. The extreme weathers of this time, however, are forcing us to recognize that planetary temperatures have increased at double the global average. Every year since 1998 has been warmer than the twentieth-century average. [xv] As a result of this sudden departure from temperatures typical for the past ten thousand years, sea levels are rising, erosion due to the retreat of glaciers is accelerating, sea ice is disappearing in the Arctic, on the coasts, along the mighty St. Lawrence River, and even in Lake Ontario, one of the continent's Great Lakes.

Global warming is the direct result of human activity. This is the conclusion of 97% of the climate science community including researchers from geology, astrophysics, oceanography, atmospheric physics, and many other disciplines. In that planetary devolution can be traced to myopic cultural and religious stories, we must realize the need of new frames for seeing.

Gaia Centre's window walk, an Earth-literacy experience, was a tour of ten window frames hung at various places around the acreage. Some frames had ripped screens, some had panes that were cracked, or glass that was broken. The message. of course, was in the medium itself: our view of nature requires repair. At each frame along the walk, one found a new story. Here are four of the stories from the Windows On Gaia walk.

Window on Trees

A weathered rectangular frame with peeling yellow paint hangs askew in the big oak at the bottom of the old cattle road that leads to the lake. Its eight panes have long been empty. Through it, one's eye is focused on trees which are most often seen only in terms of board feet, soft or hard woods, cords and face cords.

> The frame directs the eye to the Birch, Poplar, Maple, towering White Pines, Black Spruce, and Balsam on the other side of the lake. These varieties thrive because of

the bio-region's short, swampy summers and long, cold winters. What we don't see, as the old saying goes, is the forest for the trees. But if we could, we'd know this is the all-important Boreal Forest that sweeps in a broad band south of the tundra and north of the grasslands all across North America and Eurasia.

Moving along the leafy path, one might be too occupied slapping at black flies to note the critical role trees play. It's the intense insect activity – a direct result of the profuse plant growth and burst of photosynthesis in these high latitudes in summer – that make this region's dense canopy a migratory destination for many species of birds.

There's so much we never see unless we trip over it. Take tree roots. Unable to penetrate the four-million-year-old Precambrian rock plateau called the Canadian Shield, they grow horizontally, popping up occasionally from where they run below the surface of the soil. Then there are rivulets trickling down through the Algonquin Watershed below the leaf cover. There's the Snowshoe Hare – white in winter, brown in summer – it's always camouflaged.

The reality is, unless we know what to look for, there's more we don't see than we do.

To truly see the forest for the ecology, we need a multidimensional framework. The reality is nothing exists apart from everything else. Everything manifests within a set of dynamic and complex biological relationships that span the breadth of time, species, and environmental conditions. As we move on, my hope is we will do so with an ecological framework and see ourselves as part of a unique and fragile ecological system.

Window on Water

Where Little Cameron Lake kisses the shore, a second window frame floats among the rushes. At first glance, it appears as a pleasing re-creation of a Monet painting. Double paned, it calls the eye that usually just skims along the surface to take a deeper look at one of life's basic elements.

> Biologically, water tells an intimately personal story. It makes up 74% of our planet and 70% of our bodies. We need 64 ounces of it daily to thrive. 95% of all life exists below some watery surface.
>
> Ecologically, it tells a bigger story. Only 2.5% of the planet's H_2O is fresh water. Two-thirds is frozen in glaciers, ice caps, and permafrost, or held in the planet's aquifers. Less than 0.03% of the total amount of available fresh water is on the surface. All the chemical reactions that sustain life happen in water. With its unique capacity to take different forms, it has shaped our planet's history as it shapes our daily lives.
>
> Water is not limitless. When we drain underground aquifers to irrigate crops, it is lost to the hydrological cycle for thousands of years. Stolen from natural water systems to sell in plastic bottles, it's lost to that community's future. By 2050, water scarcity is predicted to be our number one problem.
>
> Religiously, water's been a symbol of the divine and a holy element used in purification rituals. Rivers, fountains, and waterfalls have been named as holy places. To the Indigenous, water is not only the source of life, food, and livelihood, it is a right. In 2018 in Canada, however, more than one hundred First Nation communities lived with water advisories.
>
> How do we see water? To the environmentalist, water has rights and must be protected. To Nestlé Canada, the infamous bottler of water, the elixir of life is just another foodstuff. It is best valued and distributed by the free market, they say. How do we see water?

Anyone who takes the Window-walk must ask themselves this question. "Through which framework do we view our rivers, streams, lakes, and oceans?"

Window on the Seasons

In the Crabapple tree hangs another window frame because this creature has many stories to tell. It was the first Autumn after we'd moved in. The old tree, to our urban eyes, was ornamental. Then one afternoon, a neighbour knocked on the door. She was a granddaughter-in-law of the first homesteader. Did we intend to turn the tree's apples into jelly, she wanted to know. She and her mother had made Crabapple jelly for thirty-some years from this tree, she told us. As it turned out, she not only harvested the produce, she taught us how to preserve it. Being new to rural living, we had been blind to the tree's legacy of abundance. From later that winter, comes yet another story.

> It was February and I'd been tobogganing with four-year old Jillian. Giving me, the new kid on the block a tour, she pointed to the Crabapple's icy branches. "This, she explained, used to be a tree."
>
> By mid-May, the once-upon-a-time tree was magnificent in pink, ruby, and white blossoms. Surrounding it was a shimmering aura of precious pollinators – the exotic Eastern Tiger Swallowtail Butterfly, along with a number of the eight hundred varieties of Bees in Southern Ontario.
>
> In early June, Crabapple had clothed itself in a fulsome grandeur. In and out of its canopy, Yellow Warblers came to court, mate, feed, rest, or for choir practice. All summer, Woodpeckers – Downy, Hairy, and the Redheaded – foraged for arthropods along its trunk. Professors of the RRR philosophy (reduce, reuse, and recycle), they ate only what they needed. The rest they stored in a laboriously drilled system of sap-coated holes for another day.
>
> As August waned, branches were so heavy with crimson fruit they drooped nearly to the ground. Red Squirrel, Whitetail Deer, neighbour Pat, and the grandkids shared in the harvest.

By October, there was enough jelly for my little neighbour's Thanksgiving dinner. Once again bare in November, Crabapple settled in for a winter's nap. But even then, she welcomed Black-capped Chickadees and the Red-Breasted Nuthatch to dine on the nutritious lichen that wrapped her branches like a lacy shawl.

It's fifteen autumns later. My playmate is at university discovering many more ways by which to view her world. Volunteers from the local apple-share program help with the harvest. Crabapple has become a valued teacher guiding me in the lesson of creation: for everything there is a season.

Tree-planting programs right round the planet speak to a higher consciousness. Young and old are coming to see trees for what they are: air-purifiers, living beings, seasonal companions, and spiritual guides.

Window on Soil

At the edge of the farmhouse lawns stands a wondrous circle of young Birch. In this mystical space are benches for listening, waiting, watching, and more. A long rectangular frame rests on a couple of fallen branches about a half-dozen inches off the ground. Covered in semi-opaque plastic, the old window once served to winterize the farmer's garage. Often hidden under maple and oak leaves, it's overlooked by the casual visitor. But then again, who ever looks down to really see the soil?

Soil – beneath the thick leaf cover – is another world. In every cubic centimetre, billions of micro-organisms work to break down last year's foliage. The by-product of these natural systems is nitrogen-rich soil, source of nutrients, plants, food, and medicine. Anything but *inert* or *dirt,* vital and alive, it is the Mother few of us know.

Crucial to life, it must be recognized that soil is disappearing at unprecedented speeds. Twelve million hectares per year are lost to housing developments, highways, shopping malls, and services. Twenty-three hectares per minute are being lost to extreme drought and desertification accelerated by global warming. On that same land, 20 million tons of grain could have been grown. The figures show that 52% of agricultural land has been compromised due to erosion, contamination, deforestation, agribusiness, urban sprawl, over-cropping, over-grazing, and improper irrigation practices. Topsoil covers only 8% of the planet and less tomorrow unless we recognize it for what it is.[xvi]

Soil is not a commodity price can buy. It doesn't come from Walmart or the nursery. In our harsh climate, it can take 500 years for rain on rock and wind in trees to make one centimetre of the stuff. To accumulate enough substances to make the soil fertile, it takes 3,000 years. It is time to see land as holy, full of life, life-giving, and beyond price.

In the sacred circle of Birch, Window Walkers are invited to take a handful of cornmeal and return it to the planet saying – "may there be new eyes for seeing the soil as Mother."

Window on Food

On the door to the vegetable garden is a framed mirror. Many of our guests get its message, you are what you eat. Fewer, however, are able to identify from the foliage alone the kinds of lettuces, herbs, and root vegetables growing there. Even fewer are familiar with the nutrients gained from different vegetables. The story of the food they were about to eat, this we told at the kitchen island. Billed as a Gaia-glorious meal, a lunch that honours the magnificent power of Earth to feed and heal us, it began with this invitation. "Let me introduce you to your food."

> Brandishing the showy orange root with its feathery fern top with one hand, I lifted the lid from the blue and white soup tureen with the other. "Carrot soup, source of carotene, it brightens our organs and our skin and is full of anti-oxidants which are more potent when slightly cooked."
>
> Stirring, I coax the arousing aromas to come forth. "Cinnamon, the great copycat spice, contains a chemical that mimics insulin to help the body turn sugars to energy. Turmeric helps digestion, eases women's menses, and moves harmful toxins that age the liver."
>
> Moving from dish to dish, honouring each one's nutritional offerings, we meet our food in a new way. Some shift anxiously fearful the soup will be cold, simply from hunger, or trapped in the fast-food culture. I try not to feel rushed and to take the time it takes to learn how the food we eat is part of an elegant Earth system.
>
> It takes research and time to develop respect for the food we eat. But by the time each has their Gaia-glorious meal in front of them, appetites are keen, spirits are wakened, and the way they look at their food is changed forever. I know because I've been on the other side of the table.

Cosmology, ecology, spirituality – we must find new frames for seeing ourselves as part of the planet. We must tell stories other than the humancentric, political, cultural, religious, and economic ones that are so rapidly leading to ecocide. Learning to see the fullness of Earth again, this is the aim of the Windows Walk.

Across the four acres of the farmhouse land, other window frames direct the eye into the meadow, a hidden landfill site, and up into the branches of the old-growth White Pine we call Grandfather. At first glance, a visitor probably sees shabby-chic country decor. But each derelict frame, like another generation's chalk and blackboards, is a timely teaching tool. Each one holds a Gaia-centred story to re-frame the world we think we live in and correct what has been a dangerous case of environmental myopia.

New Frames for Seeing - the Window of Awe

My children helped me see the world with fresh eyes, whether it was the canopy of green and blue above their carriage, or the rushing army of ants they toddled after. Later, their calls from the back seat to play "I spy," reminded me again to view the world through windows of awe and wonder. Years later when I watched my son-in-law's utter amazement at seeing his newborn son for the first time, I realized awe is a portal to love.

A skeptic might say our planet is in trouble because the species has lost its awe to the glitter of the manufacturing world. But some are finding it again as shown in this email from my now-adult daughter.

> "I'm in a cafe right now having a chai and looking out onto another cloudy day over the bay. G'awed, it rains a lot here." Remembering how in the past I'd get upset at her casual use of the "G" word, she asked, "Do you like my new word? When you spell God as G-A-W-E-D, it escapes much of the religious dogma and yet still acknowledges something creative out there that has the potential to amaze me no matter how many times I look."
>
> She went on to share her plan to take the back roads to London, Ontario. "Sometimes when I drive through the country and look at the skies and witness how it changes the way we see the land, I do think there could be god/s."

The email was from Jill who lives and sees life as an artist. Her outlook allows her to see what most miss, what she called the "something creative out there." Like ancestors who conveyed their spiritual experiences with paint on cave walls, or through the words of great Psalms, Jill created a unique picture-word, a neologism, G'awed. I loved her word for its ability to convey that flash of consciousness and surprise when we suddenly see the sacred nature of our reality.

Awe. As mother and clergy, I'd tried for years to inspire both my offspring and pewsters to look for God within the natural world. But creating experiences that spark an inward and involuntary response to the outward and unseen blessings of our planetary existence was nothing I could orchestrate. Now, when I'd stepped out of the church, my daughter, "without buying into any of the religious dogma" was finding it everywhere. Nothing like children to keep us humble and help us laugh at ourselves. And isn't laughing at oneself just another state of awe?

But what, if not religion, will provide the lenses necessary to correct what I've come to understand as society's spiritual and moral myopia? How else would one explain the dumping of two hundred and twenty million tonnes of hazardous waste into rivers, lakes, and oceans annually. After hosting retreats in which humans reconnected with humus, what gives me hope for the future is my trust that nature herself will give us new eyes for seeing. So it is, I write Earth's stories.

I spy with an evolutionary eye!

These are evolutionary times. Thanks to X-Ray technology, our generations can take a photo of the knee and see the cartilage is torn. We can see what once was invisible. It is good, a goodness we take for granted. The reality is, the eye with which we see and the machines that magnify what we can't are the result of the evolutionary process. Evolution itself is a lense for how we view our world.

> It was not just another day. It was the day, some five hundred and forty million years ago, when Gaia would first gain sight. It happened in the deep darkness of the ocean. A cell emerged that, with the first photo-receptor proteins,

was able to sense the presence of light. And it was good. Good because Sea Squid could detect shadows as signs of movement. Good because it was that day, Earth began the slow journey to consciousness – the consciousness of relationship.

It was another evolutionary day when the Limpet Snail, with the first parabolic reflector eye, could not only detect curves and movement, it could recognize what was danger and what was prey. And it was good.

Another day, when the Nautilus Mollusk emerged able to discern distance with the first rudimentary eye, it could choose its path across the ocean floor. With additional sight, the hunter and the hunted, could better strategize. And that was good.

As time did its evolutionary dance, the eye became more complex. The day that Earthlings emerged with a compound eye made of thousands of small, independent photo-receptor units, each pointing in slightly different directions, that was a great day. They could not only distinguish brightness, colour, movement and the speed of its predators, they could take in life's options. But the day, some five hundred thousand years later, I think it was a Wednesday, the day the human primate gained 20/20 vision and could distinguish fuchsia from gold rose with a sophisticated camera eye, that was the day Earth could fully appreciate its own beauty. Since that day, it could never again be said, it's just another day. And it was very, very good.

When I look at this planet with evolutionary eyes, it would appear Gaia, in her human form, is ever-evolving in consciousness. Some talk of the *third eye.* This psychic ability, also known as intuition, they say enables them to sense the purity of the energy-field above a grove of mature trees and the Amazon Rainforest as the living, breathing being it is. We are part of a species. This in itself is a major realization for our times. Coming to regard our species as part of Gaia, and Gaia as part of a cosmic dance, that is coming to yet greater consciousness. Universe, some say, is becoming more conscious of itself through us. And that is good, for what's needed, if we are to recover as a planet, is for you and I to better appreciate the privilege, potential, and power to cooperate with our own evolution of consciousness.

Correcting our Myopia

Life, Theilhard said, is a case of see or perish. From the moment we open our eyes, with each new image and the words we are given to explain what we see – mommy, daddy, bird, tree – we gain an ever-widening view of our world. Parents, religion, education, the market – by ascribing value to these images – teach us whether something is disposable or to be cherished. But a time comes when we have to make up our own minds. Sight, one of the primal senses, Jill reminded me, is key to our relationship with the environment.

Not unlike a child, our species has grown up because of new images and new ideas. The year before Jill was born, humanity saw Earth as a whole planet for the first time. Televised, the photograph of the Blue Pearl launched an unprecedented paradigm shift. Now, we are a society that has language, YouTube, videos, tweets, and NASA photos that daily expand our awareness of Spaceship Earth and the conscious Universe. As ecological and cosmological perspectives add to the ways we view the world, we gain evermore perfect eyes.

Jill, as an artist-activist, is an Evolutionary. Her canvases document the awesome and awful landscapes of our times. In *Global Landscapes, an Oil Series,* she shows forests with a background of deep Myrtle, Hunter, and Chartreuse greens. Over it, however, she laid down a black wash to show how

Earth's beauty is marred by oil spills. In another series, *Rural Transitions,* atop pastoral scenes of barns and fields, hives and nests, she imposed high-density residential and industrial structures. Development, she sees, is directly related to the disappearing pollinators, songbirds, small family farms, and the Greenbelts of Southern Ontario. Artists create window frames on society.

Seeing the third rock from the Sun as G'awed's country informs what Jill brings to the canvas. In turn, her work dares the viewer to see both the ugly devastation of colonialism and the ongoing colonization of the natural world. Radicalized, she now paints and creates that others might also see with new eyes, grow in ecological consciousness, and also take responsibility for Earth's future. In this way, the experience of awe has made Jill an Evolutionary.

My own evolution in consciousness came about by returning to the land. By simply being in and with the natural world, I put myself in the way of awe. Under the night sky, I learned cosmology without telescopes. In the ever-shifting wetlands, I learned ecology without professors. In the forest, I observed art without artists. Floating in the ancient waters of the kettle lake, I experienced spirituality without priests or priestesses. Out of the religious institution and in nature, I learned awe cannot be learned or commanded but is an involuntary response. Awe is what I define as my spirit's applause to the magnanimous creativity, interconnectedness, and beauty of existence.

The eyes, it's been said, are windows to the soul. But it's awe that connects the soul in one part of Universe to the soul in another. Today, the soul of the blossoming Crabapple calls me to waken to deep time consciousness. When I look at what Universe has manifested outside my window, I am in awe at the Grace, artistry and soul of the evolutionary process.

There have always been some who see through the lenses of awe. They are called Mystics. When we live as Mystics in awe of the unmerited, all-surrounding Grace, something evolutionary happens. Awe stirs wonder; wonder frees gratitude; gratitude acknowledges existence as numinous, deserving of reverence and dedicated protection. Mystics may be the ones who lead us into the Ecozoic age.

From infant to child, to adolescent, to adult – ours is a story of the development of the ever-more-perfect eye. It's a story of consciousness, of how sight is the beginning of insight, and insight is the beginning of a deeper connection. I tell you Jill's story that we might put on artist's eyes and see with awe. I write of awe as the evolution of consciousness and believe on that day when the Earthling sees through the lens of awe, wonder will well up, the mind will kneel before the cosmic communion, and the heart will want only for Earth's best future.

The first thing I put on in the morning are my evolutionary glasses. And I must say, in this post-urban, post-clerical time of my life, watching for the something wonderfully creative that's always there, and believing humanity is evolving and can consciously evolve, I see life more optimistically.

Evolutionary Wisdom

- Seeing is the beginning of Consciousness – for everything there is a season.
- Seeing through a framework of awe is a spiritual practice.
- Seeing through an ecological framework changes life from a collection of objects into a communion of subjects.
- Seeing through an evolutionary framework is a prescription to correct social and moral myopia.

For all who had courage to face the mosquitoes, the spiral labyrinth through the woods was an initiation into the new sacred story. The Totem Pole of All-Our-Relations, both the entrance and end of the Cosmic Walk, marked the present moment. Thirty Stations of the Cosmos stretched along the 13.8 billion year evolutionary time line.

CHAPTER 4

Stories from Grandmother Universe

The Universe story is the quintessence of reality. We perceive the story. We put it in our language, the birds put it in theirs, and the trees put it in theirs. If you do not know the story, in a sense you do not know yourself. Pierre Teilhard de Chardin

Her Birth Story

Nothing I did felt like enough. I hosted Gaia-centred programs, adopted a Gaia-glorious diet, swore off air travel, and drove a hybrid car. Despite taking climate change seriously in both big and little ways, I awoke each day with a sense of urgency – there's something more I'm to do.

Vocational arousal. This was how Barbara Marx Hubbard diagnosed my condition. Her explanation was exciting: "the intelligence that has been and is creating everything is awakening in you as your own conscious intent to evolve." [xvii] I wasn't suffering anxiety, I was evolving.

This emergence wasn't happening just to me, of course. It's happening in our species in our lifetime. Barbara's name for this new species was *Homo Amore Universalis* – those that know themselves as cosmic beings and capable of loving the whole Universe. We can cooperate with the process, she taught, by consciously centring our lives in universal love. And there it was, the prescription for my condition. Daily dancing with evolution. Daily grounding myself in infinite love. All that remained was discerning just what that meant in practical ways for me.

Telling creation stories was something I could do. Telling the new creation story, as Berry had said, was what the world needed. To tell it, however, I had first to learn a new language. While the terms were strange at first, the dancing quarks and streaming gases had a tale to tell as mystical and magical as any legend of a world built on the back of a turtle or myth of people shaped from clay. Full of mysterious beings – Supernovas, Eukaryotes, and Hominids – no evil demons, fairy godmothers, or angels were needed to merit my attention or hold my ear. Strangely enough, the scientific terminology made the cosmos more real and intimate than I'd ever imagined.

The more entranced I became by this story, the more I came to embrace it as mine to tell. I was discovering my work as a storyteller. I told it to Gaia Centre retreatants in the labyrinth. If it rained, I told it in the living room. In the telling something happened. I stopped speaking in the third person. I began to narrate the history as my own and to speak as though I was the keeper of a family's story. A new grandmother, I began to recognize myself as an elder with wisdom to pass along. One day, the macro and micro stories collapsed into one and it felt natural to call myself Grandmother Universe.

Here, then, are three of Grandmother Universe's stories.

I am Universe is a series of five short vignettes about Beginnings from the Cosmic Walk.

Grandmother's Outlandish Love Affairs is a four-part creation story driven by love.

Grandmother's Power-Full Treasures tells how one parent, anxious for his children's future, discovers the cosmogenetic powers that can help him navigate these unstable times.

I am Universe

The new sacred creation story from cosmological science does not have one beginning and one ending. As Grandmother Universe leads listeners through the Cosmic Walk, she tells a story of many beginnings. It is a tale of cosmogenesis for the state of the cosmos is always manifesting yet another genesis. It is an empowering story for it tells of the cosmogenetic powers that are ever expanding and sustaining the Universe – centration, allurement, radiance, synergy, cataclysm, emergence, transformation, and more. Lastly, it is an explaining story revealing the laws that govern creativity's process – differentiation, communion, and autopoiesis.

In the Beginning

Garbed in her fiery orange coat, Grandmother Universe led her listeners into the centre of the spiral woodland labyrinth. There she lit a lantern in memory of the Big Bang and began to tell her birth story.

> In the beginning, at a time before time and a place before space, thirteen point eight billion years ago, give or take a day or two, I was born. Though some say hatched, and others say exploded into existence, I like to think I came to be in a dramatic, singular cataclysmic, flaring forth of helium and hydrogen. In short, my birth, like yours, was a magnificent cosmic event.
>
> Born from what? That's the question. There are many theories including multiverses. The sole image of my origins shows a smooth background radiation. Exactly where I came from remains a mystery. What isn't a mystery is this: what I am is a storyteller ever unfolding to you that mystery.

Only a century ago, humans believed me static and eternal. Then I revealed to you my ever-expansive nature, although, you might say, it was discovered.

A physicist and Archdeacon, Georges LeMaitre, along with astronomer and cosmologist Edwin Hubble, theoretical physicist Dr. Albert Einstein, and many others were involved. Observing distant galaxies rapidly receding both from Earth and one another, they concluded two things. First, Universe is ever-expanding. Second, if everything is moving forward, everything must have a past which could be run back until all matter was concentrated in a primeval atom. Today, humans believe I/Universe am 46 billion light years in diameter, still stretching and growing.

Call me expansive, I like to say, I'm curious. Describe me as ever-becoming, I'll tell you I'm exploring my infinite potential. What's my passion? You won't be surprised when I tell you it's creating, creating, creating.

But, perhaps I got ahead of the story. Let me introduce myself, I am Universe.

In the Beginning was Light

Picking up her lantern, Grandmother Universe moved to that place that marked the birthplace of stars, thirteen and a half billion years ago. She lit another lantern to honour the coming of light and told yet another piece of her tale.

What gets me up in the morning? My penchant for novelty. In fact, it's one of the laws I live by, the law of differentiation. One day I'm a cosmic web. The next, from atoms concentrated by gravity and transformed by nuclear fusion, I'm a cosmic web with stars. But I get ahead of myself.

In the beginning, I/Universe, was but a hot dense sphere expanding and cooling. Talk of your hot flashes. Following my birth, I was in a turbulent state being rocked by nuclear fusion reactions. In that brief time masses of burning hydrogen and helium were created. When they eventually cooled down, the first stars were born.

Enormous and fragile, many of the first stars quickly became supernovae that detonated within a million years. In their explosive deaths, oxygen, carbon, gold, uranium, and other heavy elements were scattered stretching space and time.

But that is not the end of the story of stars. Oh no, for I/Universe have a penchant for novelty. In fact, the law of differentiation is one of the laws I live by. I gathered the stardust into new stars and planets, I brought forth suns and soil, created humus and humans.

Some would tell you a star is an astronomical object consisting of a luminous spheroid of plasma held together by its own gravity. But that's too impersonal and cold. I'm here to tell you, stars shatter the darkness, warm the soul, and hold the secret of what and why you are here.

Allurement, the Beginning of Communion

Her story of stars told, Grandmother Universe directed her listeners' attention to what shone above. Sometimes it was Sun, Earth's day star, source of light, energy, and life itself. If it was a cloudless night, she would point out Polaris, commonly known as The North Star. Located almost directly above the North Celestial Pole, it marks due north, she'd say. It has guided the first peoples and your ancestors to this land. Then, picking up her lantern, she moved further along the cosmic walk to the birthplace of galaxies, some twelve and a half billion years ago. Here she lit yet another lantern before she continued.

It can be said, humans are creatures of their allurements. And is it not true that Cindy's passions draw her to animals in trouble? Did Carol, when she was new in the neighbourhood, not follow her intuition and find herself in a circle of belonging? Lisa was attracted to Nancy. Tanya and David longed for children and gave birth to Meredith and Gavin. Allurements, they guide us like the stars guided sailors, settlers, and explorers.

But governing it all is a law, the law of communion. Why is there is an attraction to belong, to be part of something bigger than ourselves? What is it that drew the first stars, planets, dust, and gas into a galaxy? It is the cosmic bias for community.

Sun and its solar system belongs to the spiral-shaped Milky Way galaxy. The Earth and its moon, the sun in its orbit, everything is held in the compassionate curve of gravitational attraction dictated by the law of communion. Call it interdependence or seamlessness, communion is one of the laws I live by.

Andromeda, your neighbouring galaxy, is expected to collide with the Milky Way around 4 billion years from now. The two will eventually merge into a single new galaxy called Milkomeda. Even now, the law is at work.

I am what I am today – more than one hundred billion galaxies each containing more than one hundred trillion stars – thanks to the law of communion.

Chaos, the Beginning of Creativity

A sense of awe and intimacy was palpable as the storyteller led her listeners through the Universe story. The silence was filled with wonder and anticipation as they made their way through the woods to that place marking four billion years ago. Grandmother lit yet another lantern to honour life's earliest beginnings.

> As mineral-rich rains fell from the early atmosphere, Earth's blistering surface cooled into a crusty surface. Deep pockets in the Earth crust filled to become oceans. When lightning struck deep into the chemical-rich waters igniting the first cells of bacteria, that might have been the end of my story except for the law of autopoiesis.
>
> The mixture of necessity and change causes creativity to bring order out of disorder; systems reorganize not only to maintain themselves but evolve at the next level of organization. In other words, I/Universe, in all my forms, have the capacity of self-creating.
>
> Cells, in response to the environmental chaos, necessarily rearranged themselves into algae. In another time of climate crisis, algae became crustaceans, and so it went. Crawling, creeping, swimming, rooting, reaching deep into the ocean floor, and high into the ether, life, driven by climate change, evolved into plant, then animal, then hominid. Climate Change, it's an evolutionary driver; self-creating is the evolutionary response.
>
> Ask yourselves this. How was it, sometime between 2 million and 700,000 years ago, the brain of genus Australopithecus, about 400 cubic centimetres, doubled in size in genus Homo erectus? The answer, dear ones, is why I have hope that Homo-sapiens sapiens will survive the current extinction. So you too must have hope, for I/Universe have declared all my human and non-human forms to be self-creating. Because of the law of autopoiesis,

you are capable of bringing out of disorder order, and out of chaos creativity. You can cooperate with yet another evolution of consciousness.

The Beginning of All Tomorrows

Grandmother Universe had led them to the threshold. They gathered at the end of the cosmic walk which was also the threshold of the future. She lit yet another lantern, sign of the creativity in each of her listeners. Her last story began with an age-old question.

"What makes us human?" Looking up from the sink of fresh rhubarb, the woman watched her five year old march alongside a cotillion of ants not realizing she'd given voice to her thoughts.

Her own mother, without looking up from the pouch she was sewing for the marsupials burned in South Australian bush fires, answered with a story.

"In the beginning, *AA,* a small-brained hominid called *Australopithecus africanus* laid the still-warm body of a squirrel in front of his pregnant mate. Some half-a-million years later, *Homo habilus* stretched his six-foot-tall frame after a morning knapping sharp, flat blades. Some five hundred thousand years later, *Homo erectus* pulled the animal skin close against winter's winds and dreamt of a tool that could fell trees to build a shelter for all seasons. A million years later, a woman entered a longhouse and turned a squirrel roasting on the spit. And so time passed until a *Neanderthal* Shaman, one morning, shook her rattles to signal the day had come to bury their clansman. The family put stone tools in the shallow grave and sang him on his way. All the time, life was becoming human.

Was it Monday or Friday, we don't know, but some one hundred and fifty thousand years later, a *Homo sapiens* family donned garments sewn from hides and decorated with jewellery; they packed utensils honed from stone, and set off in search of arable land, running waters, and plentiful game. Moving out of east-central Africa, moving into the Middle East, moving into Europe, traversing oceans into Asia and Australia, humans sought their future. Deep in underground caves and high on steep, stone cliffs, thirty thousand years ago, humans painted stories of the great hunt, the terrible war, and the big sea.

It was only two centuries ago, our ancestors boarded a ship in Glasgow. They sailed for weeks until they landed in the Port of Mont Royal. From there, they travelled by canoe and carriage to the Meeting Place, our home city of Toronto. Suddenly, her granddaughter's squeal of delight interrupted the story.

Perched on a low branch of the Crabapple, she called to them with all the awe and playfulness of childhood. "Look at me, I'm on my way to the moon."

"Will you be back for lunch?" her mother asked as she made her way to lift the child down to safe ground. "There's going to be rhubarb crisp."

"Yes, and I'll tell you all about the moon," was the promise.

So, what makes us human? Grandmother Universe answered with the certainty of age. Stories, she declared, they help us to see the past, be in the present, and imagine the future. Storytelling shows us who and what we are. The future belongs to the storyteller. It might be that without stories, the species might perish.

Then holding her lantern high, she led her listeners out of the woods.

Grandmother's Outlandish Love Affairs

Life's big questions may never be answered satisfactorily. Where did we come from? Why are we here? Are we alone? Both the Judaeo-Christian and scientific responses fall short. Christianity's origin story credits all the magnificence of this world and the next to a distant deity whose banner over us is love. In the hills and valleys of everyday, this is comforting. In times of war, pestilence, and outright evil, the idea of a loving god is confusing. It also fails to explain the quantum mechanics of how the dust we came from came to be.

Post-modern science explains how we came to be with details of atoms, quarks, gravity, and nuclear fusion and more. Yet, it fails to provide any existential motivation, meaningful purpose, or essential nature of life. Neither origin story fully satisfies.

Until recently, many of us have felt we had to choose between two origin stories. Did we believe the biblical story – in the beginning, God created – or the scientific account that begins with the Big Bang? Historically, religious who studied science and Scientists who'd taken religious vows have been silenced by the powers-that-be. Priest and paleontologist Pierre Teilhard de Chardin is a case in point. For his claims that humanity was evolving mentally and socially toward a final spiritual unity, he was forbidden to publish his writings. Until now.

Now we can access de Chardin's insights. "We must put the story we perceive into our own language," he said believing only when we can tell the story as our own will we know our own story.

Cosmologist Brian Swimme and Father Thomas Berry did just that. To foster a more personal connection with the evolutionary history of cellular life, they put the story of the first prokaryotic cells in mythological language. Naming them *Aries, Prometheus, Sappho, Viking, Engla* and so on, they characterized our ancient ancestors. Their story showed us evolution was not, as Darwin said, a random process, nor was it about the survival of the fittest. Rather, ours is a story of adaptation, reorganization and self-creating; it is about diversifying to live; it is about resilience that comes from co-creating, from communion in community.

In an inter-spiritual language, here is another of story of Grandmother Universe. It's yet another attempt to answer those questions of who we are, why we're here, and how we'll move ahead.

> Once upon a never-before time, Grandmother awoke with an alarming insight. Earth is warming, ice-caps are calving, oceans are rising, and deserts are spreading. Plunging jet-streams are making wild, weird and extraordinary weather ordinary. With population numbers compounding, these are urgent times; and the times for the grandchildren will be even more tumultuous.
>
> Rising to put on the new day, the elder could not take off her deep sense of urgency. She felt she must do something. But what? Impatiently, she waited for clarity. One month, two went by. Each morning she rose, asking herself, "What am I to do?" Until one day when she awoke to find her house full to the rafters with children of all ages and colours. Butchers and bakers, computer and candlestick makers, they came from all kinds of work.
>
> "Ah, you've come." Her sigh of relief embraced them like a summer breeze on a smothering, still day. "You can call me Grandmother Universe," she introduced herself. "Some of you may know me as Lady Wisdom. Some may call me the Collective Unconscious. Sometimes I am referred to as Holy Spirit, sometimes Gaia, and some just call me their intuition. I'm known by many names and I answer to them all."
>
> Then and there, in the presence of the children she knew what a grandmother's to do. "I have a story for you. And I know you want to hear it for you have been born in this time and come to this place to do just that. Your world is in trouble for lack of a good story. Schools, churches,

politicians, manufacturers, bankers ... no where can you find the one story you need but here. Here then is the story of my four great love affairs."

Her listeners' eyebrows reached for the sky.

"So, you think a grandmother with four love affairs outrageous, do you? Is love not the origin of life – the point of life? Does awe not cause you to fall in love at least four times a day? Of course! And if you don't have four great loves in life, this story is especially for you." Her voice gentled then and she began to recall for them her life. "Yes, I have had four great loves in my life. Love of Universe, love of Earth, love of Life, and the love of Humanity. And from each one, I have gained great wealth."

This time eyebrows peaked even higher.

"Do not confuse wealth with stuff," their elder cautioned. "The wealth I gained is love's own wisdom. In these times of peril and promise, it is the powerful wisdom of love you seek." And with that, she began her story.

For the Love of Universe

"Once in a never-before time, a time before time and a place before space, Universe flared forth. Time and space, matter and dark matter, sound and vibration, energy and gravity, think of it. All that matters came out of nothing, fecund nothingness, raw potentiality.

In an explosion a million trillion, trillion degrees hotter than Sun's centre, Universe was born. They say it was the size of a grapefruit. First there were quarks and anti-quarks. A second later, electrons and positrons were created and annihilated. Except, one in a billion particles survived. Before it was three minutes old, temperatures fell; most of the helium nuclei that will ever be was formed; neutron and proton emerged and in a wondrous fusion became the hydrogen nucleus. Think of it, everything that is came from those one-in-a-billion particle survivors. Survival is in your nature.

Over the next three hundred thousand years, the young Universe of matter and gravity, light and energy grew. From gigantic filaments of ever-streaming gases was woven a cosmic web. At just the right speed, Cosmos, like a parent's heart for her children, stretched and expanded. A millionth of one percent faster or slower and nothing would have survived. Who can think of this and not marvel at the intelligence and bias for life that is at the heart of everything."

Grandmother paused to catch a breath and savour her awe. Then she went on.

"When electrons joined with protons, Universe gained atoms. Concentrated by gravity, masses of atomic energy became primal stars. Solar systems, galaxies, the Cod fish, schools of Cod, you and your grandchildren, each and everything is a concentration of light radiating out and beyond its self."

She paused to give her listeners' imaginations time to percolate, to envision the good things they might create with their own atomic energy. In a moment that could have been eons, she went on.

"Some of the first concentrations of energy were stars. The giant reds, Supernovas with iron at their core died explosive deaths. Scattering their very essence, the elements of iron, gold, calcium, carbon, selenium, zinc, and more seeded a next generation of stars. Through death, Universe expanded. And, if you can imagine, it's still expanding."

Unable to imagine it, her listeners were silent. When one, a gardener, suggested it must be like a cauliflower grows larger by reproducing itself in fractals, Storyteller applauded.

"Allured to the Infinite More, the stars gathered into galaxies. Birds, bees, elephants, humans with knees – all gather into flocks, hives, herds, families, and cultures.

Think of it. Everything, from stars to starfish, belongs. Together, each contributes to the Infinite More.

Take Sun. This spectacular god of burning gases appeared in a halo of argon, neon, titanium more than four and a half billion years ago. After half a billion years, it had surrounded itself with a system of planets including Jupiter, the oldest and largest, Earth, the youngest, and Mercury, the smallest. Together they became something greater than what was possible alone. Like a Grandfather giving his life's possessions to his grandchildren, every day Sun spends twenty billion tons of its life energy on its solar family, and will do so for billions of years to come. Think of the abundance, the generosity. Who could not be drawn to such a self-giving love?"

Her question caught them by surprise, they'd never thought of Sun as loving.

"From this love affair, I receive so many jewels of wisdom. The essence of being is energy. The state of being is belonging. The way of being is self-giving, contributing to the Infinite More. Bedecked in such gems, how could I not be attracted to such a purpose?"

Overwhelmed with gratitude, Grandmother took time to compose herself before going on.

For the Love of Earth

"We'd met in Sun's great round dance. She stood apart from the rest and was blossoming quickly into a unique being. A young planet, she would become a supreme beauty, a garden oasis in the desert of space. Earth!

She was born from a grand marriage – the union of a Supernova's galactic fragments and the pure potentiality of Universe. In the beginning, the young planet was a molten sphere, an electromagnetic kiln in the icy cosmos ever baking a new reality. Wrapped in a novel atmosphere, a shawl of cosmic winds and streaming rains to cool her biosphere, she was an exquisite sight. In the rolling contours of her crusty surface, roiling seas gathered. Her hydrosphere made her unlike any other planet in the galaxy. But it was not her beauty as much as her unique and infinite potential that captured my admiration."

Her listeners understood completely.

"Becoming, becoming, becoming." This was Earth's motto. When her heaviest elements fell, she gained an ocean floor. When her lightest elements rose, they gathered into land and continents. At every turn, she became a being of greater complexity. She was always becoming her next self. Her youth was shaped in the age of bombardments, asteroids, and stellar storms. From each chaos, she brought new order. Every destruction she used as a portal of emergence.

Once a planetoid, even larger than an asteroid, tore off a quarter of her body and flung it into space. Using gravity, she held that fragment that should have been lost forever close. Today her Moon, your source of light in the darkness, the mistress of ocean tides and seasons of growth is a shining example of her power to see the possibility in cataclysm. It would be from Moon's surface, four billion years later, Earthlings would first see their planetary home for the living, breathing, ever-becoming being she is.

How could I not love her and her emergent and resilient nature? So engaging was the burgeoning young Earth, I thought I would never take another lover. But that was before there was Life."

A sigh moved through her like a Chinook that comes suddenly through the mountains melting winter's snow to warm the cheek. After, she picked up the threads of her tale and began to weave one more chapter.

Loving Life

"Life was born in a gigantic petri dish of dancing chemicals – the first ocean. With a pioneer spirit on an evolutionary path and infinite potential for diversity, Life was exciting. Everyday was a dance with peril and a date with promise. She appeared for the first time nearly four billion years ago. Like an actor in a Shakespearean drama, she has been reappearing in a different guise ever since.

In the beginning, Life was a simple prokaryotic cell called *Aries.* Ignited by lightning, she was a dynamic concentration of energy. Fortunately, she was able to recall and repeat the very events that had brought it to life, and so she was prolific. Unfortunately and all too soon, there was both an excess of bacteria and a shortage of hydrogen with which to feed Earth's first population.

Emerging as a cell called *Promethio,* Life prospered through a process of photosynthesis. Born of genetic mutation, this agile cell was multi-talented. Fortunately she was able to capture Sun's photons by emerging with a Chlorophyll molecule that could turn photons into food, and store it for the future. Thanks to her powers of self-organization, she produced the oxygen that sustained Life for over two billion years. Unfortunately, the day came when Life, threatened by over oxidization, again was forced to re-organize itself and mutate.

Enter a cell called *Viking.* Fortunately, through a process of symbiosis, *Viking* could siphon vital energy from a cell called Engla at the same time as it was injecting and strengthening it with DNA. Together, they became Vikengla, another version of Life. Life thrived because of one law – the whole is always bigger than the sum of the partners. She was ... awesome!"

The story generated smiles all around. Most had never thought of Life as a Love story.

"Then the nucleated *eukaryotic* organism emerged on the scene." Grandmother's voice took on a tone of sheer excitement. "Its unique strategy of survival – respiration – was most alluring. After taking in its essential oxygen, the cell could emit any poisonous excess. Its offspring, *Kronos,* a predator cell, lived by ingesting other cells. Brilliant! Life was always finding ways to sustain herself. I was enthralled by her intelligence.

Sappho's way was to evolve through meiotic sexuality. With its two nuclei, each with its own set of chromosomes, this was the first cell to release ovum and sperm. And can you believe it, against all odds, even in the expanse of the ocean, ovum and sperm found mates and birthed Sapphos, Sapphinas, and Sappherellais.

To date, there are two hundred different types of cells in the thirty-seven trillion cells in your human bodies. Three hundred billion new cells are created each day, and two hundred million in the time it takes me to tell of it. It was this singularity of Life, ever in pursuit of more Life, that I loved so passionately.

Facing every threat with some form of adaptation – respiration, predation, death, differentiation, sexual regeneration – Life was always taking on another form. Eight hundred million years ago, the first multi-celled animal, a being of some ten thousand cells and a merger of countless strands of DNA, emerged. Using calcium and phosphorous to shape the first protective epidermis, Life became the Jellyfish! It was wonder-full!

After only six hundred million years, Crustaceans travelled the oceans. With jaws, backbones, fins, and eyes, Fish and Trilobite were better able to hunt, escape, court, and mate.

With this ever-emerging Life, every century was a surprise. She kept me interested," reported the Grandmother with a wink.

"Our time was full of firsts! A half billion years ago, when freshwater green Algae merged with oceanic Fungus, the first plants and insects on land appeared. They would transform the planet. When a lobe-finned fish with lungs and a warm body was able to hatch in the ocean but live on land, the first reptiles and amphibians emerged. Who wouldn't love a Five Lined Skink?"

When her excitement waned into a sombre silence, a voice in the crowd asked,

"Were there hard times too?"

"Ah, yes, the Permian Triassic mass extinction happened two hundred and fifty million years ago. One of the most deadly, yet, it opened the way for dinosaurs. From three feet tall to three tons, they ruled for the next hundred and seventy million years. Then, sixty-five million years ago, between the Cretaceous and Paleogene periods, when another mass extinction occurred, Life saw it as an opportunity to diversify. She brought forth vertebrates, bats, whales, rodents, cattle, and primates. Even the worst times, Life used to experiment. Imagine dragonflies with eight-foot wingspans, and millipedes eighteen inches long.

The best time, however, was just one hundred and fifty million years ago. Life grew in consciousness. When the first bird sang, she found her voice. When plants first flowered, she became colourful and fragrant. When mammals that reproduced from within could nurse their offspring externally, Life had learned to love herself. Always changing, I was never bored."

Clapping, as though applauding Life itself, she concluded, "It was a marvellous affair! I fell in love four times a day and with the turn of each season. With the buds of spring, the flame orange of summer's Oriole, autumn's umber death, and the lacy woods of icy winter. No two days were the same. I was enamoured of innovation. So, it was predictable, when Life's Human experiment came on the scene I would inevitably begin a love affair such as the world had never seen."

The Love of Human Consciousness

She leaned forward into her audience's deep yearning and continued. "Like any epic romance, my fourth great affair began in the folds of time. Earth's surface was shifting, continents drifting, passages were opening allowing the polar waters to escape. Great floes of ice sank to the ocean depths and travelled on the currents to warmer climes. Temperatures plummeted. Gaia was thrust into an Ice Age. Lush forests became dry savannas. Primates that were tree dwellers became ground hunters. Like a prelude in a great opera, it was an axial moment of preparation for the entrance of a unique and marvellous character.

With a larger brain and more-complex nervous system, Hominid looked on its environment reflectively. A rock became the means to a meal. Using what was at hand to survive, the creature became *Homo habilus.* Ever in pursuit of a friendly habitat, these beings with the power to reason, made their way from one bioregion to another. Conscious of their surroundings and with powers to adapt, the young species held my interest.

Millions of years later, *Homo erectus* took centre stage. Like the young child whose play is fashioning dreams into realities, furs became cloaks, hides became shelter. He captured and carried fire, flinted tips, carved weapons, bonded into bands to hunt. In community to prepare, preserve, and share food, she worked to live. Using powers of innovation, steering the course of civilization, evolving through the ages to an unprecedented level of self-consciousness and a vastly expanded range of emotions, the Human being was compelling.

Like no other, the Human sought intimacy with the land, its minerals, and plants. Conscious of beauty, he fashioned jewellery. Conscious of nature's songs, she fashioned instruments. Sensitive to the geography, he gathered into cultures, each with its own language, storytellers, educators, traders, hunters, midwives, and healers. I was completely smitten by this being's powers of differentiation and ever-changing psychological landscape.

It was, however, as Neanderthals and *Homo sapiens*, the Human was most able to return my love. Some descended deep into the Earth to connect with me. Others climbed to the highest mountains. They sang to me, thanked me with paintings on walls and papyrus. They struck laws and shaped religions in my name. It was all a reflection of their growing consciousness of my beneficent presence, and I loved them for their gestures and attention. But it was short-lived."

As when a cloud blows in over the hills turning a sky-blue day grey, the storyteller's mood changed.

"Coming into adolescence, Humans became self-absorbed. They experimented with ever-greater independence, took ever-greater risks. In the last fifteen thousand years, and especially in these last centuries, self-awareness expanded dramatically. Copernicus discovered that Sun didn't rotate round the Earth, but that Earth rotated round the Sun. Darwin discovered his species wasn't created in a day but evolved through time. Einstein declared evolution – of Universe, Earth, Life, and Human – is on-going. Through the ages, most recently the industrial, transportation, technology, and communication ages, my beloved Human came to understand the quantum nature of reality. She created an international study lab in space and wove a world-wide web of instant information. More and more, he questioned who and what I was. The more absolute about my nature she became, the further he withdrew from my love."

Her listeners, feeling her sadness, waited in silence. After some moments of remembrance, Grandmother went on.

"In the rosy sunset of the Cenozoic era, today I see the Human shadow. No longer searching for external validation, he has made decisions apart from the wisdom of Heaven or Earth. I see the atrocities she has waged against her own and other species. I see him hurrying yet a sixth mass extinction of life. But some see the errors of ways they once called advanced. Some spend their lives on the best of struggles. And I love them for their conscious evolution."

Her tone was proud. Her countenance hopeful.

"What I love most is the Human's capacity for becoming. In fact, many are becoming my co-creators. You have sought me out; come to hear my story because your hopes are more real than your fears. Awakening, you are recognizing yourselves as expressions of a loving Universe, as beings with the powers of life and death, as a species both vulnerable and vital. I am falling in love with you, with your infinite potential, yet again."

She spoke tenderly as she looked into the face and heart of each listener. "You've come because your world is in trouble for the lack of a good story. My story is your story. It is a love story. Some might say four love affairs are outrageous. But to do so is to miss the point: love is never afraid to relinquish what was and to embrace what can be. The affairs of love must always make room for infinite potential. Within you is the potential to fall in love with the probability of the possibility. Adapt, evolve, and become more than you are today."

Moving among them, becoming an urgency in their souls and a fire in their bellies, she spoke deeply to each one who had sought her out and come to hear her story.

"Fall in love again and again, and again and again dear ones, four times a day. With what your Human self's becoming, with Life's persistence, with the diversity of your Earth family, and with Source – your creative and intelligent Universal Self. With each and all of these, fall outrageously, extravagantly, erotically, and unabashedly in love. Then dear ones, knowing the story, you will know what to do. As the birds tell it in their language, and the trees tell it in theirs, go and tell it in yours."

Dedicated to the grandparents and grandchildren of this evolutionary moment

A Storyteller's Reflections

Coming to know myself as Grandmother Universe was the latest step in a dance of deep time connections. In the same decade that I discovered Earth as Mother and myself as a child of stars, I met my biological mother and the Scottish family I didn't know I had. I sent my DNA sample for testing and learned my genetic history was 51% Ashkenazi Jewish. A coincidence? I think not. It's a cosmic moment, a time of awakening. We are coming to know ourselves as multi-layered, multi-storied, mathematical beings. This story I tell trusting that when the grandchildren understand they are part of a love story, they will live into their place in cosmological history co-creating its next chapter in love.

Coming to know myself as Grandmother Universe was the latest step in a dance of deep time connections.

Grandmother's Power-Full Treasures

The Universe is permeated by cosmological powers that wove us into being and we are those powers in a new form ... coursing through us moment by moment. To become aware of these powers is to touch the source of Life. Brian Swimme

The one thing elders still long to do is pass on what they've learned. We believe it would make the next generation's life easier. I'd like to pass on Swimme's teaching of the cosmogenetic powers.

Learning of them, working through theory and art to identify them in my own life, I am as familiar with the ten cosmic powers as the four directions of creation. They've given me another layer by which to know myself, both as part of a cosmic story and the Earth story. Allurement, cataclysm, emergence, transformation, synergy, homeostasis, and the rest – the ways in which Universe moves and has its being are also and always at work in and through my life.

One of the gifts I find in knowing there are cosmic powers at work is objectivity. Consider the ongoing mass extinction. Absolutely, I view this and feel it to be a terrible tragedy. Cosmology teaches me this is a cataclysmic event, cataclysm being a destructive means by which to create something new. I take comfort in knowing cataclysm and emergence act as partners in the cosmos.

Knowing the cosmic powers has also been useful when I sit with climate deniers. Then I try to remember the power of homeostasis may be working through them. Homeostasis is that tendency in the cosmos to maintain internal stability in any system. It's been described as the impulse to protect the status quo and what it loves.

Yes, I'd like to pass on the knowledge and gifts of the cosmic powers. The reason being that in one instance they call me to take life less personally, and in the next they call me to be more compassionate. And so I offer this story.

The crackle of dry leaves meeting eager footfalls told her she was not alone. Her daily tryst interrupted, she rose from where she lay in the embrace of Grandfather White Pine's roots. Her greying eyes pierced the woodland shadows to find a man and a small child kicking at last Autumn's now brittle blanket. They were following the spiral path that led directly to her heart-place.

"I was hoping you'd come. And here you are," she called across the woods.

Her neighbour Mike's dark brows rose quizzically and disappeared under his tell-tale red cap with a moose on its brim. He nodded – his signature greeting. Noting three-year-old Mark's fascination with each unfolding Fiddlehead fern and yellow Dogtooth violet, the elder knew she'd ample time before they arrived. Closing her eyes, she returned to her daily conversation with the towering Conifer. They'd been meeting this way for a decade now. It started that misty morning she'd felt, as much as heard, those same words addressed to her, "I was hoping you'd come."

"You were hoping we'd come?" Mike's curiosity was piqued.

"Well, like most grandmothers, I have a story I'm longing to tell." She answered with a mysterious smile and indicated a place for them on the pungent forest floor. "It's a story full of treasures," she said with a tempting tone. "Treasures I've gathered over my long life."

"Treasures!" Young Mark's wide green eyes riveted on this curious woman whose friend was a tree. A smile crept around his father's often-sombre features.

"Just how long is that long life?" he teased.

"Long enough to know the difference between stuff and treasures," she parried. "Fourteen billion years long. But because of these times, it's time I tell it to you."

Folding his willowy body in two, Mike sank easily to the ground and pulled his youngest onto his lap. Usually a man of few words, unusually he had a lot to say.

"These are exceptional times. Oceans are warming, ice-caps are calving, due to extreme weathers, floods, fires, and droughts. Species are disappearing before my boy will ever know they existed."

Grandmother's eyebrows arched her surprise. Not at his words – everyone was talking about the unusual weather. That the climate concerns had become too heavy for the quiet woodcarver to carry alone – that was her surprise. It was her turn to nod. As though an unspoken agreement had passed between them, they sat in silence honouring the despair of parents and grandparents everywhere. Mother Earth had probably travelled one hundred thousand kilometres round the sun before she spoke again.

"There's never been such times. Not for your generation or your species. Parents will need to discover the treasure chest of powers they didn't know they had to navigate the coming centuries." Her visitor looked up from watching his son examine a pine cone. Joining in what he thought an old woman's game, his nod encouraged her to continue.

Her scarf, so bright it could have been cut from the burning stars, covered her hair and draped round her shoulders like a rabbi's prayer shawl. Eyes closed, head bowed, leaning into the yearning between them, she spoke in whispers, the language of mystery.

"The treasures I speak of are the vast powers of the Universe. They are as much in you as in the stars and planets. Powers of creativity, they hold the potential to turn fears into possibilities."

Mike realized the neighbour wasn't playing. Again, his nod invited her to go on.

"I'm talking about the creative strategies of existence. By the sheer fact we are beings of a creative Universe, they are deep within that pine cone, the molecules of this tree, the squirrel chattering above us, your beautiful child, even in your aging neighbour." She rested back against Grandfather Pine.

Mike, a potter, carver, and builder, believed in creativity.

"Universe is permeated by these creative cosmic powers," she continued. "They brought Universe into being and are coursing through you and me as we speak."

Freeing his wriggling child to follow his imagination, Mike asked the question of all millennials.

"What are my powers in a planetary disaster?"

"I like to think of them as the many faces of creativity," she replied. "Centration is the first. Both the cones he's stacking and Mark are centrations of energy. Everything we are, see and do is a centration of energy. Mark's energies are focused on …"

"Building a tree," the three-foot high sculptor had a big imagination.

"Like Sun's focus is being Sun, your focus is being a good parent." Mike felt understood. He visibly relaxed.

"What else are you concentrating on these days?" she asked him.

"I'm carving – charcuterie boards, spoons, spreading knives – when I'm not tending the garden. Being laid off, having a garden's essential. I enjoy growing things."

"It's by using our power of centration, we pursue our heart's desires." She leaned closer as though to share a secret. "Like an apple needs a peel, an egg needs a shell, and the planet needs its atmosphere, everything requires a membrane, a container within which energy can centre itself. Your intention, farming for example, is the membrane that concentrates your energies, tells you what to let in and what to omit from your life."

"I wouldn't mind checking out the Farmers' Association for information," he offered.

"That excitement in your voice," noted his forest muse, "tells me gardening is not only a deep longing in you, it's an allurement." Mike's puzzled face prompted an explanation. "Another creative power of Universe, allurement is what draws stars into galaxies, plants to reproduce, me to tell stories, you to market-gardening."

Just as suddenly as his allurement had surfaced, it withered into cynicism. "Nobody can spend his days carving spoons, growing pumpkins, and walking the woods with his son. Grow up, learn a trade, be responsible. That's the story I grew up with."

"There is another story," she spoke now in flannel tones. "When we accept that we have a part to play in the unfolding drama of life, we will draw our particular lifework into being." She paused to let the idea take root. "Could you imagine that being laid off was not only disastrous but an opportunity to concentrate on your dreams?" She took his silence as an invitation to continue. "Cataclysms happen! But what if I told you from a negative can come the positive?"

Jobless at the moment, the young father unleashed his fears. "The negativity, hatred, and violence – it's everywhere. I don't see much positive. Some say these are end times."

"These are worrisome times for a parent." She chose her next words with care. "As a Grandmother, I find comfort in the cosmic paradox: at the edge of cataclysm waits creativity. From disorder comes new order. End times are thresholds to never-before times. This is the cosmic story."

"Story!" Hearing one of his favourite words, Mark came running and jumped into the lap of his neighbour. With no better encouragement, the storyteller continued.

"Onec upon a time, sixty-five million years ago, Mother Earth was struck by a mean, monster meteorite. Airplane-sized dinosaurs, eight-foot-long dragonflies, tree-sized ferns, and some 70% of life disappeared. It was a great and terrible tragedy. And yet, suddenly there was the opportunity for the emergence of the very animals we love today ..."

"Lions, and tigers, and bears!" Mark, quoting last night's movie, was off again.

"Where is the treasure in global warming?" his father asked skeptically.

"If there is a treasure in this crisis," she began, "it will be that humans discover the power of inter-relatedness." As one, they looked up to find the red squirrel pelting them with pine cones. Then the elder asked a searching question.

"Do you believe in a caring Universe?"

"No!" Mike's reply came so swiftly and fiercely, so clearly from the depths of his being, it pierced her heart. Her compassion flowed forth in the form of a story.

"Once upon a time, in a land yellow by day and black by night ..."

"No, it's a land far away!" The child was in her lap again. She went on. "In a yellow land far away, where rocky cliffs pierce empty skies and dry thirsty riverbeds cut through cracked dusty valleys, there was sadness. The land was lonely, forests were injured, vegetation was scarce, and the deer, many, many deer, were hungry."

"Why?" the child demanded.

"There were no wolves. The great grandparents had killed them all. Now, some seventy years later, the land was overrun with moose, mule and white tail deer. Bring back the wolves, the children cried, and they did. As deer became fewer, grasses and trees like the Aspen, and Cottonwood flourished again. Birds returned to nest in their branches. Beaver came to prune the saplings, build homes, dam streams, and create ponds. Otter and muskrat, trout and toad, they came too to make their homes in the ponds. The coyote, rabbit, weasel, and mouse populations multiplied providing meals for fox and hawk, eagle and raven. Bear came back for now there were carcasses and berries aplenty. The dry and dying yellow land became green and was happy again thanks to ..."

"Wolves!" Intuitively, Mark knew the answer. Smiling, the storyteller went on.

"But even more wonderful, the forest roots reached down anchoring the banks of the river. No longer did rain fall only to splash and pool on the hard ground before it returned to the skies. Now the waters collected and swelled. Rivers flowed and were healthy. Wolves brought back the rivers and the once-yellow land lived a long, long time."

"Hurray!" Mark scrambled away to look for wolves as his dad wondered at the sheer elegance of this inter-related world. Storyteller, after resting against Pine and listening to Breeze's adventures for a time, spoke again.

"We grew up hearing how humans are caring, weather and forests are wild, how animals are to be feared. This story is too small. It doesn't tell how, over time, planet and cosmos take care of the future."

"Can you really use the word *caring* to talk about the Universe?" Mike asked. "Or is it just a word that sounds good in a story?" In a flash, the boy was back in her lap.

"Far, far away," Grandmother resumed, "there are stars – hundreds and thousands, millions and billions of stars. One by one, by thousands and hundreds of thousands, stars came together. Like families, galaxies hold stars from birth into old age. In the Milky Way Galaxy, stars spill their light across the vast darkness, expanding and stretching Universe."

"Like I stretched our family when I was born?" The boy stood on tiptoes and ran off.

"If Universe had expanded even one millionth of a percent slower, it would have imploded and recollapsed. If it had expanded even one millionth of a percent faster, Universe would have diffused into dust, unable to bring forth structures such as stars, galaxies, and planets. That we are part of a Universe that is expanding at just that rate essential for life to emerge points to synergy. Synergy, that power of cooperation for life, is deep in the heart of Universe."

A builder, Mike understood synergy. He knew wood had to be joined in such a way if a project was to last. He warmed to the possibility of a cooperative Universe. The woman, whose friend was a tree, continued.

"Synergy is at work all around us. See Fern. If it weren't for the bacteria attached to its roots, it wouldn't be able to access the nitrogen in the soil. Synergy is Fern's treasure. Even one cell of skin on a finger is living and supporting the survival of several trillion other cells. That kind of deep cooperation is built into the body of Earth, the human body, and the cosmos."

Mike's face said he wasn't ready to shed his cynicism. She went on.

"You want to know how, in a caring Universe, there can be so much violence in the world." Could his unusual neighbour read minds too? He wondered. "Conflict is neither the nature of the Universe or a sign of a deity's judgment. It's a sign that somewhere, somehow, something in the system is out of sync. And when something is out of sync, it's time for something new to emerge. Emergence is one of our story's greatest treasures." Like he'd heard his cue, Mark climbed into her lap yet again.

"When Earth was just a young planet, space was a dangerous place. Asteroids whizzed this way, planetoids that. Flying fragments from exploding stars collided here and stellar dust storms swirled there. A monstrous planetoid, bigger even than Mercury or Jupiter, became caught in the young planet's gravity and struck Earth a powerful blow."

"Wham!" Mark crashed one fist into another.

"A quarter of the planet was torn away and launched into space. A disaster, right? Not completely. That very same gravity caught hold of the hurling magma and held it close. In the cold of the cosmos, over three hundred-and-eighty-thousand kilometres away, the once-fiery fragment hardened into Moon. Now it is Earth's source of light in the darkness. Disaster or treasure?"

"Treasure!" The child thrilled to this story. The elder continued.

"In time, the atmosphere, four hundred and eighty kilometres thick, wrapped right round the planet like a scarf protects us from the cold. When winds brought clouds that poured rain onto the planet, the water puddled and swelled into oceans. When lightning bolts struck, the cells came to life. Earth is the result of emergence; emergence waits at the edge of every crisis."

Mike was smiling as Mark changed laps and settled in for a nap. He was enjoying this visit. He'd never heard of the powers of the Universe, not as a child in school, nor as an adult in university. He was soothed by his neighbour's tale spun from the latest science and her faith in a caring Universe. Leaning against a Poplar, a species that had rushed in to rejuvenate the land after a fire, he posed another question. His voice was quiet so not to disturb his child, or perhaps because the possibility was too awful to speak aloud.

"Do you think we'll destroy the world?"

"Some believe there's a new kind of human emerging in our time. Like other species, ours too is driven by self-preservation. I believe the crisis is driving our next evolution." It was a thought Mike had never entertained. She delved deeper. "Why wouldn't our species continue to evolve? The nature of nature is transformation. Why I recall a time," and she launched into a story from four billion years ago.

"Every day there were more bacteria until Mother Earth had so many bacteria she didn't know what to do. One day, she went to the cupboard and the cupboard was bare of hydrogen atoms. So, the cell rearranged itself to include a chlorophyll molecule. Now it could turn solar energy into carbohydrates. Using its power of transformation, Life evolved to include the process of photosynthesis. And that's how Earth survived its first environmental crisis."

"Are you suggesting humanity will survive overpopulation and global warming by evolving?" His voice was incredulous.

"We've done it before. Look at Buddha, Confucius, Mohammad, Jesus. They evolved beyond selfishness. Today Greta Thunberg and Vandana Shiva are examples of our ability to be selfless and self-confident enough to call for Eco-socio-economic systems going forward. Millions are part of a grassroots global communication net for ecojustice. Some nations are banning plastics. Artificial Intelligence technologies use algorithms to monitor endangered species and land-use patterns.[xviii] We are becoming a new kind of human being. There have been more than twenty species of humans, to date. Why not another one?"

Mike was captivated as Grandmother continued to spin her story.

"Unlike the caterpillar's journey from larva to cocoon to butterfly, the human will have …"

"Will she have wings?" Mark had returned from dreamland where all things are possible. Grandmother Universe went on.

"Our next evolution will not be physical. The new human will have higher consciousness."

Mike spoke quietly to his son. "No wings." Then thinking of his brother Ben married to Peter, a neighbour Dave who'd become Deana, and Jody Wilson-Raybould, the Indigenous woman who'd been named Minister of Justice and Attorney General of Canada, he added, "But they will have more love than ever before, Buddy Boy." The Father's hopes for his dreamy boy were palpable.

"Do you feel the powers of creativity more keenly these days?"

Mike thought how being laid off, he'd had time to read about permaculture, and envision bigger gardens. But, thinking he should be out working, he hadn't done as much as he wanted.

"Follow the energy! Whatever you feel passionate about or feels urgent," Grandmother went on, "can be an allurement no matter how impractical. If it feels like you're trying to get the planet to spin the other way, it's probably not a genuine allurement. How was it you chose to visit this morning?"

"Mark said he wanted to see Grandmother Universe," he skirted the question. Hearing his name, the boy wakened asking if it was lunch time. His spirits lifted, Mike turned to leave. His hungry boy, far along the spiral path already, was calling.

"Look at me. I'm a tree! Look at me!" The child held branches on either side of his body.

"There's a child awakened to his radiance," the storyteller remarked.

"A Peony blossoms pink and sweet! A Dolphin leaps up and beyond its watery world! I throw new cones! A child calls, look at me!" Grandfather Pine chimed in. "Seems to me the sheer delight at being star stuff has to burst forth at some point."

"May that dear child never lose touch with his starry imagination," she replied.

"And may fathers rediscover theirs," added her friend-who-was-Tree.

Nestling again into Pine's welcoming roots, Grandmother found her way back to the magical world of hopes and dreams where children with branches for arms, and adults with light streaming from fingers dance in a forest of power-full treasures.

Dedicated to parents everywhere.

This story was based on a real conversation. Written for all parents who worry at the uncertain future, may it remind them of their evolutionary legacy, the Cosmic Powers. May they find their own with which to create a new world order.

After the stories.

Claiming my identity as Grandmother Universe changed me. I no longer think first of myself as Canadian or Christian. In the midst of conflicted climate conversations, I think of myself as part of an awakening species. While many despair at humanity's carelessness toward the planet, I trust we are evolving. You might think me too optimistic when I say the evolutionary story gives me hope. Or too positive for claiming the cosmic powers as treasures to discover, embrace, and use to take up our response-abilities in the challenges ahead. But like schools teach citizenship, and Sunday Schools teach the Ten Commandments, I believe cosmology, by teaching the powers of the Universe, can help us realize we are Universe in human form, participants in the future.

Having come to know myself as Grandmother Universe, I find I am more hopeful in these dark times than many of my friends and family. What's the difference? Awareness. Aware of my self as an expression of Gaia, conscious of the Big Bang as more than a sitcom, as my origin; these ideas help me feel part of, rather than victim to, the changes happening at this time. Believing evolution is neither a theory nor a threat to faith, I'm free to talk to trees, to feel held by the land, and called by the fullness of the Moon. Oneness is not some existential concept; it's what I experience in the lake; it's both the quantum reality of my body with the larger planetary-body; and it's the sacred singularity of all that is. Accepting my story to be billions of years long is humbling. As a manifestation of the Universe and a grandmother within it, I am a new kind of human.

As a Cosmic Story Storyteller, the story has changed me. It has taught me I am both smaller and more significant than I can imagine. It has shown me to be but a single step in a dance of countless steps that precede and will continue after me.

Like all grandmothers, I know the story I have to tell holds wisdom. I want to tell it to the next generation for so many reasons. That they might not repeat our mistakes. That they might recognize themselves part of a family older than they can conceive. As it is with grandmothers, I am ready to tell my story whenever the listener is ready.

But here is an interesting part of being the story's teller. I am not skilled in the art of storytelling. I am not brave to be its voice. I am not trained to be its dancer. It is the story that is doing the telling, the dance that is dancing, and the music of the spheres that is vibrating. The story has told me, we are not just humans having an environmental crisis. We are the human family having an evolution of consciousness.

Evolutionary Wisdom

- The stories we believe are the stories we live.
- Owning our 'evolutionary storyteller,' we become evolutionary elders.
- Stories evolve.

CHAPTER 5

Emergence

Out beyond ideas of wrong doing and right doing, there is a field. I'll meet you there. Rumi

Out of the pulpit and into the woods – I hadn't seen that coming. Like the caterpillar can't foresee the cocoon, I had never imagined I would someday move out of the Christian circle of faith. But why didn't I see it coming? Jesus' story teaches only by dying can we return to Source and become the fullness of what we are. Evolution, it seems, was not only inevitable, it's part of faith.

If choreographed as a ballet, these last two decades I've described in these chapters would have to be titled, "Emergence." A natural process in the evolutionary story, emergence means leaving one stage and form of being to enter another. But no butterfly ever said shedding one's cocoon was simple. Moving away from a two-thousand-year-old culture, freeing myself from the very patriarchal structures where I'd had a sense of belonging, identity, and vocation – it was a sticky, wriggly, and emotional struggle.

There was, however, a gift in the struggle. I had all the teachers I needed. Green Nuns and mystical priests, Eastern

Buddhists and Indigenous Shamans, Scientists, Information Technologists, and futurists – they showed me the spiritual work of every time is growing beyond its separating stories. They taught me the work in this time is moving beyond wild-Western consumerism, paralyzing petro-economics, an anthropocentric story, and a Heaven-bound religion. They demonstrated that the moment for stepping into a field of expanded consciousness is this one.

There's never been a moment like this one. Global warming is a reality looming larger ahead of us than behind us; there's no escape. All that remains is the challenge to be human in a new way. Like pioneers with all the fears and excitement of living in unmapped territory, we're stuttering to speak a language we've yet to create. Aware we can't make the same mistakes about God and creation that caused the Anthropocene age, we're critical, even rejecting, of religion. We're hopeful for but can't really imagine the Ecozoic age ahead. Threatened by hardships we cannot know, some are beginning to recognize we're more vulnerable and more creative than we knew. All in all, consciousness is expanding. Unlike the undeniable instinct of a caterpillar, we can cooperate with the emergence of a new kind of humanity or not. It's a defining moment.

Becoming conscious of Consciousness, learning of the evolution of consciousness, realizing we can consciously cooperate in the evolution of consciousness – so much has changed for me since leaving the pulpit. I no longer think about God in a static way as a creator made in man's image. These days I refer to that sacred other with brand-new terms. The Universal Intelligence that governs all that is by the laws of differentiation, autopoeisis, and communion. The Evolutionary Impulse that builds and sustain the cosmos with the powers of centration, allurement, cataclysm, emergence, synergy, homeostasis, and transformation. Consciousness, the driving force that has manifested in plant, animal, and today is becoming conscious of itself in the human. But my very favourite understanding of that ever-expansive energy described as divinity is Evolutionary Dancer.

Becoming more, that is the choice before me, before all of us. Choosing to seek ever-greater consciousness, to become more fully who we are, to say yes to all we can be – this is a way to move beyond despair and into hope-full action. When news of poor choices for the planet deplete me, I remember so many whom we've met and hosted. What they taught me was to live on the trajectory of more consciousness.

The Green Party's Elizabeth May – apart from all she has done to raise consciousness in Canada, helped write this line into the global Earth Charter: "This is a time of peril and promise." Caroline McDade put the Earth Charter to music and sent it into the world as a CD. Rebekah Hart from Montreal came to teach Joanna Macy's practices, The Work That Reconnects. Becoming more – more conscious, more inter-connected, more active for change, more evolved – this is the choice that turns hopelessness into creativity. When Barbara Marx Hubbard invited a young woman from the Occupy Toronto sit-in to speak to our conference on Conscious Evolution, she showed us conscious evolution happening in our city.

The environmental crisis is an opportunity to consciously choose personal and social evolution. That is what the evolutionary dance invites, become more.

At the end of these chapters and following on my dance outside the church, I'm optimistic. I've learned that now is the time to use technology's powers for the common good; now is the time to govern, manufacture, and cultivate with as much compassion for nature as we have for humanity. I've met outrageous mystics who fall in love four times a day – with Cosmos, Earth, Life, and Humanity. I've danced with elders, adults, youth, and children who are pelting the future with possibilities. I'm hopeful the cataclysm that is climate change will be followed by the emergence of something more. I believe love is the ultimate nature of the Universe.

Once I thought I'd never step out of the circle of the church. Then I thought I'd never step back in. Little did I imagine the path of one-Universe consciousness always spirals back upon itself.

PART 2

In

Out of the Woods and Back IN the Church
Evolutionary Stories for Climate-Conscious Pewsters

CHAPTER 6

Back IN the Stable

A person works in a stable. That person has a breakthrough. What does he do? He returns to work in the stable. Meister Eckhart

In the beginning, I ignored the invitation like a bathing suit two sizes too small. Would I provide occasional leadership at a nearby church? I scratched the dates and contact information in my daytimer and tried not to think about it. But thoughts kept popping up.

I didn't really fit the mold for Christian clergy anymore. How could I just pick up like nothing had changed? I had changed. How could I return and still be authentic? It was true, I no longer believed what the church expected me to believe. I could no longer say what the tradition expected me to say. Yet I longed to say with integrity what I believed. Doesn't everyone dream of the day they can get back into that swimsuit?

Allurement, one of the ways Universe creates more future, is hard to ignore. Even in the midst of Gaia Centre's work, there'd been times I'd thought about returning to the miracle and muck of congregational ministry. I'd missed the rituals, studying the wisdom teachings, applying them to current issues, sharing them with others. I'd missed the community life.

Alluring too was the audacious congregation extending the invitation. A close-knit group of elders, they'd refused to close when told they were too small to be viable and imagined a unique way forward – a roster of Sunday-leaders. Like those early cells of life that avoided extinction by evolution, they were resilient. They were intriguing.

Beside these allurements, there was the wisdom of my teachers. "What does the stable hand do after she's had a breakthrough? She returns to the stable." When I'd first heard Matthew Fox speak these words, I'd cringed and quickly filed the mystic's truth in the back corner of my consciousness. When Miriam MacGillis counselled, we must take the New Story back to our tradition, I heard her message – with consciousness comes responsibility. Certainly Barbara Marx Hubbard, author of *The Revelation,* an interpretation of Christian scriptures through the filter of the evolutionary story, had taken it as her duty to teach the New Story to Christian religious. Despite my hesitation to return to ministry, the teachings and allurements were pulling me in another direction.

Then, one morning I wakened from a dream with a clear vision for a four-Sunday series titled, *Consciously Becoming.* The intent – bring the stories of evolution and Jesus together. They'd be like partners in a tango, each one subjugating to the other's distinct curves and thrusts, but never humiliating the other.

I wrote up a proposal. In it I even listed the titles of the four reflections: Becoming More Human, I Spy With My Evolutionary Eye, Evolutionary Elders for Adventurous Churches, and last, Christ the Universal Human. I sent it to the congregation and waited their response. They accepted.

With a mix of anxiety and anticipation, I approached the church door once again. Bringing my newfound treasures – the Medieval Mystics, Earth-literacy, Creation Spirituality, New

Cosmology, and Conscious Evolution theory – I hoped I'd be welcomed. And I was.

One might say my coming to Kinmount United Church was a destined *pas de deux.* They were the Little Church That Would go forward. I was the clergy who would not go back. It was a dance of synergy. My focus was no longer the typical Sunday fare – how to be a better disciple or more active member. The challenge was how to become the next human species. My sacred creation story was not only from Genesis but cosmological science. My mission – never about the salvation of souls – was Cosmos-consciousness and a whole-Earth spirituality. My blessing was the congregation itself. Having chosen life, not closure, they were open to innovation.

This is how our metamorphosis began. As tradition had it, the clergy descends from their elevated pulpit to sit, tell a story, and talk to the children. But there were no children. I was telling children's stories to elders. The telling turned to my listening to their spirit-full life-experiences. I proposed an evolution in the weekly order – replace a heady doctrinal sermon with reflections to spark congregational conversations. When it was approved, I moved down from the chancel, they unscrewed some pews from the old floorboards, and we gathered in a circle of mutual inspiration.

We were discovering a new model for being church. Without a contract, they were free to ask me back – or not – and I was free to accept – or not. I didn't become a stakeholder and they didn't become corporate controllers or a captive audience. What we did become was an experiment in Evolutionary Christianity.

Those four Sundays stretched into many over many years. It is from those rich and deep meetings come the next chapters. Each one is a gentle waltz between the evolutionary and Christian stories through the seasons of Advent, Christmas, Epiphany, Lent, and Easter.

Going forward, some words may need clarification.

Universe is a word which can be confusing. Too large for us to experience or even imagine, it has been the domain of a few specialized professions. Up until now, we've understood ourselves to belong to our family, nation, religion, or political party. But now, science is inviting us to know ourselves, and everything else, as manifestations of and belonging to the Universe with a capital 'U.'

Pewsters is a new word. Because not everyone in the pew identifies as Christian today, nor should they have to, I suggest we need an additional word. Like jurors sit in the jury box to hear evidence and pass judgment on a person's innocence or guilt, pewsters, I suggest, sit in pews to listen to interpretations of wisdom texts and reflect on whether they make relevant and compassionate connections to the social and environmental reality of the whole-Earth community.

For other unfamiliar terms that help express the genre of Evolutionary Spirituality, see the Glossary at the back of the book.

So here we are, about to step through the simple wooden door of that little heritage church on the hill. No glass or fancy carving, stained brown, one might think they're entering a pioneer village building. But having pushed past my doubts and fears to get here, let me assure you the very opposite is true. This was the door to the future church. So whether you're from in, out, or on the fringe of Christianity, welcome to the stable door.

Evolutionary Wisdom

- We don't have to fit.
- Dreams are messages from Consciousness.

... whether you're from in, out, or on the fringe of Christianity, welcome to the stable door.

CHAPTER 7

The Advent'ure

Deep in the hidden process of our metamorphosis, we can see a natural design – an evolutionary pattern – traditionally called God – to guide us toward the next stage of transformation. Our Conscious Evolution is a way to learn how to cooperate with these processes toward chosen and positive futures. Barbara Marx Hubbard

Opening the Door

Turning the knob and pushing open the rustic wooden door, I was pumped. This wasn't a step into the past. The twenty-some elders that made up the congregation were open to more than the standard fare. They'd accepted my proposal for a series on faith and the evolution of consciousness. This was the beginning of an adventure. I moved from the cloakroom through the swinging door into the dimness of a still-empty, lovingly-tended sanctuary. I was back.

It was the first Sunday of Advent. For Christians, that's New Year's Day without the hats and horns. From *adventus* meaning coming, Advent is a spiritual season observed over the month of Sundays before Christmas day. For some, it's about preparing for Jesus' second coming in glory to judge the living and the dead. For others, it's a time of anticipating his birthday celebration, and for still others, it's a time to focus on becoming one's Christ-like self. And for everyone, it's when we find chocolate in the calendar.

Enter any sanctuary in Advent and chances are you'll find mitten trees and food baskets waiting to be filled. Whether it's to honour that Jesus identified with the poor or emulate his life of self-giving, it's a time of heightened social awareness. What's not acknowledged, however, is the impoverishment of the planet. My hope was to broaden and shift the focus from social justice to ecojustice. After all, what good does it do to teach a woman to fish if the waters are contaminated?

Attitudes towards climate change among the Kinmount pewsters were probably like those everywhere at the time. Some believed there's lots of time to change. Some saw it as part of the natural environmental cycles. Some felt powerless to make a difference. Others were happy to leave the matter to the saving power of God, industry, or technology – whichever came up with a solution first. And for one or two the environment, like politics, wasn't an appropriate topic for Sunday.

The challenge, as I saw it, was to find a relationship between the Bible's call to love and live in Jesus' ways, and the demands of creation to live sustainably within the planet's means. The solution, as always, lay in the power of stories.

Two kinds of stories were needed. Stories that were known and traditional, as well as the unfamiliar and evolutionary. Both became part of each gathering. We let go the practice of reading from Jewish Scriptures, Psalms, Gospels, and the Epistles – an intellectually exhausting experience – and came up with one stream-lined for the reality of our times. One traditional plus one evolutionary, that added up to enough to guide our thought-stretching, heart-opening conversations through Advent.

The Traditional – The Bridesmaids' Tale

This is a text often read at Advent for it's emphasis on anticipation and preparation. Here is a paraphrased version of the story.

> According to custom, the bridesmaids awaited the bridegroom's arrival. After many hours of waiting, however, the bridesmaids fell asleep. Finally at midnight, they were wakened to shouts of joy announcing the groom's much-delayed appearance. Five of the bridesmaids had prepared for just such a situation. They'd filled their lamps with oil. Lighting the lamps, they escorted the groom into the banquet hall. Five, unfortunately, had come unprepared without oil in their lamps. Having left to fetch fuel, they returned to find the doors to the wedding party had already been shut. (Matthew 25:1-13)

Seemingly a harsh parable of preparation or punishment, some historical background may be helpful. It was written in the first-century, in a corner of Judaism called the Matthean community. The parable posits the temple leaders, who had rejected Jesus as the Messiah and bridegroom, as the unprepared bridesmaids. The faithful bridesmaids, of course, were understood as Matthew and the Jesus-followers.

But what if the teaching story is read within the context of the global warming crisis? What if it's read in a way to shift the church's focus from personal salvation to planetary sustainability? Then the parable might sound something like this.

The Evolutionary Bridesmaids' Tale

> The window of opportunity is closing. It is the midnight hour. Time to usher in a new way of being. Be prepared. Do not deny global warming. Be awake. Awake to the sacred in the air we breath, the oceans we sail, and the soil

we plant. In good consciousness, the time to welcome the coming Ecozoic Era is now before it is too late.

Retelling and interpreting the church's teachings in a way to inspire action in our own times – this is part of an evolutionary and relevant Christianity. When the tradition frees itself from the focus on saving souls and securing their entry to a heavenly eternity, then will it see Christ crucified in the dying coral. Then will it hear Christ's call to care for the ill in the voices of climate scientists. Then Christianity will have awakened to serve the new age.

To live out this parable in our time, however, the church must have fuel in its lamps. I am talking about the wisdom of modern science. And from the new science, it must tell twenty-first century parables, teaching stories grounded in the sacred ways of cosmology. In these times, one story is not enough. Another Advent and another story is in order.

The Evolutionary – Becoming Advent'us

"I will become ... I will become ... I am becoming ..." But not having any idea what it might actually become, all Creativity could imagine was, "I will become more!" And so it was Creativity, on fire with potential and longing, danced, reached, stretched, and expanded ever more. Flames became gas. Particles of matter became quarks, neutrons, protons, hydrogen, carbon, and more.

Even when Creativity became Universe, it was becoming more Universe. So it went for billions of years until one day, four-and-a-half billion years ago, on a Wednesday I think it was, on a planet not too big and not too small, Creativity became Bacteria.

Bacteria was Creativity on steroids. Always adapting, morphing, and evolving, it was ever becoming more than it was the day before. So it went for eons and eras in the depths of an ocean that was neither too hot nor too cold. A single-celled amoeba one moment, an Octopus with eight arms that could reach twenty feet the next.

Creativity, you see, was adventurous. One day only a few million years ago, on the continent shaped like a giant ice cream cone, life that had become fish, reptile, dragonfly, tiger and chimpanzee became something more. Homo-genus Advent'us – hunter of food, carrier of fire, tool maker, thinker – the one who is always becoming something more. And so it was Advent'us learned to cook and dreamed of the day it would have its own TV cooking show.

Bo led in a round of applause. Yes, this was a church that unabashedly clapped to express gratitude, awe, and delight – signs of divine encounters according to Creation Spirituality.

Not surprising, Paul and Desmond, the retired clerics jump-started the conversation noting the differences between the two stories.

"In the Bridesmaids tale, humanity awaits some superhuman God to intervene. It's a monotheistic story – God and the Universe are two different realities."

"The modern myth's based on pantheism – a philosophy which treats the Cosmos as synonymous with God. Creativity is another word for the divine. The divine is creative energy, not separate from but ever becoming something more in and around us."

"There's no closed door!" Beaumont or Bo, as he's called, spoke thoughtfully. Bo liked the new story. The parable, however, ended with some shut out of the kingdom and a sense of doom. He liked to think God's not finished with us yet.

The conversation introduced the principle of cosmogenesis – nature is ever-evolving, ever-beginning, and always becoming the next new thing. The evolutionary story doesn't close the door on potential. It doesn't mean there aren't planetary limits to global warming. It means there's no limit to the Creativity in the Universe and it's ability to turn crisis into emergence.

As we rose to go out into the December chill, we carried some new thoughts. Advent meant something new. The divine energy is becoming more conscious in and through us. We're becoming more able to live equal to our Christ-potential. In that everything exists in a state of ever-becoming, Advent is not a prescribed month of Sundays; all time is an Advent'ure.

Saying our goodbyes, reactions to this evolutionary treatment of the texts were mixed. Sheila, a former nurse, embraced me in one of her famous hugs. She was excited by this new way of thinking. John leaned in to whisper how he would always believe in Jesus as Saviour. So graciously, the retired engineer and successful inventor told me not everyone was comfortable with the marriage of tradition and cosmology. Driving away, I was content. New ideas had led us to revisit our beliefs. It seemed appropriate to be doing this work in this land the first peoples had named the Kawarthas – the land of reflections.

Becoming All We Can Be

It was another Sunday in the season of Advent. This week's story, the legend of Mary, was both familiar and a favourite. In a nutshell, it goes something like this.

The Traditional – Becoming Magnificent

> Neither Jerusalem's great priests or powerful politicians had stood up to Caesar. The harvests of fishermen and farmers alike had been appropriated to feed the foreign legions. Taxes from Jerusalem's widows and sick swelled Rome's coffers. The tribe's mood was dark.
>
> It was into such darkness an angel came to Nazareth, the most insignificant of towns. More surprising, it came to a girl-child, the most inconsequential of beings. The girl's name was Mary, a variation of Miriam, meaning

bitter for they were bitter times. The angel's message was also surprising. "You will bear God's messiah, a saviour to your people."

She would bear the messiah! Good news for the nation. For Mary, not so much. She was betrothed to Joseph. She could be stoned for breaking the marriage contract. "How can this be?" she asked. No kidding. It's a question the world, missing the point, has been asking ever since.

The point being she, least of the least, lowest of the low, gave birth to a child of God. As the Wisdom book says, the sun shines on rich and poor, good and bad alike.

To sum up, Mary became Mother Mary and took her place alongside all the she'ros who'd ever sung the wondrous song, the Magnificat.

"Blessed am I, for I have served God's work. I will not be seen by history as cursed but blessed. Through me God's promise has come true. He will deliver us from evil, defeat the powerful, empower the powerless, feed the hungry and sick, dismiss the greedy and rich. He will rule with mercy which shall run like the waters – forever." (paraphrase of Luke 1:46-55)

Despite what we learned in Sunday School, the story is not about the mystery of one girl's impregnation, or a distant deity's power to save. It's about the fecund and regenerative nature of all life. It's about the nature of the cosmos; how out of crisis, Creativity brings new life. Her song was to Israel what O Canada is to Canadians – a national anthem, a profession of belief in a higher power, a vision of a just and merciful society. Told to heighten consciousness and inspire greater democracy – it was a good story in its day and has inspired countless numbers since.

But could we tell it in language that speaks directly to our own dark times?

The Evolutionary – Manifesting Magnificence

As the coffers of conquering manufacturing corporations and fossil fuel industries swelled to overflowing, the land receded, seas sickened, and Earth's vitality plummeted. In only fifty years, Earth's temperatures had risen and her condition had become chronic. Adventus, a mere child as species go, was frightened; life, as they knew it, was threatened.

Into this darkness came a wizard. His magic lay in tales woven from science, cosmology, and hope. He came to the maiden species, Adventus.

"Fear not, for you Adventus are blessed in all the Universe. You will waken to your creative power and co-create a new age."

Blinded by their dependency on an ever-increasing gross national product and fear of economic recession, Adventus questioned the wizard.

How can this be?"

The wizard raised his arm and a sea of salt poured from his fingers onto the ground forming a great and giant spiral of salt.

"Blessed are you to be part of the Milky Way Galaxy.

One hundred thousand light years across, that's a major road trip of almost one and a half billion billion kilometres, your galaxy home is beyond comprehension. Made up of some three hundred billion stars,[xix] you are like grains of sand in the sea. Blessed are you by the gift of immensity."

Bound to the ways of individualism, Adventus felt insignificant and powerless.

Drawing a finger about halfway out from the centre of the salt spiral, the wizard continued.

"Sun's place is here. Just the right distance out from the centre of the Milky Way. Any closer and it would suffer the violent waves of X-rays and gamma rays. Any farther away, it would be at risk of colliding with shooting stars, orbiting asteroids and comets. Blessed are you with the gift of place."

But the species Adventus had forgotten their dependence on bioregions; they were strangers to place.

"Earth's place is a Goldilocks place. At just the right distance from the Sun, its temperature allows water to dance from liquid to solid to gas. Carbon is catalyzed and life is sustained. Any further away or closer to the Sun and Earth would be at risk. Blessed are you with the gift of place."

When wizard tried to pick up a single grain of salt, he failed.

"The Milky Way galaxy travels beside the Andromeda galaxy and within the Virgo Supercluster of galaxies. Nothing exists alone. Everything is held in a compassionate curve of gravitational attraction. Blessed are you with the gift of communion."

Myopic, Adventus could not see the bigger picture. Impatient, the young species could not understand its purpose, what it should do.

"You are not alone but part of the Sun's solar family. Travelling around the centre of the galaxy about three hundred and twenty two million kilometres per second – and it still takes about two hundred and twenty-five million years for one revolution – you cannot rush or slow time. Just a few million years old, you are becoming what you can be. Blessed are you with the gift of time. If the Evolutionary Impulse has been working for almost fourteen billion years to bring you forth, be assured, you are pregnant with purpose. Blessed are you with the gifts of time and place."

At this, Adventus was full of song.

"Blessed am I, for I am the vessel of the Evolutionary Impulse, a manifestation of magnificence. I am not cursed; generations to come will bless me. I say, Yes! Yes to my part in a holy, holy, holy planetary and cosmic community."

Dedicated to Larry Edwards, Professor of New Cosmology.

Sheila's smile told me she'd seen the parallel between Mary's story and a humanity pregnant with potential. Wendy, so overwhelmed by the immensity of the cosmic reality, whispered of how small, insignificant, and humbled she felt. I was grateful to be able to say how humility is the teaching of both the biblical and evolutionary stories. Be it individuals, congregations, or species, everything is a whole part as well as part of a larger whole.

Two great books had shaped our Advent conversation. *Quantum Theology* by priest and scientist Diarmuid O'Murchu and Luke's gospel in the Bible. In his story, Mary's anticipation of giving birth teaches us none are too insignificant to contribute to a better future. It's a truth echoed by modern science: "all are holons within larger holons dancing between dependence and independence ... each must transcend simple self-rule and integrate ... itself with the holonomy imposed by the larger life form, Planet Earth."[xx] In short, we prepare to give birth to our best, most Christ-like selves by accepting we are not too small to affect the whole; we are the whole. Our environmental crisis is a challenge to church and society to discover our place in the planetary community; to say yes to the evolutionary process, and to become all we can be.

Becoming Greater

Ultimately, what do we think is the essential purpose of Christianity? The question was one philosophers, atheists, and teenagers had asked for centuries. To the third Advent conversation I'd again brought two stories. This morning, I elected to begin with the older one from the epic of evolution.

The Evolutionary – Ever-greater Than Before

A long time ago in a land far away .... more precisely, four and a half million years ago in the Afar Depression of Ethiopia, there was an animal, *Ardipithecus,* by name. Ardi, meaning ground or root, and pithecus, meaning ape, was the beginning of a new human being.

Ardi had a big toe for grasping branches and travelling the treetops, small canine-like teeth for a fast-food fruit here or a bite of foliage there. It was a good life and Ardi was happy.

Then the weather changed, drastically. Food became scarce. Ardi's survival instinct said, adapt. As his teeth became larger and stronger, Ardi became something newer and greater.

Meet *Ardipithecus ramidus*, Ardi R for short. Unfortunately, her brain, being a fifth the size of your brain, wouldn't have caught the joke. But Ardi R was just right for her time – four million years ago. And just right for her place in the forest of Kenya at Allia Bay along the Omo River where life was sustainable.

Then the weather changed, drastically. Ardi R was challenged by drought and hunger. She too evolved to survive.

Hello, *Australopithecus anamnesis* or Ardi A. Being less of a swinger, Ardi A was more of a walker. She needed stronger hind legs to hunt on the wide-open savannas, and a more robust lower jaw to eat what she caught. To meet her, you'd think her part-chimpanzee, part-human. She, however, didn't think herself part of or preparation for anything else at all.

Enter *Australopithecus afarensis.* She emerged already becoming *Australopithecus africanus*, who emerged becoming *Australopithecus robustus,* who, a million years ago, became *Australopithecus boisei*, who prepared the way for *Homo erectus*, who was but a step behind – da, da – *Homo sapiens.*

This species evolved just three hundred thousand years ago. And there have been some great ones – Abraham, Sarah, Moses, Miriam, Mary, Jesus, the Buddha, Gandhi, Rachel Carson, Vandana Shiva, David Suzuki, Maude Barlow, Barbara Marx Hubbard, Matthew Fox, you, and me, to name a few.

Now the weather is changing drastically again. The sixth great extinction is happening. To survive, the-animal-that-once-became human is becoming its future self. And again, it will do even greater things.

The story's end signaled the conversation's beginning.

Matt had been through his share of wars, economic depressions, and hurricanes in his four score and more years. A serious reader, he was familiar with the idea of crisis as that which drives change. He cited some examples. Penicillin was invented after the first world war. The polio vaccine was found to prevent polio. Evolution, he imagined, is coded within us. But, he wasn't sure how the story addressed the question, 'what's the purpose of Christianity?'

It was the perfect lead-in to my second story. From the first century, it had been written by an evangelist we know only as John.

The Traditional – Greater Than Before

"Have you lost faith in the future?" John challenged his ragtag circle of rejects. No longer part of the synagogue, the once-bright hopes of Phil, Tom, and the rest of the so-called Jesus-followers had faded like morning dew in the noon-day Sun. They had indeed lost their faith. John challenged them to stay the course.

"Live the life, the truths, and the ways of the rabbi Jesus: inclusivity, equality, love. Remember his promise: you'll do even greater things than he'd done. Have faith, God's presence was within and among them."

But Thomas had doubts. Philip wanted proof. John was incredulous.

"You still don't see that the divinity in him is in us too?"(paraphrase, John 14)

The circle had great empathy for Tom and Phil. Like them, living in the shadow of the valley that is global warming, many had lost faith in the future. Like them, they too found it hard to believe the promise: you will do even greater things.

The challenge to be and do ever greater things than our ancestors is ageless. In the twelfth century, Meister Eckhart wrote to foster faith in the human experiment. "God is in all things. Every single creature is full of God."[xxi] It's an empowering belief.

In the twentieth century, Theilhard de Chardin wrote of the Christ as the omega point that humanity was evolving toward. To believe this is to believe the human-to-come will have a greater capacity to love the whole as much as she loves herself.

Living mystic, Matthew Fox writes of the isness within. He called it the Cosmic Christ that's not yet fully born. When we understand Christ as a "principle of cohesion in the universe," a pattern evident in the Jesus story but not limited to him, [xxii] then we'll be able to accept, as beings that are part of an evolving whole, we're ever-becoming able to do greater things.

Both of the morning's stories invited trust. Trust in the comic pattern of cohesion, trust that chaos drives evolution, trust that the Universe is filled with the holy pursuit of greater beings.

Rosemary shared how, after having to forsake university for an unplanned teenage pregnancy, she became a mother, activist, and clinical counsellor. She did greater things than she'd ever imagined. Sheila spoke as a mother whose daughter took her own life and whose granddaughter turned her life around. Faith in greater things she knew to be what gets us through hard times. Virginia marvelled how young folk had come together across international borders to demand endangered oceans and the rights of water be put on political agendas.

It was an inspiring conversation. But what, I nudged them, did they believe to be the essence or purpose of Christianity in all this?

Joyce was smiling, sure sign of a new idea bubbling up.

Jesus called followers to do greater things. We can assume he was referring to the pursuit of a just, social society. The work of the church is to call humanity to become its better self.

It was my insight too. Christianity's purpose is as one of evolution's vessels of Consciousness.

The harder question may be, if the church isn't aiding the next phase of our transition from Homo sapiens sapiens to *Homo Amore Universalis*,"[xxiii] is it still Christ's church?

Becoming More

On the fourth and last week of the Advent season, I shared this true story.

> "So, David, what are you going to be when you grow up?"
>
> The five-year-old was impatient. Waiting in the church office for his mom to prepare materials for her upcoming Sunday school class, he clearly would rather have been playing in the snow. Thinking to distract him, the office manager asked the question all adults ask children when they don't know what to say – what are you going to be when you grow up? Expecting some variation of astronaut, firefighter, or policeman, she was surprised by his reply. In a voice that betrayed his impatience at a question the answer to which seemed obvious, he said, "I'll be more me."

David had a reputation for being precocious. It's a word that often discounts the wisdom of children. But what if we saw him as an Evolutionary? He was born, after all, into the technology, communication, scientific, and information age; an emergent age when everything's becoming something more.

Emergent is not the way the Christian culture sees the world. Call it a false loyalty to tradition or a recalcitrant response to science, but the church in recent centuries has not been what David's generation would call evolutionary. Until now, it has been inattentive to Earth's ecological limits. But perhaps more alarming, it has ignored the need for stories of a divinity proportionate to the now-known immensities of the Universe.

A conversation about grandchildren burst forth like flames from smouldering embers touched by a low-flying wind. There was awe for these children born with the world at their fingertips. There was fear for teens who only engaged through social media. But mostly there was hope for a generation that, more greatly than ever before, spoke a global language of technology and faced challenges of planetary proportions.

As I reflect on the story today, it strikes me, youthfulness is what the stories of David, Mary, Jesus, and the human species hold in common. What would it mean for Christianity to embrace its youth? Could it mean a new-found sense of healthy self-doubt, humility, and adventure?

Opening the door to bring the Universe news to church has been an existential adventure. Advent became more than a four-week yoga class for the spirit; it became the nature of existence itself. The discovery was what David had known intuitively. As planetary beings, we are growing up to become more of what we were born to be. Perhaps the most significant revelation was recognizing that the question we ask of our children is the question our children are asking of us, the question humanity is asking of the church: what are you going to be when you grow up?

It's a question that doesn't close the door on the church's teachings but invites a deepening of faith. Faith being the conviction that one has purpose and place in this global climate emergency. Faith being the "soul-level moral imperative to evolve for the sake of the future of the evolutionary process itself."[xxiv]

Surely this is the purpose of Christianity, to teach a gospel of potential. I admit that once I would have said the church's work was to spread the teachings of Jesus. But I've come to believe the work of the church, and of all religious and spiritual traditions, is that of becoming.

Becoming what? Becoming more fully one with the divine whole. In fact, now I see the very nature of our divine existence to be that of becoming. Life, it would appear, is in a state of perpetual Advent.

Since first receiving that invitation and submitting that four-part proposal, there have been many Sundays spent with Kinmount circle. These reflections on Advent have been gathered over many visits, each one beginning by pushing open that simple, age-darkened door. It has been good stepping back into the church, the fears and hopes of *Homo sapiens*, and the challenges and possibilities for the Earth-family. The gift I gained was a deeper understanding of Advent as an Advent'ure.

Evolutionary Wisdom

- The whole Universe is an Advent'ure of becoming.
- The call of the Advent'ure is to live in a way equal to our 21st century potential.
- It is essential to think of ourselves as part of a youthful species and that species as part of Earth.
- There is a moral imperative to evolve for the sake of the evolutionary nature of life itself.

The wizard raised his arm and a sea of salt poured forth to become a giant spiral galaxy, our Milky Way home.

CHAPTER 8

Conner's Cosmic Christmas

The aim of scientific language is to provide exactly defined and unambiguous statements about reality; that of poetic language is to communicate reality itself, as experienced by means of imagery, evocation, tone, and the ambiguity – or rather ambivalence – of paradox, of symbol ... the cutting edge of great poetry is sharper and digs deeper than that of any prose. Teilhard de Chardin

Opening the door on Christmas

Crossing the parking lot rapidly disappearing under a duvet of snow flakes, the air tasted of frosted Pines. The white clapboard church – its steeple piercing the night, wreath-hung door, and candle-lit windows – appeared straight out of a Hallmark Christmas card.

It had been an adventure getting through the blizzard. I wondered if others would venture out. Tending to last minute details, sounds of a child's voice, stomping feet, and muffled good cheer in the cloak room dispensed with my worry. Soon Conner and his family pushed their way through the swinging doors and into the sanctuary. As others followed, the little building filled with the magical cheer of Christmas Eve.

Mom guided the four-year-old to the stable. It had been built by Mr. Denman when she was a girl, I heard her say. The little boy's eyes told me this manger wasn't like the one at home. It was as big as he was. And there's the baby Jesus, Mom pointed to the doll on the straw. No crib, no onesie, not even a blanket, Conner winced and turned away. He was looking for something, probably some sign of Santa, or gifts under the tree. His brow furrowed. He'd found nothing to explain why Mom said, "This was what Christmas was all about."

Dad was looking around too. He eyed the pews arranged in a circle, then the table in the centre – a slice of an old-growth Cedar that had fallen to a tornado a few years back. He noted the giant beach ball that looked like the Earth. Aren't those your Mom's old blue curtains, he asked his wife pointing to the backdrop above the stable. Hung with twinkling lights, dollar-store stars, moons, and spirals, they assured him, things were different this year.

The boy wriggled to the back of the bench. When a man with a white beard who looked like Santa in his play clothes came to shake his hand, he was wide-eyed. You remember Reverend Desmond, Mom told him. He baptized you when you were a baby. Conner knew about baptism. Grandma said that was like when she watered her plants; it helped him grow up to be strong and happy.

I saw the child's large brown eyes sweep the room once again. Looking for other kids, I imagined. Not seeing any, he turned on his Leapfrog Laptop and settled into his own world.

"In times such as ours, surely Christmas Eve must be different." I began the service.

Conner looked up. Not unlike other children before him, he was probably reasoning out that if the woman at Applebees was the hostess, I must be a Revesse. I smiled at him.

"Approving more pipelines from the Tar Sands, Canada has further endangered Mother Earth and infringed on the lands of the First Peoples. Levels of carbon dioxide in our atmosphere are still rising. A healthy environment has still not been included in our Charter of Rights and Freedoms. To serve the grandchildren of all the Earth family, tonight must be a Cosmic Christmas."

Dad's eyebrows raised to new heights at the strange phrase. The little boy glanced to the door as thought I'd just signaled Santa to make his big entry. Disappointed, he went back to his game.

Pointing to the tray of votive candles on the table, I invited folks to offer their prayers and intentions for a different world with the lighting of a candle.

Conner seemed fascinated as folks went to the table, lit candles, and said what they wanted for Christmas. A granddaughter to be well. An end to shooting in the Middle East. Some just said thanks for new babies or family or health. He was especially surprised when Mom went up.

"I pray this Christmas Eve brings Santa and Jesus together for Conner."

Her prayer was the challenge of every Rev. and Revesse in every church on this night. I found myself on my feet, lighting my own candle, expressing my own prayer:

"Tonight, may we bring Santa, Jesus, and the Cosmos together for children everywhere."

Opening the Story

Then it was time for the story. It's what had drawn them from their cozy wood stoves and half-finished tortieres just as it had drawn folks every Christmas eve for centuries. It didn't matter that Jesus' birth was never historically recorded or that no one knew whether the birth occurred in April, March, or September. No one fussed that the date had been chosen to coincide with the mid-winter Roman Feast of the Unconquered Sun. They simply came the night before Christmas, a date established to be December 25th in 274 C.E, to hear what over time has come to be called the Christmas story.

It didn't matter to most pewsters whether they heard Matthew's account or Luke's, whether Jesus was of the house and lineage of David, a descendant of Father Abraham, or could be traced to Adam, the first human. On this night, no one questioned how reports written more than three decades after the crucifixion could be accurate. No one wondered if there was a connection between the time the birth narratives of a Saviour appeared and the time Judaism's Great Temple was destroyed. The literary agendas and historical ambiguities were not what made so many folks Christian on Christmas Eve.

People come for the story. It's poetic use of language evokes the mystery of all reality; it speaks truth to ageless questions: How will we go on? Are we of value? Is there hope? The poetry of story and the cutting edge of poetry are sharper and dig deeper than fact to the truth of wisdom itself.

The Traditional – The Birth of Jesus

When Rome occupied Israel, politicians and priests protected their own power first and the people not at all. Into this darkness an angel came to Mary, a girl-child with no power at all. She would give birth to a son of God, the hope of Israel, whom she was to call Jesus.

When Joseph, Mary's betrothed, heard she was with child, he was angry.

Fearful, the girl sought safety in the home of her cousin Elizabeth. After years of being barren, she too was pregnant. Her son would prepare a way for Mary's boy, Jesus.

When Joseph had a dream in which God reassured him he too was part of the plan, he agreed to proceed with the marriage.

> Late in Mary's pregnancy, Rome ordered everyone to go to the city of their ancestors to be registered. Joseph went up to Bethlehem taking Mary who rode a donkey. Finding no room at the inn, Mary gave birth in a stable. She laid the baby in a manger.
>
> Angels announced the messiah's birth to shepherds in the fields. Shepherds, the least powerful of all!
>
> Magi, following the child's star and seeking his birthplace, caused great alarm at the palace when they asked where they might find the babe born to be king? (paraphrase, Matthew 1,2 and Luke 1,2)

This is not *the* Christmas story. Woven from fragments of two different accounts, it is, however, what most would tell as the Christmas story. The fact is that on Christmas Eve no one's a scholar and everyone's a mystic. No one questions the feasibility of a star stopping in its orbit, or if there were three or four wise men, or any at all. It's of no consequence that many religious cultures have stories of deities becoming human.

What matters is not the true story but the truths this great cosmic romance gives one's sacred imagination. In a time of peril there is promise. No child is born to be just another number in a census. Every life has purpose and power. These are the compelling truths which Conner's Mom brought him to hear.

My hope was to reinforce these truths with a second birth story. This one fashioned from the poetry and miracle of postmodern science and the creative power of ritual.

When I announced I had a second birth story to tell, the circle was surprised. It was not a better story but an older one. Unrolling a wicker garland that I'd prepared as a timeline of the Universe story, I held out one end in the little lad's direction. Would he like to help? He jumped down and took one end. Reverend Desmond jumped up to take the other. As they took their places at opposite sides of the circle, the garland unfolded to reveal trinkets and toys hanging from one end to the other.

Moving to stand beside Desmond, I began my story.

The Evolutionary – The Birth of Everything

"Once upon a time before time, firey, holy creativity flared forth and Universe was born." My hand rested over a cluster of red-velvet leaves – flames from the Big Bang.

"As Universe grew, it brought forth its first stars."

I drew my hand along the garland to a cookie-cutter star, then further along to a clump of tinfoil stars.

"In time the stars gathered into galaxies. As the cosmic web stretched out, microscopic molecules of gas appeared. With these Universe would shape wonder after wonder."

My hand moved to stop over some Lego pieces. I'd moved more than half the length of the garland when my hand stopped above another cookie-cutter star. This one was hung with many coloured Christmas balls.

"From stardust, gases, time, and gravity, were born more stars. And planets. Spinning around one very bright and generous star, the Sun, the planets became a solar system, a cosmic family. One planet, however, was different than others. It was covered with water."

"Earth!" Conner, chiming in, pointed to the blue ball.

I smiled my thanks and took up the story.

"One stormy day, almost four billion years ago, lightning struck deep into Earth's dark waters.

And what do you think happened?"

"It created a charge of electricity," declared Desmond.

"Yes, and the very first cell of life was born." I spoke with the awe of a grandmother who'd held a new-born grandchild. "These microscopic cells gave birth to a wondrous array of sea animals and plants. Some with shells. Some with skeletons." I drew my hand along the time-line to a sequence of miniatures toys. At each one, Conner called out its name.

"Snail. Fish. Tree. Bird. Dinosaur. Horse. Ape." I stood now less than a foot away from him. The story was almost over.

"Earth, with its sky above, oceans, and lands below, was full of life. It was an ecological system, an Earth family. When drought, flood, ice age, or planetoids happened, the plant and animal Earthlings migrated to find more-liveable locations. One day, some five million years ago, the family received a new species. Human beings became part of the Earth family."

Conner didn't need instruction. He rustled the cut-out paper-dolls.

"Abraham and Sarah, Maryam and Mohammed, the Buddha and Maya, the mother of Buddha – there have been some wonderful humans. Tonight we're celebrating the birthday of another wonderful human."

"Jesus," said Conner, pointing to a miniature manger.

"Jesus' teachings are important. *Love your enemy. Love God. Love your neighbour as much as you love yourself.* They teach us the way to become the best Earthlings we can be."

Conner's eyes were wide as full moons when I pointed to a miniature figure in red. It hung inches from the boy's fingertips.

"Nicholas, sometimes referred to as Saint Nick or Santa, followed Jesus teachings. He loved giving gifts to children on Jesus' birthday." Conner's Mom was smiling. The boy was too.

He pointed to a tiny plastic telescope, the last thing on the story-garland.

"Just as wise ones have always looked to the stars, scientists today look to the Universe.

And what do they see?" This was Desmond's cue to answer,

"Everything in the entire Universe is part of one holy family."

"What do you think Jesus might teach today?" My question was met with a wonder-filled silence. After seconds that seemed liked eons, Rosemary spoke with all the wisdom she'd gained from sitting with Alice Williams and others from the Curve Lake First Nation in the Truth and Reconciliation circle.

"Love your *whole* family as yourself."

At the garland's end, the boy was wide-eyed. I bent until we were looking at each other, face to face. I had one last question.

"What part of the holy family am I looking at right now?" The boy's eyes were bright with the fire of all time and space. He was so excited he could only whisper.

"Me!" The applause was spontaneous. With his wonder-filled *me*, the child had preached the cosmic message of incarnate and inter-connecting love.

In times such as ours, surely Christmas Eve has to be a little different. The incarnate creativity that gave birth to Universe, polar bears, Jesus, and Santa cannot be left in the manger. It must be freed into the child-like hands of our species. The elegant intelligence that only can be described as the law of love, ever-connecting all past and future, cannot be limited. In this axial moment, we must expand in consciousness to know ourselves as star-stuff and Earthlings before we know ourselves as Christians or Canadians. Then, we will know the cosmic power of our love.

Closing the Door on a Cosmic Christmas

And so another Christmas Eve took its place on the garland of time. Bundled up from tuque to boot, Conner, his parents, and all the grandparents made their way into a world frosted with fresh snow. Each took away their own story to tell.

For Conner's mom, it was how her prayer had been answered. They had brought Jesus and Santa together for her boy. Conner's dad would tell the guys at work of the drive through deep drifts, how it wasn't an old-fashioned Christmas, of grandma's curtains, and a garden garland of Lego, stars, and his son. Desmond would tell his family how, after fifty years a cleric, his Christmas gift was discovering that the nativity story rested comfortably within the epic of evolution.

Proud of their little congregation for pushing the envelope, Matt and Virginia would go home to phone their son's family in Vietnam. They would tell how Christmas Eve had been less about what happened while shepherds watched their flocks by night two millennia ago, than the potential of their grandkids to find a way through the environmental crisis.

This cosmic storyteller, also known as the Revesse, would write one day of the night she proclaimed God to be the creative and evolutionary energy that's still birthing more Universe.

What a thrill it had been to proclaim Jesus and all that swims and slithers, soars and runs to be stardust, particle and proton, electron and neutron. The Universe story freed Jesus to be the avatar and incarnate teacher he was. What gratitude I felt for a story that weaves past, present, and future together.

The Cosmic Christmas Eve came to a close. Its evolutionary stories had been told. Once again, by aural alchemy, the words transformed lives; the creative powers of hope and love were born. But this year was a little different. This year the hope and love was not for humanity alone, but the whole, holy planetary family.

Evolutionary Wisdom

- Jesus' nativity story is cradled within the epic of evolution.
- Jesus was made of spirit and stardust, particle and proton, electron and neutron in the same way all that walks, swims, slithers, and soars are made of stardust, particle, and proton.
- As the birth of Jesus promised to bring peace and goodwill in the global human family, so the birth of today's generations must bring peace and goodwill to the Earth-family.

In times such as ours, surely Christmas Eve has to be a little different. The incarnate creativity that gave birth to Universe, polar bears, Jesus, and Santa cannot be left in the manger. It must be freed into the child-like hands of our species.

CHAPTER 9

Evolutionary Epiphanies

Awareness of our capacities for conscious evolution is the key revelation of the 21st century. Barbara Marx Hubbard

Opening the door to Epiphany

Inside, the furnace roared in protest. Outside, all was wrapped in January's icy shroud. Early arrivals sat as though numbed to the core. Setting the coffee table, even Cathy and Rosemary seemed somnolent. As more frosted faces arrived, I thought of Angaangaq, the Eskimo-Kalaallit Elder and wise man from Greenland. Having watched three-mile-thick glaciers disappear in just five decades, his people had sent him to the south to melt the ice in the heart of man. What, I wondered, could warm the dear hearts and gentle pewsters to the evolutionary import of our day?

It was the first Sunday of 2011. Bold headlines proclaimed the dangers of hydraulic fracturing. Fracking, a method of extracting oil and gas trapped in shale and other rock formations, involves pumping water, chemicals and sand underground at high pressure fracturing the rock. This releases the gas or oil which flows to the surface where it's collected. To some, it's an economic saviour. To others, an environmental nightmare.

Accessing fuel by fracking involves major risks to fresh water. The up to one hundred million litres of water that can be used in an average frack can end up contaminated with high levels of methane and toxic hydrocarbons. Studies show leaks and spills create long-term water pollution and threaten all life forms. What wisdom would melt the ice in the hearts of those who dare to risk poisoning the future?

At 9:45, Matt put his hand to the new nylon bell-pull. The original twisted sisel had broken off in Sheila's hands a few years ago. The story still brought laughter. But that morning, the deep dong song of the cast iron bell announced the Feast of Epiphany!

The wheel! The light bulb! These were someone's epiphanies, the 'aha's' that come in the middle of the night awakening the world to the possibility of a radically different tomorrow. Democracy! The Parliament of World Religions! An Earth Charter of Rights! Such epiphanies are visions of life at a higher stage of consciousness. While some ideas can be turned into reality quickly, others take a very long and often painful time to manifest.

Epiphany Sunday is one of the oldest, and originally the most important of the Christian holy days. Today, I'd venture to say it is probably the least known. Regardless, since the fourth century on the twelfth day of Christmas, the church has celebrated two evolutionary ideas. Divinity is not separate from but present with us in and through Jesus. And God's love is not just for the chosen tribes of Israel, but the whole of humanity, for male and female, Jew and Greek, free and slave alike. These two major breakthroughs opened a path to the non-duality we seek today.

We can trace these ideas to a certain story by a certain evangelical author called John in a very particular time. This is that story, though it is told here with a few twists.

The Traditional – The King's Epiphany

> In the days of the corrupt Herodian monarchy, Zorastrian priests from Persia, what is present-day Iran, arrived at the palace in Jerusalem. They'd come to offer tributes to the one born to become king of the Jews. Unaware of any such child, Herod feared an uprising in the making. Demanding his own wisemen search the books of the prophets, they found this in the writings of Micah: a shepherd-king, a leader that protects the people, would come from Bethlehem. Being BGPS, that is to say, before Global Positioning Systems, Herod's officials gave the magi directions to the out-lying hamlet, but not without a proviso. After they'd found the child, they must return to the palace with his whereabouts that Herod too might bring gifts. Wink, wink. Finding the place where Jesus was, the esteemed visitors presented gifts fit for a king – gold, frankincense and myrrh. Then, warned in a dream of Herod's duplicity, they gave Jerusalem a pass and steered their hump-backed steeds home another way. (paraphrase of Matthew 2:1-12, Micah 2:6)

It's a great story! It doesn't matter that there's no historical record of any such visit. It doesn't matter that it was written to criticize Israel's response to Greco-Roman imperialism. Isolationism was a blatent betrayed of the Torah's hospitality laws. Pointing out how the powerful, to protect their power, can misuse it, the myth teaches universal truths. For this reason, though many don't know about Epiphany, most remember the story of the wisemen and its call to live with a more wholistic consciousness.

The story has particular significance for the church. The role of the Persian priests is to set the stage for the book's ending – the Great Commissioning. Sending Jesus' followers to all the world with a message of God's unconditional grace and inclusiveness, the story announces the emergence of Christianity as a global religion. (Matthew 3:13-17) Revealing an epiphany of evolutionary proportions, love is to be unconditional, it's a great story.

But what aha does it hold for today's church? Can it shed light on how we're to respond to the encroaching demands of the natural world, that *non*-human world we have regarded as *other*? The answer – with holy hospitality – is easier to express than embody. Learning what it means to love the Earth as ourselves calls for a conscious evolution of consciousness. But this is the work, this is the conversation we must have, both as church and society, if we're to become co-creators of the future.

What does the future mean to you? The question, like a sudden deep freeze in the forest, brought an uncharacteristic silence upon the circle. It bid a deeper conversation than most.

Desmond was the first to speak. Slowly, from the depths of his sacred imagination, he told how the question summoned up the image of his grandchildren playing free of the threat of war or global warming. His grandaughter, a visiting pianist that morning, was surprised. She and her friends, she took me aside to say, were too busy thinking about university and jobs to worry about the environment.

Dorothy's voice was sad. When she'd tried to envision peace in the world, images of violence took over. Bo said the furthest ahead he ever thought was about what's for supper. It wasn't really true but it brought some comic relief. Wendy confessed her preoccupation was with her future health and housing. That brought nods all around our circle of elders.

In short, when it came to thinking about the future beyond our own, it was difficult. We were preoccupied. We felt detached and powerless.

What we celebrate in the season of Epiphany are the gifts, the holy aha's and evolutionary insights that breakthrough our powerlessness and show us another way forward. This I know because life told me so. And so I told my story.

The Evolutionary – A Clergy's Epiphany

> It was November, 2010, the day after a major Gaia Centre conference. I'd been settled in a friend's study to relax while she cooked. Instinctively, my hand reached into her library and pulled out a book. Neither its subject nor its author were familiar. *Conscious Evolution. Awakening The Power of Our Social Potential* by Barbara Marx Hubbard. By suppertime I was at chapter five and totally enchanted. With each page the reality of an ongoing evolution of human consciousness became clearer. By midnight, I'd scratched down a string of new thoughts that would frame my future.
>
> Reality is always evolving. This is an evolutionary moment. Humanity's evolving again. Some new humans already exist. Jesus was a prototype of what humanity can be. Kinder, more inclusive – the new human will care for the non-human world. They will no longer project their creative power on a distant deity but claim it. The entire book was a feast of epiphanies.

All the new ideas I'd discovered outside the Christian culture began to add up. Cooperating with and participating in this evolution of consciousness, the future becomes meaningful, and the present purposeful. This was the epiphany I found in Hubbard's book. Sharing it with the church was my work. Returning was my way of cooperating with the necessary evolution of climate consciousness.

Climate consciousness was the gift received from yet another guest's book, *Sea Sick, The Global Ocean In Crisis.* Author Alanna Mitchell is a newspaper journalist and environmental reporter.

Her stories about the accelerating crisis in the world's oceans were both captivating and horrifying.

The place where life began, the oceans are in crisis. Oceans are larger than our atmosphere; it is where 99% of life exists. They are the true lungs of the planet where most oxygen is produced thanks to phytoplankton. All this is in crisis.

Human activity has altered Earth's oceans – temperature, salinity, acidity, ice cover, volume, circulation, and the life forms within them. Because the climate is regulated by the ocean's currents, winds, and water-cycle, sick seas are now a threat to what and who will survive on land. The book's gift was this: the climate crisis is also an ocean crisis.[xxv]

Three epiphanies had brought me back into the Christian circle. The climate crisis can also be described as an ocean crisis. The environmental crisis is driving an evolution of consciousness. Consciously cooperating with the evolution of a new unity-consciousness, we can find another way home. And so I'd come home to my Christian family to say climate science required and offered another way to be church.

Having revealed my own epiphanies, I laid out the reality according to the new science.

If the mean global temperature rises three to four Celsius degrees, sea levels could rise up to eighty centimetres. Unprecedented numbers will be forced from their bioregions.[xxvi] Current estimates of climate-migrants range between twenty-five million and one billion people by 2050. Canada, like the rest of the world, must decide whether to be governed by a fear-full fortress mentality, or find its way guided by exceptional grace and hospitality. We are faced with a wave of cultural change in Canada the likes of which we've not yet seen.

On June 27th, Multiculturalism Day, Canadians celebrate that more than 20% of our population is foreign-born, the highest of the G8 countries. We are made up of more than two hundred ethnic groups, speaking as many languages, and practising a multiplicity of religions. But this is only a fraction of the holy hospitality that will be needed of us in the future.

What is the way of the church in these times? This was the question. To extend our understanding of hospitality, I'd brought another epiphany story.

The Evolutionary – A Society's Epiphany

In the days when the fossil fuel industry was king and ruthlessly wielded power over the natural world, a wise woman from the west came asking hard questions. "When will humanity leave its polluting phase behind? When will they live into the fullness of their collective potential? When will a new humanity be born?" For she had seen the collapse of stock markets and the corruption of democracy and knew the species had arrived at a dangerous threshold across which lay its demise.

On hearing her questions, the oil and gas barons were troubled and all the automotive and manufacturing CEOs with them. Fearing a threat to the gross national product, they called the environmental scientists together and inquired of them when such a shift might take place.

In due time, they said, for they had seen in the recurring patterns of evolution that it is the nature of nature to transform. The crisis of global warming, rising waters, and dying oceans, they said, foretells our species' new birth. The new human species, they said, would be co-creators with the evolutionary process. Self-organization for ever-greater life is the way of the Cosmos, they said.

Even in this evolutionary moment, they said, a safe future fuelled by sun and wind is unfolding. Even now, they promised, a world without microplastics and fed without pesticides is being born.

Quickly, the wealthy rulers paid others to produce other truths. They bought newspapers and information organizations to silence the truth-speakers. But the wisdom of Gaia could not be muzzled.

> The wise woman from the west offered her wealth of wisdom to the world: "Your planet is a co-creative evolutionary being. Humanity's potential is evolving. Consciousness, what some call God, is evolving. You will go forward because you will find another way."
>
> Then the people opened her gifts and began to find ways to cooperate with their Mother.

Where was the holy hospitality in the story? My listeners looked puzzled. I confessed the story wasn't about hospitality in the traditional sense of charity or making room for the needy. The generosity and openness needed in these times is to Gaia-centered economics, green technology, and ecological agriculture practices. These would allow the next generations to attain alternative energy, sustainable manufacturing, and organic foodstuffs. Innovations, inventions, and adaptations that honour the needs of Mother Earth, these must be the way of the future.

Epiphanies can and do happen in every age. They come bringing visions that give birth to yet another evolution of consciousness and greater inclusivity.

On the celebration table that morning, there was no toy treasure box. There were no ornate perfume bottles remembering the biblical story of the magi's gifts of gold, frankincense, and myrrh. Instead, there were three bags proclaiming the gifts of an Evolutionary Spirituality – epiphanies suitable for twenty-first century co-creators and divine beings. Their labels read: an Ever-Evolving God. An Always-Evolving Religion. The Gift of an Evolving Humanity. We began to unpack them.

The Gift of an Ever-Evolving God

"God is a continuous coming into being."[xxvii] This was the surprising conclusion of a collaboration between an artist and rabbi. In their book, they presented many familiar images of the divine: a pillar of light, a judge, a rock, a shield, the Madonna.

The comment sparked conversation as to just where we'd imagined such images came from?

Having escaped an enemy's attack by hiding in a stoney outcrop, perhaps shepherds had returned to the tribe telling how God, their r*ock and shield,* had saved them.

After a powerful thunderstorm had devastated the crops, perhaps a priest explained how God, the Almighty Judge, had punished them because Josephine had failed to keep the Sabbath that week.

Experiencing the divine feminine energy rising in the world, seeking equality, and demanding their rights, women began to return to the ancient names for the divine – Sophia, Shekinah, and Mother.

The morning conversation was revealing. We'd always believed it was humanity becoming aware of the many natures of God. Now the rabbi was telling us God was always becoming more conscious and more present to us. This was theology through evolutionary eyes.

The artist and co-author of the book also wrote how the sacred presence of God is "in every mode of the Universe: stars, winds, water, turtles, whales, humans."[xxviii] Did we agree?

Matt observed how many more were seeking and finding the sacred in the woods than in the pews these days. Ursula said she was most conscious of a divine presence in the forested ridge above her home. For Wendy, watching the sun rise over her land was a sacred experience and an experience of the sacred. Colleen, freed for the moment from the prison of Alzheimer's, surprised us with an answer, "With my horse!" It was unanimous, every aspect of Universe was a revelation of the divine. Though this idea was something our hymns proclaimed, it was unusual in our Jesus-centric theology to start talking about it.

Was it mere coincidence that as we awakened to the collapse of the eco-systems, we became more conscious of nature as sacred. Could the evolution of human consciousness be related to the evolution of Holy Consciousness? Why couldn't the nature of divinity be ever-evolving? The discussion, in leading us to more questions than answers, ushered us into the realm of possibility.

An ever-evolving God – it was a new idea. We could only imagine the epiphany was meant to help us look at the Earth in a new way – as incarnation of the sacred and our sacred home. We could only trust the gift would inspire a new relationship with the planet, that we would take loving and protecting it as a daily spiritual practice.

The Gift of an Always - Evolving Religion

Opening the second gift of Epiphany, we found another surprise. We'd never thought of religion as evolving or Christianity as an evolution of Judaism. We turned to the earliest records of the house churches. A never-before melding of cultures, genders, and classes, they included Jews, Roman, and Greeks, men and women, slaves and free. The extraordinary inclusivity was a multicultural phenomenon that contradicted the norms of the day. Texts suggest participants in those unique circles were challenged to "be transformed by the renewal of your beliefs." (Romans 12:2) It could definitely be said Christianity emerged as a new kind of society shaped by a transformation of consciousness.

Looking at those first small circles of Jesus followers scattered across the Mediterranean with evolutionary eyes, we saw something we'd never seen before. They weren't unlike the first single cells that gathered round a nucleus and were transformed into something brand new, a nucleated cell. We recognized, for the first time, our tradition as an evolutionary social system. This was the second gift of Epiphany.

We shouldn't have been surprised. Hadn't our own ideas evolved since delving into the new science? Everything's an expression of light from the Big Bang. All living things emit a constant stream of bio-photons travelling at the speed of light. Radiance is the primary language by which Universe makes things happen. Thoughts have matter. The new information had brought new meaning to the old teaching, don't hide your light under a bushel. We came to understand our prayers as energy radiating out and beyond us. It changed our prayer practice.

We stopped hiding our prayers under a tradition of silence. We began speaking them aloud as we lit candles to symbolize our intentions radiating into the world. The community played an important role. After someone's intention, story of gratitude, or desire for help had been shared, the circle sang. "Send forth the light of our community."

In choir circles, singing's understood as another form of prayer. What the church called Prayers of the People evolved into a variation of what Noetic Science knows as Intention Experiments. But ours was no experiment; we became a circle creating resonant fields of love and light in word and song. Prayer shifted from something we directed to a distant super power to a communal act of transformation.

What we prayed for also evolved. One morning my expressed intention was for "strength and resilience for endangered species – four-legged, winged, crawling, or swimming." Desmond was surprised. He'd never prayed for the non-human ones before. As society's consciousness of the life beyond human life evolved, so our prayers did too.

How we addressed God and described the divine power also changed. When I used phrases like Intelligent Evolutionary Impulse or Heart of the Universe, Ria commented, it's all very wordy. She was right. The evolution of a new consciousness requires trying out new language to express new ideas. One scholar put it this way, "Everyone who is intent upon surviving – with worth and dignity, and living rather than passively accepting life – must sooner or later pass through the agonies of emergent consciousness."[xxix] To survive and thrive, we must expect religious language to reflect and affect a transition in consciousness.

The transition is happening. New branches of Christianity are springing up. Sisters of the Green Mountain Monastery,[xxx] a brand new Catholic community, is devoted to the care of the

Earth. The Order of the Sacred Earth[xxxi] is an inter-spiritual organization requiring only that one pledge to be the best lover and protector of the Earth they can be. Creation Spirituality,[xxxii] a tradition recovered from Christianity and found in many classical religions and indigenous spiritualities, became a new denomination in 2015. New systems of belief bearing a new cosmology, Gaia consciousness, and the vision of greater planetary resilience are emerging. This is another epiphany and gift in these times.

The Gift of an Evolving Humanity

Humanity's an evolving species – this was the third gift. After at least twenty species of the human, some believe another one's on the way. The difference in the next specimen will not be of a physical nature. Bo couldn't resist a comment: You mean we won't have an additional *digitus secondus manus* for quicker texting? The next evolution, it's said, will be one of consciousness. A humanity conscious of itself as both cosmic being and as a species. A species conscious of itself as part of a single, ecological community of existence will be a new *genus* of humanity.

But wasn't there already evidence of such humans, of this evolution of consciousness? The circle had examples. They named technological and information innovations, growing interest in the scientific, spiritual, mystical, and paranormal. Virginia named the International Court of Justice and United Nations. Desmond noted the World Council of Churches. John, pointing upward called out, the International Space Station. Paul named The Council of Canadians and the banning of fracking in many provinces. Our examples affirmed what futurist Barbara Marx Hubbard had believed – the new humans are already among us. She called them *Homo Amore Universalis*, beings who love the whole of existence.

Perhaps modern magi are part of our changing world. The circle named animal activist Jane Goodall, Canadian science journalist Alanna Mitchell, and others who are teaching society to seek another way home to the wholeness of life. These leaders of the new consciousness, the daring hearts and thoughtful people of Kinmount, they are the wise-ones of our living story. For them and the ongoing epiphanies, I am thankful.

Closing the door on Epiphany

As Mother Earth spun our community more deeply into Sun's bright rays, talk turned to the magi's choice to go home another way. What would another way look like for us?

For Desmond – a former missionary to India and participant in colonial Christianity – another way was honouring all religions. Trusting the sciences, added Rosemary. Sheila talked of trusting in that something larger than ourselves. She was talking of faith, what the geologian Thomas Berry described as "that dynamic ... which has guided the unfolding of Universe since the beginning ... and awakened in us our present understanding of ourselves and our relation to this stupendous process."[xxxiii]

The festival of Epiphany over for another year, Matt rang the bell. What did the village hear? In the past, a bell ringing mid-week would have alerted neighbours to an unusual occurrence. Five rings might have called folks to fight a barn fire, three rings to a barn-raising. On Sundays, it was a call to worship. Donated over a century ago by Mr. Craig, co-owner of the village lumber mill, the church bell that morning was heeded by few.

Given that the life of the planet is leaching away, surely church bells everywhere need to ring out with these epiphanies. God is evolving. Religion is evolving. Humanity is evolving. Another way is possible.

Evolutionary Wisdom

- Honour Father Universe and Mother Earth.
- Remember the Earth is sacred and keep it holy.
- You shall not steal Earth's resources from your grandchildren's future.
- You shall not kill – forests or oceans, soils or atmosphere, bees or any beings.
- You shall not make God a separate and otherworldly deity.
- You shall not make idols of humanity, profits, or progress.
- Be evolutionary in your thought and word for, like pebbles in a pond, they have agency.
- Those who have eyes to see, in the flashes of Consciousness, see God.
- Love religions, spiritualities, and science as vessels of evolutionary Consciousness.
- Love your atmosphere, hydrosphere, and all Earth as yourself. This is the green rule.

Sophia, Divine Wisdom. Artist Mary Plaster
www.maryplaster.com

New systems of belief bearing the gift of Gaia Consciousness and the promise of greater planetary resilience are emerging. This is the epiphany and the gift to the Church at this time.

CHAPTER 10

Freed from Contentment

Our flashes of freedom are actually the awareness of our coming state of being as a new norm. Barbara Marx Hubbard

Opening the door on Lent

Lost in my thoughts, I didn't notice the mid-February ice. Half-way up the accessibility ramp I recognized that for every two of my steps forward, I was sliding back one. The source of my preoccupation was a disturbing dream. It had wakened me to a novel understanding of Lent which I'd recorded in my journal:

> I was working happily round a kitchen when two prison guards came from behind, lifted and carried me into a seemingly endless and colourless hallway. How odd to be content in a prison. How strange to have to be carried out.

> More guards, carrying a slim, gay man wearing a beatific smile and a Basque beret atop wispy white hair, pushed by me. Odd to be smiling on one's way to death, I thought. I knew, as one only knows in dreams, the man was gay and on his way to die. I also knew his fate would be my own. Odder yet was his last word. It echoed back to me in a joyful and grateful tone, "Freedom!"

Freedom – what a welcome insight to Lent! Originally a pagan festival of preparation for Spring called Lencten, it had been re-purposed by the early church as a time of penitence and self-denial in preparation for Easter. The reason for the season, of course, was the doctrine of Original Sin. One of the cornerstones of Christianity, the belief was that humans were born in need of Christ's redemption and that Jesus suffered on the cross for our salvation. So for forty days, from Ash Wednesday to Palm Sunday, the faithful engaged in a wide range of ascetic practices, everything from fasting to self-flagellation. The goal, of course, being admission to the eternal kingdom.

Growing up in small town Ontario in the '50s, my experience of Lent was somewhat modified. Roman Catholic family and friends abstained from candy, meat, and bad habits like swearing or cigarettes. There was, as far as I know, no whipping, just extra guilt. My Protestant denomination didn't acknowledge Lent until the '60's. Then, wooden crosses made of six-foot two-by-fours and draped in reams of purple cloth stood front and centre. Additional mid-week services and Bible studies related to one social injustice or another became the norm. The mood was sombre. In my congregations of white, Anglo-Saxon, middle-class, privileged, and entitled folk, we soberly lamented the suffering of the underprivileged. We regretted our livelihoods depended on the impoverishment of others. Though the truth was, we were all prisoners of a corrupt global economy, Lent to me equalled guilt.

Creation Spirituality, however, liberated me from that sin-salvation story. Driving to Kinmount that morning, I believed

Christianity needed to focus less on the eternal life of the soul and more on the sustainable life of the planet. The dream that morning was a reminder. I could not continue to content myself or others with a faith because it was familiar. I must face the death of old beliefs and accept the environmental crisis is carrying us all into the unknown.

I opened the church door with a new approach to Lent. We would no longer focus on giving up food as a way to develop compassion for those without so to gain a seat at the heavenly table. Instead, we would explore the issues of food-convenience and food security to better understand how our individual and present-day choices could contribute to a sustainable Earth community.

India's Dr. Vandana Shiva shares Jesus' passion for food for the poor. The Hindu woman campaigns to contradict what we've been asked to believe – agribusiness produces higher yields, prevents famine, saves resources and, therefore, saves species. The opposite, according to the scientist, is true. The global advocate for sustainable farming reports the findings of her studies. An industrial farming operation based on a single crop, such as wheat or maize or cattle, requires 300 units of input to produce 100 units of produce. A traditional farm that produces multiple crops, however, be it beans, legumes, fruits, vegetables, maize, or livestock, produces 100 units from 5 units of input. That's 295 units of wasted inputs and a decline of 5,900 units of food. That, she declares, is a formula for starving people, not feeding them.[xxxiv] Add to this system the interests of the transnational supermarket chains, and we get impoverished subsistence farmers and a spiritually depleted economy.

It doesn't take a mathematician to see the energy spent on preaching forgiveness for the sake of one's personal salvation might be better spent on the evolution of consciousness regarding the food we buy. Food has always been part of religion. There have been laws to define what was clean and what was unclean. Bread, wine, and water are honoured as symbols of the sacred. Fasting for ritual purification of body, mind, and spirit has been a spiritual practice. In today's genetically modified food industry, the bread on the kitchen table must be regarded as sacred as that served at Holy Communion.

Convinced of society's profound need to be free from the colonization of farming and a culture of consumer convenience, I entered the church hell-bent on the reformation of our relationship to food. The conversation that morning, according to the comics in the circle, was meaty. It was no longer enough to give up red meat, salt, or sugar for good health. Now, we had to grapple with the burgeoning controversy surrounding ultra-processed foods.

Concerns were wide-ranging and complex. Teabags release billions of micro-plastic particles into our cups. Should we buy milk in plastic bags or cartons, with or without bovine growth hormones? With cheap, chemical-laden food-like products, it's difficult to acquire quality nourishment. Living at the 45th latitude with a short growing season, Virginia reminded us, we're prisoners to the food industry. Many can't afford to eat real food, and more don't take time to think about what the food they eat does to the body. The psychological and physiological stress of our diet is real. Our generation's food issues are overwhelming.

Lent, however, was an opportunity to look at the deeper issues – the beliefs our culture holds religiously. Humanity holds God-given dominion over the Earth. (Genesis 1:26) Animals are commodities. Progress makes it possible to have any food any time of the year. The more we consume, the better it is for the economy. These beliefs allow us to troll the supermarket aisles not counting the costs of refrigerated transportation to the atmosphere, or of solo-crop agriculture to the biosphere. The conversation revealed just how we've been contented prisoners to destructive ideas.

A time for spiritual inventory, we named the pillars of the agribusiness as entitlement, greed, profits, and impoverishment. We acknowledged we are inextricably interconnected with the planet; we recognized our food for the animal and plant life that it is; we noted our false sense of self-sufficiency.

A time for renewal, we sought to recover a sense of awe, gratitude, and humility. We acknowledged the importance of a more plant-based diet, cooking seasonally and as locally as possible. We discovered a spirituality of food is essential if we're to break free from a lifestyle based on eco-injustice.

No one could argue with the ethics of food, Matt began. Their village had been the first in the region to have a farmers' market. His daughter-in-law's samosas were a big-seller. But that was a three-month deal. Until society recreated themselves as a garden-culture and everyone became a part of the food system by learning how to can and preserve enough in the Autumn to last through the Winter, the topic of unethical food put us on a very slippery slope. His wisdom reminded us that our conversation was not only part of an evolution in consciousness; it was about the reinvention of our faith.

As the first Sunday in Lent came to a close, folks gathered as usual at the refreshment table. There was energy and companionship enough to nourish us all. As we reached for Cathy's delicious muffins made from bananas grown by the multinational Chiquita corporation in Central America on deforested land using thirty-five pounds of pesticides per acre, and drank our cups of micro-plastic tea, the dream of life locked within the prison of contentment seemed very real.

Opening the Door on Sin

We must yearn first for our own evolution beyond the separated state. Barbara Marx Hubbard

With each swing of the door separating the sanctuary and cloakroom, a refugee from the winds and mud of March arrived. It was another Lenten Sunday, another opportunity to seek a consciousness of freedom.

Attentions went quickly to what was different. The crucifix, symbol of Jesus' suffering and central to the Lenten season, was missing. In its place was a derelict window frame. Multi-paned, it illustrated our compartmentalized society which separates religion from science, education from spirituality, healthcare from the environment, and so on. Pointing out the window's cracked and missing panes, the message was clear. The worldview of dualism was broken and in need of replacement.

Displacing a philosophy or lifestyle is no small challenge. Society has been steeped in dualism since the Greek scholar Plato taught Heaven as separate from Earth three centuries before Jesus and almost seven centuries before the Church Fathers came up with Original Sin in the fourth century. And don't forget, in the twelfth century the papacy deemed the physical world of matter and body as the realm of science, and spirit the realm of the church. Dualism, the belief in a mechanistic universe of separate parts, is deeply entrenched.

I learned dualism as a child in the pews. With head dutifully bowed, I listened as Reverend Bugden listed the world's transgressions and led us in prayers of confession. I learned, without a doubt, humanity was fallen from grace and far from holy. (Romans 5:12) When I was older, I questioned the words of assurance, "God so loved the world that He gave his only Son that we should not perish but have eternal life." Somehow, I felt less assured of my oneness with than my separation from this deity.

This compartmentalized worldview, I believe, has helped bring society to the brink of disaster. Using pesticides that poison the pollinators to maximize crop output to optimize profits – this is the result of dualistic thinking. When we deny the nature of reality is inter-relatedness, it's because we're imprisoned in a comfortable criminal cosmology. When, to bring larger quantities of crops to market, we use immense quantities of fossil fuels, water, and toxic chemicals that have been connected to the rise of cancer, we are prisoners to the myth of separation. Dualism is the sin behind the sin.

Sin is not a word used a lot in progressive Protestantism. Having escaped denominations that denounced all manner of happy social activities as sinful, the word raised red flags for Paul and Ria.

A step back to better understand the word was in order.

In its truest sense, sin means a transgression against the perceived order of divine law. But as the gay man in my dreams reminded me, so much of what once was perceived as against divine order – divorce, women in leadership, the science of evolution, gender and sexual diversity – has become the norm. Today some see genetically modified foods as a transgression against the natural order. The point is this: sin is contextual, a cultural point of view that changes. In the context of Earth's environmental dis-ease, the denial of the integrated and interdependent nature of reality is a sin.

To unpack dualism, I told two stories.

The Traditional – The Baptism of Jesus

It was the moment for which John had been born. For years he'd lived like a prophet of old, clothed in camel skins, eating locusts and wild honey, condemning the corruption of king and priests, the poverty of the people, and the oppression of Rome. "Liberation! A liberator's coming! Prepare!" His radical message drew the marginalized from all over Judah to his wilderness sanctuary. "Be baptized, be ready!" His threat drew them into the Jordan river to wash away their sin. Then the day he'd predicted arrived. Jesus stood before John to be baptized "No, he should be baptized by the Messiah," John insisted. But it was not to be.

This was the moment the Nazarene had been preparing for. And it did not disappoint. Stepping into those holy waters, he came home to the reality of his being and a clarity of purpose. He understood himself as a child of the One he called *Adonai Eloheinu, Adonai Ehad,* part of a

> complete whole with a purpose and responsibility to the future of creation.
>
> After his mystical experience, the young rabbi retreated into the barren uplands of Judea. In the wilderness, hunger and thirst, power and wealth tempted him to a self-centred life. But in the end, he remained true to the divine order and lived as one within the whole. (paraphrase, Luke 3:22, Matthew 4:1-11)

If you grew up in the pew, you may have noted a few differences in the story. One being the absence of Satan and Spirit. If you're a true Pewster, you'll want to know why. This is an interpretation free of a worldview that posits life as a war between good and evil. It no longer projects human instincts, emotions, and actions onto external powers; it is free of dualistic theology that teaches separation of divine and human. The agenda is not to proclaim Jesus as Savior and Redeemer of a fallen creation, but as a mystic and mirror for all of us. The passage serves not to elevate and separate us from Jesus but to reveal a new cosmology of non-duality. The differences help us see Jesus baptism for the revelation of a new divine order that it is.

As important as this new interpretation of the story was that these insights were brand-new to me. Where had they come from? The answer seemed to require the next story.

The Evolutionary – The Flash of Insight

> A 360-degree panorama flashed past the astronaut's window every two minutes. Black of space, Earth, moon, black of space, Earth, moon ... Again and again, this reality flashed before his eyes. Somewhere in this extra-terrestrial experience, Edgar Mitchell had his own mystical experience. He realized that his molecules, and those of his colleagues, as well as the molecules of the spaceship in which he sat, in fact the molecules of the whole planet had all been prototyped in some ancient generation of stars.

> Everything was inter-related. In a flash of consciousness, he was free. Free from religious dualism that preached a Heaven and an Earth, free from classical science that taught Universe was like a machine of separately functioning parts. Returning to Starship Earth, Mitchell founded the Institute of Noetic Sciences to probe the profound mystery of Consciousness, that intelligence in the cosmos which is ever-integrating one form with another in ever-greater unity.

Half a century after the first moon landing, consciousness of our deeper interconnectedness is growing. You, me, one after another are finding freedom from the philosophy of dualism and recognizing the undeniable and amazing oneness of reality.

What is consciousness? That was the morning's question. While it's something we usually talk of as being raised, it's much more than a state of mind. It's also the highest cosmic frequency, the original intelligent and evolutionary force that brought atom to atom, and cell to cell. Consciousness is what's always pressing toward radical transformation for greater harmony. Some say it's the name we're discovering for God. It can be said that the Spirit that drove Jesus to become a champion of the people is the Consciousness that compels Vandana Shiva to fight for India's peasant farmers. As well, it is the force freeing one then another from the sin behind the sin to recognize the oneness of all existence.

Holy Consciousness is breaking through the brokenness of global warming. It's calling the church back to its radical roots of commitment to equity and unity, to the divine order. It's raising awareness everywhere that real justice must honour the land, waters, plants, animals, and sustain the whole planetary family. In Lent, the opportunity is polishing our relationship within the whole. That might mean freeing ourselves from the perilous paradigm of separation and accepting our response-abilities for food security. It might look like committing to a diet that is ecologically sustainable, socially ethical, and spiritually freeing. Could we, this Lent, participate in such an evolution of Consciousness?

Fred's frown told me he was dubious. And rightly so. This was not a simple ask. This was not just learning about the injustice of the agribusiness. This was not even a matter of fasting from junk food, or forsaking processed meats for a month. Freeing ourselves from a corrupted economic system, from a worldview of us and them, from a belief-system of holy and unholy, and from a lifestyle of comfortable convenience so to live at a deeper level of interdependence, this requires breaking free of sinful systems. Born in Hitler's Germany under a reign of genocide, Fred knew few were able to make a clean break of it.

Opening the Door of Sacrifice

> *Practise letting go of local self's desire to organize and allow integrated ego/essence to guide your actions all day.* Barbara Marx Hubbard

Sacrifice, one of Lent's great challenges, is a topic that carries a lot of baggage. Rosemary called it a virtue used to justify the oppression of women. Bruce, on the other hand, glorified the sacrifice of veterans like his father who'd died for their country. Parents make sacrifices for their children all the time, Matt added. There were none in the circle who couldn't speak personally about sacrifice. It's part of life.

I wondered if the circle would be willing to make the sacrifice I was about to ask of them. On the table sat the congregation's worn, leather-bound Bible. Carrying it down from the chancel where I'd found it on the lower shelf of the pulpit buried under a pile of old service bulletins, I'd thought, "It's heavy." Literally, it was as heavy as a ten-pound bag of potatoes. In addition, given the scandals of sexual abuse by priests, debates over homosexuality, right-wing conservatism, and the church's role in the Residential Schools program, any talk of the Good Book made for an emotionally heavy conversation.

Could we let go of the Bible as our sole authority for wisdom? This was the sacrifice I was asking for. Once, we revered the Good Book as the Holy Word of God. Fundamental Christians still believe in the literal interpretation of scriptures. Liberal seminaries, however, teach us to view scripture with a hermeneutic of suspicion. Questioning what we're reading, asking who was the author, what was his agenda, when was it written, is the passage an original account or a theological construct. This trend in current scholarship is changing how we view the Bible.

A case in point is Jesus' crucifixion. The biblical story is part of a historical account. The claim that his death was an intentional sacrifice in exchange for our eternal salvation, however, is a theological construct. The latter has fostered worship of a Jesus as divine and taught sacrifice as a superhuman act. In doing so, we have failed to understand sacrifice as the cosmic pattern of existence that it is.

To that end, I'd brought the evolutionary story.

The Evolutionary – Story of Tiamat

> The aged star had become a great supernova; Tiamat was in her death throes. Dying in a magnificent explosion, her essence was scattered across the Universe. From that sacrifice came not only the Sun, but this third rock from the Sun, our home. An amalgam of selenium, carbon, iron, gold, hydrogen, and more, Earth is made from the elements of stars. From that star stuff came Archaebacteria and Eukaryotes – early forms of single-celled life. In time, they too were sacrificed to the evolutionary pattern; their death gave birth to the nucleated cell, the basis of all complex, biological life. Fish in the sea, birds in the sky, and every living creature that moves on the ground are subject to the

> cycle of sacrifice. Mouse's body is sacrificed to nurture the body of Hawk. Plants and trees bear fruit to be harvested by Bear and Deer. Berries and Salmon become the body of Bear; Bear becomes the body of Raven; Raven becomes the body of Maggot. Sacrifice, it is the bond between creatures; the dance that enlivens the whole.

That sacrifice is an essential step in the evolutionary process is a freeing discovery. Part of the cosmic dance, it leads to ever-greater complexity, diversity, and resilience. Not a super-human capacity at all, sacrifice is part of nature's nature. It's an ability to respond for the sake of the whole that's inherent to everything and everyone. With this new reality, I realized, yet again, science can augment the church's understanding of what it means to be human. When we embrace science as sacred revelation, the church will be better able to guide society beyond a lifestyle of convenience afforded by a destructive fossil fuel economy.

As illustration, I raised the topic of cruise ship holidays. A wave of dis-ease swept the circle. Cheap cruises enable more folks of less financial means to see the world than ever before. Even the national church's magazine sports shiny travel ads for cruises to sacred sites. The prophets of marketing have projected thirty million persons will take one or more cruises in 2019. The issue is that most ships continue to use the most toxic and heaviest of fuels, fuels that on land are classified as hazardous waste. A mid-sized ship can use as much as one hundred and fifty tonnes of fuel each day and emit as much particulate as one million cars. Society's love of cruising is polluting our air and sickening the oceans. While there's no biblical passage declaring, you shall not cruise, the science tells a different story.

Fred, whose habit is to listen with eyes closed, was now peering at me from over his glasses. His brow was deeply furrowed. "Most folks today," he growled, "haven't ever had to make the kind of choices you're talking about." Sacrificing his privacy, he began to share his own story. Growing up in the Fuhrer's Reich, he'd been expected to be part of the Youth For

Hitler movement. His choice not to do so, to be another kind of German and another kind of Christian was hard, unspeakably hard. In doing so, he sacrificed home and family and moved to another country an ocean away. "Most people either don't acknowledge the hard choices, or aren't willing to give up the easier life." Fred had a unique perspective on the reality of real sacrifice.

The topic had reached deep into the octogenarian's life. Having moved from part of the establishment to being a foreigner in his own land, he knew the deeper meaning of the word. Having seen the majority refuse to risk their lives to protect others, he insisted that sacrifice is an extra-ordinary act. While his poignant words struck home and a deep sadness in all, in the end, his story illustrated how the human, in fact, does have the capacity to make hard sacrifices. Fred's story illustrated how one person by choosing to cooperate with the evolution of consciousness for the greater good can find freedom.

At the end of the morning, the choice to go forward with both the biblical and evolutionary stories as sources of revelation was a non-event.

That week Bill, with left-over boards from his garage, tube lighting, and Dorothy's old blue curtains, crafted a spiral reminder of the ever-expanding evolutionary story and hung it between two stained-glass windows. There was no hue and cry. The real sacrifices, we all knew, lay in the everyday and political choices ahead.

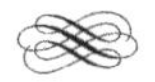

Opening to Oneness

The third Sunday in Lent brought the kind of damp cold that pierces one's peace of mind. It was the day to get to the heart of this spiritual season. Atonement – that's the Lenten carrot. In the weeks before Easter, Christians strive a little harder to do good deeds to cancel out past sins, or at least feel some remorse. That's the story. But as always, there's more to the story. The idea of atonement – we need to restore a harmonious relationship with God by wiping the sin-slate clean – is not Jesus' teaching. It was part of his tradition's temple practices.

The Traditional – Story of a Tradition

> Once a year, on the Day of Atonement, the High Priest would ask God to forgive the people. Dressing in sack-cloth, the official would take two goats, kill one, then sprinkle its blood around the inner sanctuary so to eradicate the sin. Then, tying a red cord around the neck of the second goat and laying a hand on its head, he'd call out each villager's transgressions until the guilt of the whole community was heaped on the back of the scapegoat. Eager to be rid of their sinfulness, the priest and the people would then, with shouts and stones, chase the animal away. As a result of the ritual act, harmony between Heaven and tribe was said to be restored.

Sixty years after the crucifixion, John wrote, "Jesus Christ, the one who is truly righteous, is the sacrifice that atones for our sins – and not only our sins but the sins of all the world." *(John 1 2:1-2)* And so Jesus became the people's scapegoat. It was the beginning of what we call substitution theology.

The history lesson raised eyebrows and commentary. Bo surmised most folks never knowing the story of the goats simply accepted the claim, "Jesus died for our sins." Rosemary said feminists had rejected the idea of a God who'd condone the death of his child. Bryan, a visiting clergy, claimed he'd long-abandoned the doctrine. For Matt, it was enough that Jesus' death was a reminder how every time we push evil back, we're renewed, if only for a moment. The atonement theory, Joyce observed, was also based on dualism. It was a freeing conversation.

Standing on the table was an iconic photo of the pearl-blue planet. The image, taken from Apollo 17 in the '70s, is a paragon of oneness. Oneness as the true nature of our reality was confirmed in 1918 when Max Planck discovered energy quanta. Since then the world's been trying to grasp his discovery – everything is part of an inter-connected matrix of consciousness. When we can comprehend and accept our place in a cosmic matrix of consciousness, it will replace our image Heaven, Hell, and Earth being separate floors in a three-tiered Universe. For now, NASA's photograph of the Earth was a good beginning.

Nothing is separate from what the theoretical physicist called the intelligent and conscious mind. When we can accept that, the church can let go Christ as the only way to God. Then, I suggested, we will have gained what one futurist called, "a continuity of consciousness that remembers the whole story of creation."[xxxv] A humanity conscious of the whole story! Would such a world even be trapped by the green-house gas crisis? Conscious of reality as a state of *at-onement,* would anyone even be in need of atonement? It was a hopeful vision, Matt said. Unable to hide his skepticism, I knew he meant it was a naive idea. But I wasn't daunted. If there was some grace in the environmental crisis, it's that ideas are changing. We're gaining a deepening sense of oneness. To that end I'd brought another story.

The Evolutionary – You are stardust

Neil wanted a bedtime story. It was the night after he'd been to the planetarium and he had questions. He wanted the real story about where everything came from. Mom, who'd grown up with more popular science than Sunday School, put on her best storyteller voice and began. You came from the stars. The calcium and iron in your bones – she tickled his knee – once upon a time was stardust. Your eyes are the new-improved version of the first eyes

> on the tiniest sea squirt in the deepest ocean. She kissed each eye closed. Every tear you cry returns to the ocean. Every breath you take comes from the oxygen produced by tiny ocean plants. Every sigh you sigh is carbon dioxide which the trees and oceans absorb. Your skeleton – her fingers walked up his spine making him wiggle down into the covers – came to us from the first fish. Just as sure as you come from mommy and daddy, you, along with the plants and animals, came from the Earth and the stars. When the story was finished, Neil had more questions but they could wait. That night he dreamt wonder full dreams, dreams of swimming with brother Bass and flying with sister Sparrow, dreams that led him home to the stars.

At the story's end, the smiles that only grandparents smile, ringed the circle.

"If they could grow up knowing themselves at one with all things and all things as holy," Joyce, reasoned, "they might love the natural world as much as themselves." Owner of a lakeside lodge, the woman had fostered relationships with the Earth all her life.

I added my own dream. Perhaps that Consciousness, that God that gathered male and female, Greek and Jew, slave and free into the oneness of those first inter-spiritual house churches, is dancing us to the edge of unconditional love and deeper intimacy once again.

Opening Death's Door.

The Sunday before Good Friday is Palm Sunday. Remembering Jesus as the peoples' liberator, it begins with lots of waving palms and triumphant music. It ends remembering his trial and crucifixion with the lashing of whips and pounding of nails.

The cross stood once again on the Lenten table. Bruce was visibly pleased. It had been donated by the McNamara family in the fifties and part of the congregation's story. More importantly, he regarded it as central to his faith. For me, its brassy brightness stood in glaring contrast to the old-growth cedar table, a symbol of our growing Gaia-consciousness. Desmond and Paul were less than happy. I had some explaining to do.

In the beginning, the cross was simply a sad reminder of Jesus' gruesome execution. It wasn't until the fourth century, when Rome's Emperor Constantine instituted Christianity as the religion of the empire, that it became a symbol of import. In 2006, in their latest statement of belief, the United Church described the cross as "the effectual means of reconciling the world unto God." This morning, as our ocean's chemistry is changing in ways we'd never seen, and lifeforms are being demolished at rates we've never known, the cross has something to say. We exist in a culture of death!

There is in the world a great grief. It is arising in us as if from Earth herself. And yet we seldom name it with family, friends, or sister pewsters. We are talking about global warming, but we're not acknowledging the suppressed anxiety it causes. The cross, I hoped, could help us acknowledge and hold the suffering of the planet as sacred as we hold the suffering of Jesus.

Rosemary and Paul, experienced grief-group leaders, agreed to the importance of talking about death in a context of hope. In fact, that's the Protestant party line. We display an empty cross as a sign of life's victory over death. Desmond quoted texts that teach death as a doorway to new life. "He who loves his life will lose it, he who hates his life in this world will keep it for eternal life."(John 12: 23) "A grain of wheat falls into the ground and dies only to produce much grain." (John 12:24) The latter, I pointed out as my personal favourite. It makes death to be "an explosive event."[xxxvi] And who couldn't marvel that Jesus' death was a type of an explosive event initiating a world-wide community. The cross is a reminder of this promise – death is an expansion of all life.

Along with what was, perhaps, a new interpretation of the cross, I'd brought a story from the sciences.

The Evolutionary – Death's Dance

> In the beginning, out of the simultaneous creation and annihilation of elementary subatomic particles, the dance of mass and energy began. Born out of nuclear fusion, primal stars began their journey to death. In dying, they would be scattered as stardust and seed the Universe with even more suns and planets. Death, stars remind us, is not annihilation but an expansive event. In the beginning, single cells coded with death as a way of new life, died to become multi-celled, sexual beings. Death was an evolutionary doorway. Death is nature's invitation to an expansive future, greater diversity, and deeper complexity. In the cosmic ballet, all is held in the synergistic embrace.

With the second story, I was attempting to put the cross within the cosmic dance. My hope was that we might see Jesus' death through deep time eyes and know death as a servant of more life. But more to the point was the importance of seeing the cross as a symbol for our immediate culture of death. To that end, I dared to ask big questions. Could we see the tragedy of mass extinction as a catalyst for an explosive expansion of environmental consciousness? Could we recast the cross as a symbol of freedom from the fear and apathy stirred by global warming?

The morning ended with a delicious buffet – macaroni and cheese, home-made bread, salads, meatballs, and desserts. All this for $5.00. The food, of course was prepared and donated by the pewsters themselves. The monies went to an international campaign to aid children orphaned by AIDS. In this way did the synergistic dance of death and life, life and death play out in our wee small corner.

Closing the Door on Lent

The season ended as it began – with the surprising promise of freedom. Through an evolutionary worldview, Lent had become less about penitence than emergence. We had evolved beyond doctrines that separate life into the holy and unholy. We had died to the culture of death, the sin behind the sin, and the destructive cosmology of dualism. And through it all, we were coming to a deeper understand of Jesus' death on a cross: it was not a substitute for our sinfulness but an illustration of a universal and archetypal pattern that the grandchildren of the Earth family needed us to follow. We had moved beyond slavish loyalty to our canonical text and expanded our sources of wisdom.

As well as science and personal experience, there is a world of spiritual truths. In the *Tibetan Book of Living and Dying,* we found this: "One who's learned how to die has unlearned how to be a slave."[xxxvii] It was the message of the dream! The Lenten season brought us to the ultimate paradox – death is freedom's partner. And with that, we were ready to continue our dance through the Christian seasons.

Evolutionary Wisdom

- Jesus was baptized, not into the role of a Heavenly Saviour and Redeemer, but into a consciousness and cosmology of non-duality.
- Jesus died not as a scapegoat taking away the sins of the world, but as part of a universal pattern in which death leads to new life.
- In the cosmic ballet, all things are held in the synergistic embrace of death and life.
- The suffering of the planet is as sacred as the suffering of Jesus.
- It is critical, both spiritually and environmentally, we return to the practice of sacrifice.
- The fasting required – from fast food, processed meats, meat-based diets, agribusiness, fast fashion, air travel, cruising, fossil fuels – is from humanity's self-polluting phase.
- Pollution is a transgression against the natural order.

The 21st-century creation story begins with the Big Bang, spirals into Universe, planets, life, biological life, human life, Homo Amore Universalis, infinite potential … Through the seven spirals of this evolutionary worldview, Lent, the season of letting go, seems less about penitence for past sins and more about emergence into all we can become.

CHAPTER 11

Raising Resurrection

If religion itself cannot lead the way in this denial of the denial of the Cosmic Christ, in this resurrection, ascension, and sending of the Spirit to Mother Earth by way of a resurrected humanity, then we are in deep trouble indeed. Matthew Fox

It was Easter, as foundational to Christianity as the Canadian Shield is to Ontario. Known as the celebration of Jesus' resurrection, it's a big deal. What most don't know is that the word Easter is a derivative of Ostur, the old Germanic name for the Goddess of Dawn once associated with the return of Spring.

Pulling into the church driveway, I thought of those Scots, Irish, and Dutch settlers who raised the first building in the same year Canada hammered out its Confederation. But even before that, they'd been celebrating Easter in Kinmount since 1859.

In search of farmland promised by the Colonization Homestead Act, those first pioneers had trekked three hundred kilometres north from the mighty St. Lawrence River only to find rock, swamp, cedars, pines, more rock, and harsh winters.

A town monument remembers the Icelandic settlement that didn't survive. I could only guess at the importance of those first resurrection Sundays to our ancestors.

Bill waved as he climbed the same stone steps his grandmother had climbed.

As I crossed the gravel driveway, the old bell sounded. Did the once-thriving, now-hobbling hamlet hear the great Easter exclamation, Jesus has risen? Or had it become part of their pastoral soundscape assuring them life went on as usual?

These were not usual times. Neonic pesticides threaten pollinators responsible for 75% of the world's food.[xxxviii] Mass destruction of Indonesian rain forests to produce palm oil is eradicating an entire ecosystem and a major part of our planetary respiratory system. It struck me, the global village might need to hear the resurrection promise in 2020 more than it did in the first century.

Resurrection – we can rise from death to live again. It's a complex idea that's meant many things to many peoples in different times. In the Abraham religions in the Middle East, returning to life after death was powerful lore. Egyptians spoke of Osiris who had risen from death, Canaanites of Baal, the ancient Greeks of Asclepius and Heracles. To explain the seasons, Roman mythology told how Hades, on stealing Demeter's sweet daughter Persephone away to the Underworld, plunged the land into winter. Only when she returned, did Spring come again. Resurrection is less a single religion's defining event than a universal spiritual theme.

The power of resurrection faith is remarkable. At its best, it raises a society from despair into hope and action. Such was the case when Jesus was thought to be one of Israel's great prophets come back to life to save them from the Roman Empire. At it's best, a resurrection faith creates justice where there was injustice. Believing Jesus would return from death to establish a new kingdom, his followers created communities of never-before inclusivity. Such a belief, however, can also be abused. With the slogan, "Make America Great Again," it has been used to deny the present climate reality and promise the impossible – a return to the past. In these times, the church needs a strong resurrection-faith in future ecojustice if they are to stand up to the Corporate Empire. That was the message I was bringing to the Easter series.

Inside, the one-room clapboard church looked magnificent. Rosemary had transformed the cross of death into a tree of life with purple crocus, pink tulips, yellow forsythia, white lilies, and blue hyacinths. Spring's blossoms were a testament to a resurrection story older than that of the empty tomb.

The twenty souls that gathered in the heritage church were ready to celebrate their own resurrection. Pulling together, they'd risen above a district oversight committee's death sentence and kept their congregation alive for over a decade. Jubilant, they were the ones in the 'one in four Canadians who still attended Sunday services.' Part of the 67% who believe that through the birth, death, and resurrection of Jesus, God provides new life. They were an Easter people.

Easter, not just one morning but a season lasting fifty days, was about to begin. From my foray out and beyond Mother Church, I was bringing atypical stories of resurrection. The weeks to come would be a venture beyond our theological comfort zone.

Finding what's Missing

Looking for the familiar thrill of the Easter Story in a foreign land is a story in itself. The gift may be as much in what you don't see and hear as what you do. But then, the Easter story has always been about what's missing.

> The cacophony of trumpets, guitars, and dancers clinging like smoke, we left the nightclub and picked our way

through the dark cobblestone street. The only light was that of a small fire ahead. Curious. What was going on at this late hour in the rustic village of San Antonia? Drawn like a moth to the flame, we headed for the light.

The fire burned outside the walls of *la eglisa.* It was the Easter Saturday Vigil and the street fire was what's called The New Fire, symbol of the Risen Christ.

Through the arched entrance, we saw the church courtyard was set with rows of chairs. A sprinkling of miracle seekers had already taken seats and awaited the midnight hour. Intuitively, I moved through the stone archway and took a seat. It didn't matter that I was a Protestant and a gringo with no fluid comprehension of Catholicism or Spanish. My partner, his dream of retiring into his Mexican hammock hijacked, was puzzled. But my hunger for the mystery and promise of the resurrection story shared with a faith family was not to be denied.

Inside the courtyard was quiet and still as though the nearby nightclub's noise was not allowed. Waiting for the drama to unfold was challenging. Musicians began to assemble. They looked a lot like members of the mariachi band that played in the square. Women made final additions of flowers to the alter. The table had been brought outside the sanctuary and sat on a stage built atop the front steps. The two hundred or more chairs slowly and quietly were filling up. Preparation, assembling the gifts, taking our place in the drama, waiting and watching – these were the lessons of the holy vigil.

Finally, like so many attendants before a bride, altar boys and girls carrying candles lit from the sacred fire in the street, paraded to the front. Carefully, they lit the two-feet-tall candles that stood either end of the table. The music began, the parish priest, short and swarthy, arrived bedecked in a white alb, the garb of the servant. The Mass was about to begin.

Despite it being all in Spanish, I sunk into the liturgy like a beloved family rocking chair.

"El Senor esta contigo." The Lord be with you.

"And also with you." My response came as natural as breath.

"Al Amanecer del primer día de la Semana María Magdalena y la otra María vinieron a ver el sepulcro." I didn't need its translation. I knew the story – on the first day of the week, the women came to the tomb.

"Su aspecto era como un relámpago" There was an earthquake.

"No temáis." Don't be afraid.

"La resurrección." He is risen.

"Aleluya." Hallelujah, indeed. The story, inscribed on the heart of all who'd grown up in the bosom of Mother Church, was what I and the two hundred others sitting and standing in the tepid Mexican midnight had come to hear.

No one minded the service was cobbled together from four unique accounts. It didn't matter that in one, the risen Christ was a touchable body and in another, an untouchable spirit. The differences were simply the authors' trademarks. The truth lay hidden in the folds of time and the wounds of our lives.

Well into hour two, like birds that know when and where to migrate, the congregation rose and moved as one toward the host and cup. When their hungers for forgiveness, healing, or hope were fed, they returned to their seats, again, by some invisible path. This is the power of ritual; it creates patterns, paths, and one people.

Approaching the third hour, my sitting bones protesting loudly, a shocking beam of light directed our attention to the left of the make-shift chancel. As good as any movie set, a rocky outcrop appeared to project from the church-wall. In front of what we were to believe was the tomb where Jesus had been laid stood a four-foot high, too-round stone.

Then we were plunged again into darkness and the thunder of the mariachi's drums. When the light reappeared, we saw a beautiful young villager disguised in white robes. His message came straight from scripture.

"I arose, and am with you still. Wherever you may fall, you will always fall into my hands. I am present even at the door of death, even there I am waiting for you, and for you, I will change darkness into light." (Psalm 138)

No one minded the text was written half a century before Jesus lived. No one focused on the theological questions raised by talking angels, lightning bolts, or earthquakes. It was the cosmic message we'd come for: life will always overcome death.

Then the light went out and the Paschal mystery play was finished for another year. We joined the exodus of young parents carrying sleepy toddlers, and adult children supporting tired elders. As we inched our way out of the courtyard into the cobble-stoned darkness, the musicians rushed past us to don their mariachi regalia and serenade patrons of the *barras*. The young Jesus rejoined his amigos to talk of soccer. Gringos, having drunk deeply of the familiar in a strange land, went to relax into a few more days of sunshine.

The ritual, offering as it did something to everyone, was a miracle in and of itself. Literalists heard how Jesus rose on the third day assuring their personal salvation. (1 Corinthians 15:1-5) The grieving left hopeful of the eventual reunion with loved ones. Liberals and mystics, needing neither dogma nor theology, found in the images and metaphors the holy promise – light always trumps darkness. Able to sustain us all, it was a good story.

And yet, come the first news of the new day, I was bereft. In Australia, more than a billion animals had been killed in unprecedented fires. Extreme weather conditions

> have turned something familiar into something abnormal. Last night's Easter drama had offered no hope for the larger Earth family. There'd been no call to live and work for planetary salvation. I'd looked for the familiar and discovered traditional Christianity lacked relevance in these burning times.

At Easter children traditionally hunt for coloured eggs. Adults seek the promise of a safe eternity. The disciples looked for the risen Jesus. It may be comforting to look for what we know. But in abnormal times, what we know is not enough. At Easter, the Church must help us seek what's missing that today fires ravage the world. What's missing within the heart and soul of our lives? What's missing within the institutional structures of church and society? Surely at Easter we must be sent out to seek that love and power which lies as though entombed and waiting to be found.

I looked to the Kinmount circle who were facing an uncertain future. The times demanded the pioneer spirit in them rise and enter the wilderness yet again. I believed they could take the familiar Easter message – there is life after death – and rise to the present and real challenges of global warming.

A Taste of the Future

Another week in the Easter season, I brought the circle a story from my deep dive into Eco-spirituality.

> It was the earliest and blackest of mornings. Using only the light from the digital clock I saw it was the appointed hour, 4:30 am. I got dressed and began the adventure I'd come for. Following instructions which had suggested, no flashlights, I was forced to use some long-unused senses to navigate my way. With each footfall, the wooden steps

leading from my third-floor bedroom protested loudly as I felt my way down to the main floor, along the hallway, into the kitchen, and out the back door. I stepped onto the gravel path that led to the woods. It was pouring darkness.

Arms waving like antennae, I beetled forward dodging branches only to plow into wispy-wet webs. Slug-like, I inched over the rise and fall of Gaia's body. Surely, there is no darker place than a forest impoverished of stars or moon. Resisting the urge to hurry out of my blindness, I walked cautiously placing one foot after the other.

The forest floor was spongy and thick with memories. It had been laid down over hundreds of thousands of Autumns atop igneous and metamorphic rocks born of the Late Precambrian and Early Paleozoic ages. After many agonizing minutes, I stepped into an open field and inhaled deeply of the promise wafting up from the wakening soil.

Slimy grasses grabbing at my knees, I lengthened my strides toward the silhouette of my destination – an Amerindian teepee sitting in the back meadow. The crackle of the canvas flap told me my approach had not gone unnoticed. Stooping, I felt like the most devout believer genuflecting on entering a magnificent cathedral. A waiting hand guided me to my place in what was a unique pre-dawn gathering of Green Nuns in an obscure field of northern New Jersey.

Sinking gratefully into the blanket of silence, I began my wait for the prodigal sun. Any fears of arriving late I released into the realization that all humanity's coming late to the dawn of an Ecozoic worldview. All worries at being a Protestant in a Roman Catholic retreat dissolved in what united us – the cosmic law of differentiation, ecology's way of inter-dependence, and faith's promise of resurrection. These things we shared.

In that safe place, I passed one and a half hours. Sometimes my mind wandered to hot chocolate or the absurdity of it all. Sometimes I repeated a favourite poem,

"My heart is moved by all I cannot save. So much has been destroyed. I must cast my lot with those who, age after age, perversely, with no extraordinary powers reconstitute the Earth."[xxxix] Though my reasons for being here seemed muddled, I absolutely trusted I was where I needed to be.

When the tent flap was finally raised, air, fresh and juicy, rushed in pronouncing morning had broken. One by one, we moved through the portal. Step by step our procession moved over the still-waking field. My ears strained for some assurance that this was not the silent spring Rachel Carson had predicted pesticides would bring. My eyes sought even a sprout of grass, any sign that would witness to Darwin's truth, "geology proclaims a constant round of change, bringing into play by every possible change of climate and the death of pre-existing inhabitants, endless variations of new conditions."[xl]

What I did see was just as promising. We, this ragtag remnant of religious leaders, were that change. We were a variation of Christianity emerging for Gaia's new condition.

Cresting the hill, the bio-region of the Delaware River Valley stretched before us. A path cut through the winter wheat to a cairn built of stones, prayers, and visions. Filing past, each one added something: granite from the Canadian Shield, shale from the coast of Maine, dust from the drought-stricken fields of New Mexico. Each offering added to the intentions of this ritual place – Earth's resilience and a new humanity.

Returning, we crossed the still-thawing brook. Entering the lane, we marched through the tempting aromas of fresh bread and coffee wafting from the farmhouse. Resolute, we leaned toward our destination and bowed to the discipline of all ritual.

At that barren thicket, we looked for the cross bearing an image of the crucified planet that we'd laid there on Good Friday. But all signs of humanity's crimes against nature were gone. We lifted bramble, moved branches, looked under bushes unable to grasp that what had been true yesterday was not true today, But on that Easter morning, any reminders of the ways in which society made us all participants in ecocide had simply vanished.

Only when the tantalizing trill of a flute interrupted our confusion did we cast our gaze further afield. Across the woods and some distance away, a vibrant display of Spring's blessing circling the base of a giant Black Walnut tree captured our attention. Yellow forsythia, blue hydrangeas, and fiery tulips – the sight was more splendid than the most exquisite tapestry, more alluring than the most dogmatic doctrine. One by one, the tribe of rogue religious turned and moved toward the vibrant display of life.

On drawing close to where all Easter had broken through, much was revealed. Yesterday's farmers were this morning's musicians. Yesterday's gardeners this day's florists. In an instant our string of silent seekers was changed into a circle of spirits dancing round the Tree of Life. Only when we'd milked the last ounce of delight from that place, and our spirits were full to overflowing, did we turn back to our breakfast.

The kitchen island was laid like the most sacred communion table. Fruit, eggs, loaves of bread – here was Earth's body harvested for us. Juices, milk, water, teas, and coffee – there was Earth's lifeblood poured out for us. The meal was a holy Easter rite promising an abundant Ecozoic age.

A Christian community had celebrated the resurrection without denying the crucifixion of Mother Earth. That was my story. The event had spoken hope to its death and dying by celebrating the universal pattern of new life. We had mourned not the sacrifice of Jesus, but the dis-ease and decline of Mother Earth. The ritual joined hearts with humus that we might be reborn into lives of ecojustice. Free of theological rhetoric and rich with a new cosmology, the event allowed us to encounter the Cosmic Christ that fills the Universe in all its parts, (Ephesians 1:23) and rises new every Spring.

At Genesis Farm, we grounded the Easter Story in nature. An evolutionary ritual born of an Eco-spirituality, it was life-changing. Not just a retreat from tradition, it had been a venture into the future of my religious tradition.

Raised up by Science

On a third Sunday of the Easter season, I shared the story that had catapulted my faith over the walls of Christendom. I'd registered in the New Cosmology class to learn what the university syllabus described as, 'a new sacred story.' Here, as I remember and will never forget it, is the story he told.

> In the beginning, the Universe was born from the first flaring forth of energy. Hydrogen, carbon, and oxygen were concentrated by gravity into a web of gasses stretching time and space. From the nuclear fusion of these gases came the first stars. With iron at their core, some grew into giant red stars. In their explosive deaths, these supernovas scattered their essence upon the cosmos. From helium, hydrogen, carbon, oxygen, nitrogen and more, whole new generations of stars, planets, and life forms came into being. Since the beginning, there has been birth and death and resurrection.

Since the beginning there has been birth, death, and resurrection. The words, spoken with a reverence reserved for the most-sacred truths, struck my belief system like an incendiary bomb. Until that moment, I'd only ever known resurrection to be a theological concept, the power and purview of divinity; the ability that validated Jesus as the son of God.

His words shattered that revered ancient doctrine into oblivion. What was left was a new and exciting image of a universal power bringing out of death more Universe. It was a new beginning in which resurrection became a principal of cosmic creativity, and a pattern that was billions of years old.

But my tale is not complete without a word about the storyteller. Like the story itself, Larry Edwards was a myth buster. A scientist by training and a Roman Catholic by baptism, his mind was full of the Cosmos, his heart broken for the Earth, and his faith expanded by an evolution of consciousness. If there were moulds for scientists or Catholics, he'd have broken them both.

A natural storyteller, Larry, as we called him, reminded us science, like religion, is also a story.

With a charming familiarity, he spun the tale of a supernova called Tiamat. After burning for billions of years, the stellar being died in a solar explosion … "seeding the Universe with new stars," he liked to say. His deferential manner – commanding a never-before reverence for all things stellar – he'd learned from his teachers. Bryan Swimme and Thomas Berry also used romantic rhetoric to describe that particular star's death: "she may have showered sentient creatures with the radiant energy that time has transformed into living bodies and cathedrals in wheat fields …"[xli] A scientist and storyteller, Larry offered the star the same kind of respect he'd give to a venerable ancestor.

In his class, I gained a new cosmology to be certain. I learned resurrection is nothing that can be limited to the human experience. Everything – from stars above the farmhouse, to the endangered Five Lined Skink running through these highlands, to my unborn great-grandchildren, to Jesus – can be understood as a resurrection of Tiamat's light energy scattered billions of years ago. Of course, it's a little more complicated than that, but in essence, what I took away was this: everything comes from resurrected stardust.

As this new cosmology rose to prominence in my psyche, the doctrines and dogma of institutional Christianity crumbled like a sandcastle to the tides. In the wake of that event, I was free to see the Universe for the grace-full sanctuary it is. My faith was raised up by science.

Dancing Light

Seven weeks long, Easter is the longest season in the Christian year. On yet another of its Sundays, I shared one more interpretation of resurrection with the Kinmount circle. It was a brave and gentle message the retired Rev. Norm would say afterwards. High praise from one who understood the challenge of religious leadership – how to share one's changing faith in twenty minutes without stomping on the life-long beliefs of another. What Norm also understood is that sometimes it's the lived reality of the pewsters, and the popular science of society that changes the faith of the preacher. In this case, that was exactly what had happened.

On the eve of a new century, there were those in my city congregation who took the mind-body-spirit connection personally and seriously. Yuppies, young urban professionals, they sang classical church music on Sunday, studied yoga on Monday, went for acupuncture on Tuesday, and talked of light workers and energy healers at Wednesday evening meditations. Through the eyes of these *new agers,* I began to see quite a different world.

Some professed to be able to see auras, the energy-halos surrounding all plant, animal, and human life. Having only ever seen halos in religious paintings, I didn't pooh-pooh the idea, but neither did I embrace it. What I know now, from my smattering of science, is that we live within electromagnetic fields created by bio-photons. These particles of light, travelling one hundred and eighty-six thousand miles per second, travel through the microtubules in our cells and beyond our bodies thereby creating energy fields. Those with a practised and open mind can learn to see these emanations of light, auras.

Wilf's aura, I was told, was a warm yellow which was indicative of his sunny nature. That I understood. With a handsome shock of white hair, flirty blue eyes, and quick wit, the elder was popular. Folks liked to be in his company. Sixty-two years earlier, when he'd met Nancy at the CFO dance, (Canadian Forces Organization), "something happened" as he put it. Simply put, they fell in love. Their attraction was obvious. That I understood.

Today, if I attempt to explain what happened within the realm of the new science, it might sound like this. Wilf's energy, like the Sun that releases waves of photons which penetrate, warm, and transform its recipients, made folks feel good. In fact, "every organism, from bacteria to humans, appears to be in perpetual quantum communication,"[xlii] Because radiance, according to cosmological scientists, is how the Universe communicates with itself and makes things happen, we could say, there was a two-way flow of gravitons, an exchange of radiant energy between those two young people. And so it was, Wilf and Nancy, two sentient creatures permeated with the radiant energy of an ancient star vowed to communicate in light until death, which they did.

One last story comes from the day after Wilf's "resurrection." I went to see him in hospital having been called by Nancy to visit. Garbed in the iconic blue hospital gown, wired to some beeping, burping machine, the now eighty-something year old was glad to see me. Even after a near-fatal heart attack, he was smiling, excited even. He had a story to tell. He remembered moving off into a peaceful light, he said. But realizing he hadn't said goodbye to "his Nancy," he came back. Medicine calls such experiences near-death events. But isn't this yet another language for a universal truth – everything is a resurrection of dancing light?

Attempting to explain the attraction between two people using the science of light was nothing I would even have thought to do two decades ago. Why not? The answer rests in an important story.

Worship Class 101, 1987. A bodily resurrection, pronounced my esteemed professor, was the only resurrection to be celebrated on Easter. Talk of flowers springing from bulbs and winged ones from caterpillars is for butterfly-believers, he declared emphatically. A first-year seminarian, I was too timid to expose myself for the unorthodox thinker I was. The result was not only the shutting down of my sacred imagination. Every Easter Sunday sermon after that, I allowed his story to trump mine. Until the day after Wilf's light danced back to communicate one more time with Nancy.

There are many languages to describe death and resurrection – spirituality, religion, science, medicine, and law. Different cultures hold different beliefs. When science can help religion understand the phenomena of life returning from death in the language of light, however, I'm hopeful it will help change the prevailing dualistic worldview. If society was to come to see the world for the miracle of light that it is, then surely our relationship with the Earth would change. When Christians can regard not only the resurrection of Jesus as miraculous, but all the material world as an expression of resurrected dancing light, surely we would view everything as holy, holy, holy. Because we protect what is holy, my deep hope is one day we will come to love and protect, honour and obey nature until death us do part.

Consciousness Continues

What lives on after death? That must be the question the church asks at this critical time. The question captured the circle's attention. Is it Spirit, religion's term for the non-material nature of God, faithful spouses, and persistent mothers? Or can we understand that which continues to make choices and offer comfort after death as Consciousness?

Noetic Science is the study of Consciousness. I capitalize the word as I would Spirit. Max Planck, a theoretical physicist in quantum mechanics was awarded a Nobel Prize for his work that concluded matter and Universe to be derivative of Consciousness.

How is it I'd heard nothing in seminary of Consciousness as the energy that brought forth sentient creatures in the beginning and continues at the end of physical life? The answer is important. Christian education is just that, education to become Christian. It fails to look for the bridges to science or to help us understand what it means to be conscious beings.

I wanted to know more about the science of Consciousness and how it related to resurrection. The research on near-death experiences had this exciting story to tell. Subjects injected with the psychedelic Dimethyltryptamine, the same chemical manufactured by the brain in near-death experiences, reported a euphoric sense of separation and freedom from the body. Their conclusion, Consciousness is continuous, was a new take on resurrection.[xliii]

What of the nature of resurrected Consciousness? In death, as in life, it is interactive. This was the message of a Gaia Centre guest, Sid Kirkpatrick. The biographer[xliv] of American psychic, Edgar Cayce, he shared how, before the famed seer died in 1945, he'd freely provided information, accurate medical diagnoses and cures for more than fourteen thousand patients.

Cayce's source of wisdom was the Akashic Records. Described as a vast cosmic repository of thoughts, intentions, and deeds – past, present, and future – they reminded me of what's referred to in the Bible as the Book of Life. (Revelation 20:12) In truth, I'd always thought the Book of Life to be like Santa's list, a literary device to encourage good behaviour. It was a new idea that information is stored energetically in the 'Akasha.'

From Sanskrit, the word Akasha refers to the element of ether, the all-pervasive space of radiation, brilliance, or light. In

India's philosophy, Akasha is the womb from which everything has emerged and to which everything ultimately returns.[xlv] It is said to have tremendous influence on emotions, relationships, beliefs, and realities on a daily basis. Here was yet another belief system affirming that what continues after death is Consciousness.

Today, science and spirituality are expanding our views on life after death. In a deep meditation practice, Sandra communicated with her deceased husband for many months. Having read Christina Rasmussen's book, "*Where Did You Go – A Life-Changing Journey to Connect with Those We've Lost,*" she was able to discover so-called portals to the spirit realm. A how-to-manual, it advocates how we don't need to suffer the finality of death. We can share our loved ones' resurrection. Sandra's talks with her spouse eventually ended when he announced he had to move on to other work. By then, she was ready to let him go.

Have you ever received a message – in prayer, meditation, dreams, out of nowhere – from the invisible realm? This was the morning's question. When I confessed that my own family had one or two such stories, the smiles and nods around the circle encouraged me to share.

Mom's two a.m. visits began the week after her funeral. First to my father, then my sister, my daughter, and me. Each of us had awakened to find the very woman at whose graveside we'd gathered just days before standing at our bedside. She was, in her new life as she'd done so often in her old, tucking us in before she could rest. An annoying trait when I was forty, after her burial it was just too precious for words. An event I would have dismissed as my own fantasy, it was undeniable as a shared family experience.

The story freed Sheila, Wendy, Paul, and others to share. A touch of comfort on a grieving wife's back in the darkness. A reminder of bills to pay from a husband standing in the kitchen by the fridge. Joyce spoke of the place where, even after two decades, she still goes to feel close to her deceased husband.

Driving along a country road, an eagle had flown alongside Cindy's car. Though unnerving, there was no doubt it was a visitation from her deceased mother who'd had an intuitive bond with nature. Resurrection stories, we concluded, weren't limited to sacred texts.

During the weeks of Easter, predictably, the church revisits the biblical accounts of the disciples' encounters with the risen Jesus. Sharing a meal with them on the shores of the Galilee, joining travellers on the road to Emmaus and accompanying them home for supper, and of course, comforting Mary of Magdala in the garden. The stories remind us of Jesus' commitment to life. When they are used only to convince us he was the Son of God, our Saviour, much of their power is lost. Lost is the teaching of Jesus as an archetype, a mirror of human potential, in life and death. In these critical times, the church must recover the promise of the resurrection. Connection and communication is limitless. To be human is to receive messages that help us move foreward.

Messages from Eternity

That Consciousness lives on after death is something we already know. But why is it critical information to revisit in these times of planetary break-down and future uncertainty? The answer would come from yet other corners of the metaphysical world.

The phenomena of channelling was something I'd never taken seriously while in the pulpit. As a Christian, I'd never heard of, let alone studied anything about the process by which some individuals receive messages for others from those who have died. In truth, I'd actually distanced myself from those who claimed to be receiving transmissions. But once outside the church, in the Consciousness Conversations at the Gaia Centre, I was ready to explore new ideas.

Michael and Nancy introduced us to the Seth materials. Seth, I learned, didn't refer to any single entity in the invisible realm. It was the name of a collective of many energy personalities no longer focused in physical matter. Between 1963 and 1984, Seth had dictated a vast collection of practical wisdom through an American called Jane Roberts. These teachings – on both the inner reality and humanity's evolutionary potential – are archived at Yale University Library and accessible online. It was there I found Seth's instructions on the nature of life after death.

- Not only must you use your abilities after death, but you must also face up to yourself for those that you did not.
- You must learn to be co-creators – gods as you understand the term.
- You're learning responsibility – to handle the energy that is yourself for creative purposes and creation."[xlvi]

These directions, from the Consciousness that continues after death, made resurrection into something I'd never considered – a responsibility. Here was why we must ask the question, "what lives on after death?" After death, according to Seth, the obligation to use the creative energy of our consciousness continues. The contract of our lives extends beyond the grave. Expanding our potential and hope, this is vital information.

Automatic Drawing, psychic automatism, or magical art composed under the tutelage of spiritual beings – this phenomena stretched my sacred imagination even further. Gaia Centre's guest teacher was Wendy Oakes. She'd spread prints of Alma Rumball's automatic drawings over every surface turning the farmhouse into a massive undecipherable canvas of colour and form. It made for an other-worldly effect. Not unlike the cosmos before anyone had seen its constellations, I thought.

The drawings seemed to carry some mysterious power. The artist herself had never understood the brilliantly coloured figures and haunting hieroglyphics in her work. In an audio taped interview, Alma reported her hand moved by itself: "my hand just flies like the wind, just flies like the wind." Over her lifetime, she produced hundreds of these images. Alma's only explanation was that Jesus had appeared and told her to draw. Her renderings were all titled. Many were labeled Atlantis – the mythical, Utopian civilization that had been flooded. Others were of Joan of Arc, Jesus, and the creation story. Meticulous drawings of Eastern deities have since been authenticated as revered Tibetan and Buddhist symbols. Tubes coming from the mouths of these other-worldly beings suggested the art contained important communications.

A woman who'd never had a chance for higher education or to study world religions, Alma's story was compelling. A recluse who lived an hour away from where we were gathered, her life story pushed our conversation further. By talking only about the message of Jesus' resurrection, were we blind to what's happening around or in and through us? What about other art? Could we find divine communication in other than the Holy Word? Certainly Jeremy Munce, creator of The Alma Drawings film, began to see the drawings as an exploration of another plan for life. The message they brought him was to follow something greater than himself. Wendy Oake's life was also changed by the drawings. After the artist's death, she dedicated herself to bringing prints of the images to the public. The reason, she said, was to share the message she found in the images: pay attention lest we go the way of Atlantis.

Automatic drawing, formerly a suspect phenomena, was not anything I ever expected to make the subject of an Easter Sunday message. How far we've moved away from those traditional cultures that respected magical art as the sacred language of light. At the University of Creation Spirituality, art was taught to be a form of meditation, a means of communication with a higher Consciousness. In most churches, there's little room on a Sunday morning for art, meditation, or the wisdom that comes from total oneness with the Conscious Universe.

Channelling, in word or art, the concept stretched both my Easter imagination and my hope. The new-age revelation gave fresh promise to an old text, "remember, I am with you always, to the end of the age." (Matthew 28:20) I'd always understood the text's message to mean that the risen Christ was always available to believers. But in light of the new knowledge – in death, responsibility for life continues – the former interpretation felt too small. Now, we could all say to our loved ones, "I will be with you always." Speaking these words, I heard my voice soften. The hope was not to destroy but expand our beliefs about life after life.

The responses from the circle to my so-called brave reflections on resurrection were just that – brave. Open to other than the biblical stories, they were extending authority to things beyond the church – to science, to their own experiences, and to their deepest longings. In retrospect, it was a remarkable conversation; we were participating in nothing less than the resurrection of hope eternal. Ursula, a cherished Oma to a loving family, spoke quietly from a place of deep thought. "I like to think that after my death, I might still care for those I love."

Abraham, Michael, Lazarus are other known consciousness-entities communicating from life beyond life. Books and audios make their wisdom available to the masses. Here is witness to their teaching, our responsibility for life continues. But it is their purpose where I find hope – to help humanity attain enough spiritual maturity to cope with the planetary crisis and live responsibly within Earth's means.

Lifted Up or Stepping Up?

On the last Sunday of the Easter season, it's customary to read the fantastical story of Jesus being lifted into heaven. Regarded as the final act of redemption and a glimpse into the bodily resurrection at the final judgment, belief in the ascension has been essential in some corners. Though many Protestants abandoned observance of the event at the time of the Reformation, the United Church of Canada continues to pay lipservice to the story by reciting the Apostles' Creed on Easter. So, following tradition, we recalled Luke's account of Jesus being lifted into the heavens.

The Traditional – Lifted up.

> Dear seekers, I've answered your questions about Jesus' deeds and teachings in his last days. I've told how after his death he was with the disciples and urged them to wait and trust the Spirit would help them in the future. (1 Corinthians 15:6) Now let me tell you how he finally left us. Forty days after his resurrection, they went to Mount Olivet at the edge of Jerusalem. There, before their very eyes, he was lifted into a cloud and disappeared. Having witnessed his ascension into heaven, they stood dumbstruck staring into the skies. It took a couple of angels to bring them back to the work at hand. "Take Jesus' message into the world. Go global! He'll return in the same way he left!" (paraphrase Acts 1:9-11)

I made full disclosure. I'd always dreaded Easter service. The reason being, I could not with any integrity preach a literal interpretation of the ascension. Nor could I repeat the creed's declaration: "He ascended into heaven, sits at the right hand of God the Father almighty; from thence He shall come to judge the living and the dead." I didn't believe in a general resurrection of souls or a judgment day at the end of the age. A theological construct, it seemed to explain life after death as a matter of cause and effect and smack of the old childhood threat, "wait 'til your Father gets home!"

My concept of resurrection had evolved. I didn't believe there was only one definition. My ideas, you might say, had been raised up by the story of evolution. In fact, having hosted some of the world's leading Evolutionaries, I'd come to understand the story of evolution as an ascension in Consciousness, and an epic of resurrection itself. To explain, I had a story.

The Evolutionary – The Futurist and the Evangelist

"The next human is arising in and through us, now." Sitting across the breakfast table, Barbara Marx Hubbard made anthropology sound like religion, religion sound like science, and evolution sound like the morning news. A futurist, Christian, and student of science, she incorporated the gospels, cosmology, physics, quantum mechanics, biology, and noetics into her theories of Conscious Evolution. She'd written an interpretation of the scriptures from an evolutionary perspective.

As an adult, Barbara had experienced the risen Christ as a light body, an energetic presence. It changed her understanding of death as resting in peace to continuing as an energetic presence. In her eighties, she felt she wasn't dying, she was regenerating. Her future, she saw as an expression of her integrated whole self consciously guiding humanity's transition into its next evolution.

In a time of exhaustion and overwhelm at Earth's suffering, Barbara had a second experience in which she was told to pay attention to the capabilities coded within her and evolving in all humanity. With these the future human would be aware of being part of the Universe, able to materialize at will, capable of teleportation, telepathy, and interacting with light bodies once called gods. This insight into what the human was becoming directed her lifework.

She began to teach the environmental crisis as a sign one phase of humanity was ending, a new stage of science was beginning, and democracy was shifting. If society consciously chose to cooperate with their own evolution, she said, we would see a shift from dominion over to co-creation with nature. Individual creativity would turn into synergistic cooperation with the whole.

Barbara expounded these profound ideas with unabashed delight. Given I'd been schooled in systematic theology, she taught me not to take myself too seriously but delight in new ideas.

Barbara's claim that we can cooperate with humanity's next emergence stirred my imagination. Were her mystical experiences not present-day ascension stories? Was the futurist's call to consciously step into a higher plane of consciousness not a call to cooperate with the ongoing ascension of the human species? The new ideas, though more alluring than white chocolate, made preaching a traditional Easter all the more terrifying. Then I found a cartoon by Graham Wilson in Michael Dowd's book, *Thank God For Evolution.*

Picture a series of beings on an ascending staircase. First, a fuzzy blob, then a fuzzy blob with eyes, then a fuzzy hominid, then a man wearing a suit and a surprised expression. Ahead of this character, the stair case continued with a number of empty steps. The caption reads, "I wondered when you'd notice the empty steps." Brilliantly, the cartoonist mocks our myopic denial of the evolutionary reality. But even more powerful was this alternative definition of ascension. Humanity is ascending the evolutionary staircase. Paying attention, we can cooperate in our own ascension.

We co-hosted Dowd, who billed himself as an Evolutionary Evangelist, in a Peterborough church. God's love and saving grace, he declared as he danced from one side of the sanctuary to the other, is revealed in the Bible, on the cross, and throughout the entire fourteen-billion-year epic of evolution. "To ignore or discount any of these is to miss the meaning and magnitude of them all."[xlvii]

> Passion, he taught me, is the only possible response to the magnitude of evolutionary possibility and the empty steps ahead.
>
> The empty step compelled a question I'd never asked from the pulpit. What is our species becoming? It was a question that fascinated Hubbard. The new human, she believed, will "rise from our mortal earthly condition to our ever-evolving universal condition."[xlviii] This was a resurrection of a third kind. Not of the body, not of the spirit, but of Consciousness. This was about an ascension of Consciousness.
>
> Meeting the futurist and evangelist, I had come to a radically new way of thinking. From the crucifixion of Earth will rise a new kind of human: aware of its universal nature, mindful of the original unity, and conscious of its infinite potential to co-create the future.

My unusual Easter story finished, there was no uprising! There was no applause, but there was no stoning either. I'd dared to speak with integrity and no one's faith nor any stained glass windows were shattered. There were some smiles, some puzzled faces, and a few nods. A couple of retired clergy appeared elated, grateful for a freed and freeing approach to the Easter mystery.

For me, there was relief. Raised by science from the shards of a two-thousand-year-old stained glass paradigm, I'd come back to church with an Evolutionary Spirituality. I'd read the Easter story in a never-before way: not as a literal event in the life of one man; not as the central event in one religion's belief system. I'd celebrated it as a pattern of deep interconnectedness that remains from age to age. I felt relieved, hopeful even. I could now embrace Ascension Day as any day we stepped up to live with a One-Earth Mind.

Closing the Stable Door

Pulling out of the gravel driveway at the end of the Easter journey, much was changed. I'd stepped out of the doctrinal box, danced on the fringes of science, dipped into other cultural spiritualities, and told some unconventional stories. We'd gone beyond the tired debate: how did Jesus really rise from the dead – in spirit or body? And, the circle had bravely accompanied me.

During those fifty days, the stone of tradition that had long entombed my religious imagination was rolled away. Free of any monopoly I'd assumed Christianity had on resurrection, I had explored thoughts just as miraculous. Resurrection was no longer something that happens to us by the grace of God; it cannot be limited to a supernatural event in time. It is a cosmic power that's been coded within us since the beginning; it's an experience in this life, and a responsibility in the next. And ascension was less about Jesus rising into eternal life than human potential stepping into its fullness. Yes, this had been an evolutionary Easter with a poignant message for the sixth mass extinction.

As I drove away from the congregation, I marvelled. This had been its one hundred and fiftieth Easter gathering. I found myself casting a glance over my shoulder. I wasn't surprised to see the grandmothers and grandfathers – past, present, and future – waving me on.

Evolutionary Wisdom

- The Christian and evolutionary stories share a universal theme of resurrection.
- Evolutionary science is not an enemy of faith but a catalyst for its evolution.
- Resurrection encounters are not limited to the age of miracles but are the norm.
- Easter rituals can raise consciousness and inspire a planetary culture.
- An evolutionary Easter allows us to cast our gaze further afield than personal salvation.

The Church needs an expanded resurrection-belief if they are to rise up and inspire society to take back responsibility for the planet from the Corporate Empire.

CHAPTER 12

Discoveries in the Stable

Meister Eckhart had been right. The stable hand who has been to the top of the mountain must go back to the stable. It's part of her evolutionary responsibility. And I'm grateful I did. Only as the prodigal daughter was I able to recognize that critical times demand that our understandings of divinity and humanity evolve. Only by stepping back into the Christian culture did I glimpse its future. Circles! No more rows. Circles in which both biblical and cosmic stories are told. Circles where God, the Evolutionary Impulse, and Consciousness are celebrated as a new trinity.

What happened after the stable hand returned to the stable? An experiment in Evolutionary Spirituality. While naturally there were some who preferred the familiar, the circle as a whole was open to the adventure. Joyce put it this way, "Thank you for asking us to think more deeply."

By the time you read this, the dance has taken me out of that community. The Little Church That Would continues to experiment with shape and form as numbers, climate, and the Coronavirus dictate. While the day may come when it is yet another honoured Canadian heritage site, that too will be part of the dance.

But for now, as the planet undergoes significant environmental changes, the experiment that is Evolutionary Spirituality offers this assurance – there is an intimacy between the Christian and scientific stories that makes them stronger together; and together, they can make the Earth-family more resilient.

Going forward, in, out, or on the fringe of the church, singly and together, we will need an exceptional strength. I am referring not to physical prowess, but spiritual, ethical, and cultural resilience. What, you might ask, provides resilience to the individual and the community alike. And the answer will surprise you for the source of such strength is seldom acknowledged. I am referring to ritual.

In the last section, I am excited to share a discovery. Ritual can be evolutionary. While we expect rituals to preseve and transmit a tradition's beliefs, norms, and way of being, these are not the kind of rituals we need. At a threshold in the human story, what is necessary to leave our destructive stage behind are revolutionary practices, exercises that turn society's focus to the future of the species and the planet.

PART 3

On the Fringe

Evolutionary Rituals

Out, In, or On the Fringe of the Church

CHAPTER 13

Evolutionary Rituals

When I am caught in the creative swirl of Evolution's dance, I must step into her arms, feel her rhythms, and follow her energy. Only then can I come home to the fullness of who I am.

Ritual Power

In my beginning was ritual. Snuggled against mother's black seal coat, quieted by the butterscotch lifesaver from her pocket, Sunday night church captivated me. The pomp and ceremony of parading choristers in long burgundy gowns, the rise and fall of women in paisley dresses and feathered hats, men in dark suits and striped ties, the strains of Mozart and Mendelssohn, the man in the long black robe on the stage above us – everything declared it to be a time of great importance.

An adult event, I spent my time exploring the stories in the coloured glass windows: children crowding round Jesus' knee, sad women below a cross, angels atop a rocky cave. The weekly drama comforted my childhood and shaped the adult I would become.

Those 1950 religious rituals created the beliefs which shaped my reality. There was heaven and earth, good and evil, rich and poor. A good person gave to those in need. If you were one of the needy, God loved you anyway.

Traditions of my Eastern-Ontario farming community shaped my work ethic. On Fair Day, there were ribbons for the best calves, jams, and hams. Success was rewarded. After high school, some got jobs at the Nestle's plant. Others went to the newly built Community Colleges. Few went to University, a job being the ultimate goal. Stores closed on Labour Day to celebrate workers' rights and contributions.

National holidays shaped my understanding of society and citizenship. These included Christmas and Easter. The Canada of my childhood was Christian. On Canada Day, there was a parade on Main Street. On Remembrance Day, flags, wreaths, and speeches taught me to value justice and national sovereignty more than global unity or individual lives.

Rituals are powerful. They are words and stories enacted and embodied. On their own, words inform. Exchanged, they make for communication. Words accompanied by specific movements that are experienced repeatedly, however, create neural pathways, beliefs, individual identities, and whole cultures.

Ritual Resistance

It's 2020, a new decade in a new century. I live in a multiethnic and multireligious society; a technological age, generation of retirees, and dis-eased planet. Surely my rituals, be they personal, social or spiritual, must be different.

Changing rituals is not the same as updating your wardrobe. Typically, we protect and preserve rituals as a way of preserving and protecting the culture we know and love. Changes to rituals can cause conflict in families, congregations, even denominations.

"If it's politically incorrect to sing Onward Christian Soldiers, I'm out of here."

"The Bible says God abhors homosexuality. We'll start our own Church."

"Over my dead body will we take out those pews made by my grandfather."

I've heard them all. You won't be surprised when I tell you courses on Conflict Management were part of the church culture in the '90s. Books have been written on the subject of resistance to change, *Dancing With Dinosaurs* being an example. One reviewer called it a compelling argument why not to be or become a Christian. When an impatient clergy colleague waved the book at a congregational Board meeting, it was like a toreador waving his cape at the bull.

My days in ministry could have been easier if I'd had an evolutionary understanding of change and the power of homeostasis. One of the cosmogenetic powers by which the Universe has morphed, adapted, and expanded, it is the resistance to change that provides stability midst break-down. In a mammal, it's the dynamics that maintain form and function even while the species is undergoing the evolutionary process.

Evolutionaries understand and honour resistance at the same time as they facilitate the dance of becoming. They honour resistance to change as the way we protect what we love.

Dances of Becoming

To be or to become? That's the question driving an evolutionary ritual. To be the woman I am today struggling to protect life as it was – this isn't even possible. To become part of a global human species that believes in the wholeness of life, has loyalty to the planet, and a commitment to the future – this is actually probable. By grounding our rites, practices, holidays, and traditions in the story of evolution, it's possible to shift consciousness from being to becoming.

I dare to make this claim because I've witnessed the power of rites based on the new cosmology. Walking the spiral, woodland labyrinth was part of every program held at Gaia Centre and every Gaia Farmhouse retreat. For those who were willing to open themselves to the depth of the experience, the cosmic walk was transformational. These are some of the insights shared by our guests.

Wanda's image of life shifted from one with a beginning and an end to one that was spiralling, ever-unfolding with no endings. Cynthia embraced herself as stardust. Desmond, conscious of how his cosmic story was so much larger than Christianity, and regretting how his ministry had contributed to the suffering of Earth and oppressed cultures, threw his clerical collar into the Big Bang Bonfire. Walking the labyrinth at night reminded Marilyn how life's journey is always into the unknown. Khenmo had us describe Buddhist symbols of compassion, peace, and love all along the labyrinth path with cornmeal to help us meditate on what kind of energy we wanted to give back to the Universe.

One woman's experience was even more dramatic. At that place where death is honoured as one of the ways Universe seeks more future, Angelica received a visitation from a deceased friend. Reassured and freed from grief's anxiety, she invited her group to return and create a ritual of thanksgiving at that place. The ritual revealed the interconnectedness of existence between the invisible and visible planes.

For me, the significance of the ritual walk in deep time was two-fold. I came to understand myself as something more than an individual, a woman, a Christian, or a Canadian. I am a manifestation of the Universe. Part of an evolutionary process, I recognized myself as part of a species, and more importantly, part of a species that's evolving.

Context is what defines one ritual as Christian or another as Buddhist. When the context for our holiday, meditation, personal, or communal act is the deep time story of an unfinished and still-evolving creation, it can be evolutionary.

Ritual Cultures

One might assume that introducing evolution into ritual would be easier outside than inside the church. But it wasn't always the case. Some guests to the Gaia Centre being non-church-goers were suspicious of ritual which they associated with religion. The Kinmount congregation, on the other hand, was already a ritual culture. There, the work wasn't introducing ritual but introducing the evolutionary story into the ritual. In a Sunday order of service, there were many opportunities to do just that.

Candle lighting typically occurs at the beginning of any service. Words are spoken to explain what each flame symbolizes – God's presence, Jesus's love, the Holy Spirit. At the Little Church That Would, we integrated the language of science into this ritual. It looked like this:

> One: In light of the Cosmic Christ alive in all the Universe,
> All: we light the flame of divinity within and among us.

At Holy Communion, too, it was possible to add cosmology to the theology because the ritual was already in place. Then the candle lighting liturgy sounded like this:

> One: Remembering our common origins in the First Flaring Forth,
> All: we light the flame of Holy and Cosmic Communion.

Evolutionary Rituals are ways to show how religion, humanity, and divinity evolve.

As I developed Evolutionary practices, I discovered a deeper appreciation for rituals. In word and action, they actually serve to both envision and incubate the message. Rituals, I now see, are better called dances. Like any waltz, circle, square, or folk dance, they transform the one into the whole, the me into the we, and just as importantly, the creature into the co-creator. I am, you are, we're becoming co-creators of the future.

In the next example, called The Dance of Becoming, the intention is enlightenment. Used at the Winter Solstice, it is another candle lighting ritual. But there are some major differences.

Radiance candle:
When December's growing gloom dims our joy, when we huddle against the long cold nights, I/we remember: out of dark and fecund emptiness, Universe first flared forth.
We are light's creations, fire become stars, planets, mineral, plant, animal, and human. Like this flame,
I/We hold the transforming power of radiance.
Where on the darkest day can I/we become a radiant presence?

The ritual is evolutionary because it refers to radiance, one of the sacred powers by which Universe expands. Referring to radiance as a personal power, the ritual reminds us the powers of the Universe are as much within us as around us because we're expressions of the Universe. More than lip service to a distant power, evolutionary rituals lead to our becoming Evolutionary Dancers, agents of co-creation.

To aid the desired transformation of consciousness, these practices inspire and invite meditation, reflection, and deep questioning in oneself or with others.

The Allurement candle,:
As the Winter Solstice nears, Sun plays hide and seek but mostly hides. In its long shadows lurk heart's desires – health, love, peace, good work, safe children …
Also lurking is Gaia's grief for land lost to drought, raped for oil, fired, and fracked.
Allurements all, they pull us like gravity draws Earth into its place in the cosmic family.
Like flame compels one's gaze, so passions attract the future.
What is attracting me/us to become all I/we can become?

Ultimately, and most importantly, Evolutionary Rituals are an intentional response to the undoing of Earth's life-support systems. To transform the consciousness that brought about human-induced global warming, they waken us to think more deeply, live more compassionately, and to embrace more fully the powers and response-abilities within us.

Dances in Deep Time

DEEP TIME

The Great Work of our time, it has been said, is the reinvention of the human. To that end, Evolutionary Rituals serve to awaken us to who and where we are in deep time.

A new term to most, deep time is a useful phrase in many ways. It contradicts Bishop Ussher's claim in 1650: Universe came to be around 6 pm on October 22, 4004 BC. It honours astronomers' latest calculation in 2018 of a Universe that's 13.8 billion years old. Lastly, it simplifies a number so great as to be unbelievable; and it makes a story so awesome as to be inconceivable a matter of fact.

Accepting the reality of deep time is vital. It stretches our understanding of history to cosmic proportions. We think less about our biological clock and more about our specie's contribution to planetary evolution or devolution. When we grasp this, which is no small accomplishment, we discover more about what it means to be human.

Take a detour with me. Ask yourself, "What does it mean to be human?" Don't most of us think being human is something that happens to us? For many it's something we try to either endure or make the best of. But what if we think of humans as an expression of Universe, as cosmic beings with agency? Believe me, it takes even going for groceries to a whole new level.

The Dance of Identity is the name of an evolutionary ritual. It can be used to expand the import of personal milestones for an individual, family, religious or commercial organization. It's appropriate when celebrating a birthday, anniversary, an opening, or ending of a chapter in our life story. But don't miss this, the ritual magnifies the importance of the event by putting it in deep time. Showing our lives are part of the Universe story's time-line, the experience adds import to our choices.

This ceremony was part of the reinvention of work program and used in a New Year's Sunday gathering. It requires only enough space to take twenty steps in one direction and back. The path can be straight ahead and back or in a spiral. If trying this between pews, it can be done by stepping in place. The first steps, however, are away from all the stories and rituals that have defined us. Here's an excerpt from the walking meditation found at the back of the book.

We stand at a threshold moment in the dance of identity.
We turn back to where we come from.
Now consumerism, religion, nationalism, dualism –
modern humanity is not. (*take a step)*
Now *Homo-sapiens*, Neanderthal, H*omo-erectus* –
the human is not. (*take a step)*
Now animals – Elephant, Polar Bear, Wolf, Deer, Cow, Raccoon,
Fox – are not. *(step)*
Now the winged-ones – Eagle, Jay, Heron, Sparrow, Honeybee,
Butterfly– are not. *(step)*
Now rooted-ones – Cedar, Pine, Apple, Corn, Squash, Sage,
St. John's Wort – are not.*(step)*
Now Oceans – lakes, rivers, aquifers, all waters – are not. *(step)*
Now Sun and all stars – are not. *(step)*
Now Universe is not. *(step)*
(*Turn to retrace your steps and continue as above)*
Now I am no thing, raw nothingness, total fecundity,
infinite potential. *(step)*
Now I am single cell, photosynthetic cell, nucleated cell
respiring, adapting, evolving. (*step)*
Now I am algae, crustacean, reptile, tree, bird, flower,
bee, dinosaur, chimp, sensate. (*step)*
Now I am Hominid, *Neanderthal, Homo sapiens sapiens*
at threshold.

***Reflection**: Take some time to write down the ways in which you choose to identify your being.*

The surprise in this experience is that it is necessary to empty the stories, beliefs, and teachings that have shaped our self-identity before we can redefine ourselves. The power of the ritual is that it does redefine us as cosmic and planetary beings with a part in the Great Work.

Rituals for Conscious Evolution

This is what I've discovered in these disturbing and distressing times: my stories are too small; my nation's holidays too trite; my religion's traditions ignore the evolutionary possibility in the planetary crisis.

This is what I need: rites and practices that calm my chaos and transforms my powerlessness. Evolutionary Rituals meet these needs. When I am caught in the creative swirl of Evolution's dance, I must step into her arms, feel her rhythms, and follow her energy. Only then can I come home to the fullness of what I am, why I am here at this moment in time, and the choices that are mine.

The purpose of Evolutionary Rituals is to identify the conscious choices being raised by these times. Choices like, "Do I wish to become a different kind of human?" "Am I willing to let go traditional rituals that have proven to be detrimental to all life?" Such choices are portals between what was and what can be. As vessels of evolutionary consciousness, they invite a spiritually ethical, scientifically conscious, and socially sustainable humanity.

Afterwards

The Last Word

As I sit down to write a closing, Mother Earth demands the last word. It it is Good Friday, the Spring of 2020 and COVID-19 has shut church doors all over the world. Schools, factories, businesses, parks, beaches, restaurants too have been closed. To slow the spread of the disease, only essential services remain open. On this day set aside to remember Jesus' suffering, all the world is talking about the agony and death caused by a bacteria called the Coronavirus.

My reason for beginning this book, the environmental crisis, has reached pandemic proportions. By disrupting ecosystems, human activity has shaken viruses loose from their natural hosts. In need of new hosts, pathogens, crossing from animals to humans, have spread quickly. Voices, from the new discipline of planetary health, say our destruction of biodiversity in the name of progress and profit has created the conditions for the deadly virus to spread from non-human to humans.

The pandemic has slowed industry, crippled the economy, and shutdown life as we knew it. This tiny organism with the power to kill has invited our species into the mirror dance.

Now it is the first day of Summer, 2020 and Carbon dioxide levels in Earth's atmosphere have exceeded 415 parts per million for the first time in planetary history. CO^2 is the greenhouse gas scientists say is most responsible for global warming. These are exceedingly dangerous times.

I look for some sign of redemption; it's part of my faith tradition. I trust Universe to bring creative newness from cataclysm; it's part of my cosmology. I find what I'm looking for, an evolution of consciousness. It's happening thanks to the environmental crisis and this pandemic. The world has reduced non-essential, economic activity, is producing less stuff, cutting air travel to bare minimums. We've used less energy and emitted fewer greenhouse gases. I am encouraged: we can become what Earth needs us to be.

I sat down to write a final word only to realize the planet is already writing it. Though wounded, Earth is coded with evolutionary powers. Cataclysm, emergence, synergy, transformation – these same powers by which Universe manifested the Blue Pearl planet make it regenerative. These same powers working in me, I realize, stir me to write.

The news of the day isn't the plague of 2020. It's cosmogenesis: Universe is ever-seeking and manifesting a next beginning. It's bigger news even than the *Book of Genesis* which tells of only one beginning; bigger too than John's *Book of Revelation* which warns of only one end. The message of cosmological science is that the nature of reality is an eternal genesis. At this end to planetary life as we've known it, another beginning is being born out of the environmental crises. This hope dances me to the end of this book.

I didn't arrive here easily. On awakening to the fact that I was spending my one magnificent life to save the church when the church should be hell-bent on saving humanity from self-destruction, I stepped out. And what a sometimes awesome, sometimes awful world I stepped into. But most importantly, I stepped into a world of expansive thought and conscious evolution.

As I danced from liberal Protestantism into a Creation Spirituality, into an Eco-spirituality, into Conscious Evolution and integral theory each step drew me further. Where I arrived was in the vital and emergent conversation some call Evolutionary Spirituality. And just when I knew where I was, surprise! I was invited to step back into the Christian culture.

Back in the lap of Mother Church, it was a welcome discovery – Christian and Evolutionary stories can dance together. Moving through the religious and secular calendars, the Holy Word became an evolutionary word. Resurrection burst the bonds of Christianity and became the norm in a holographic Universe. Theology, Ecology, and Cosmology became the new Trinity. The Golden Rule became the Green Rule: Love the Earth as much as you love yourself. The divine presence appeared as the Evolutionary Dancer.

These pages have been my way of cooperating with the power-full Consciousness breaking into society through its breakdown. Writing this book, telling this story of my own conscious evolution, I hope will play a part in my species becoming all it can be.

The Last Story

Grandmother Universe also has a last word, a last story she'd like to tell.

> Now, dear ones, it has grown late. I feel Moon's call. She bids us turn our face to the future, to gather up any wealth you might have found in these pages and spend it on a tomorrow you may not see. From the linty lining of Grandmother's deep time pocket, here are a few gold pieces I wish to give you.

First, the golden rule of seekers: ask questions. But ask not, "How can I change the future?" Ask "What can I become?" Then become full of rage at those beliefs, laws, and expectations that would have you live too small and love too few. Become "outrageous."

Next, the gold coin of courage. This is the tender spent by the likes of David Suzuki, Maude Barlow, and Elizabeth May – the outspoken and stand-up sentries of the future. This is what will secure you a voice in conversations that decide today what will be burden or legacy tomorrow.

And here is golden wisdom, indeed. Gild whatever is your lifework, occupation, or project in the Earth community as your sacred work of art. Then will each day be purpose-driven and meaning-full.

Now, here is an acorn from Gaia's woods. This simple seed has led theologians to become geologians, nuns to become mystics, clerics to redirect their vows of obedience from Heaven to Earth. Not just an acorn, this is the seed of our becoming. Plant it deep in your soul and all your life will be one of growth and fruitfulness.

And lastly, from the very depths of my deep-time pockets is a clump of dirt. Gardeners, cooks, farmers, shamans will tell you this is your Mother, your medicine, your origin, and your destiny. Let this be the place from which you rise each day and your destination every night.

Now, my pocket is empty. No, wait, here is a thread. I pass it to you who would spin the evolutionary story further still ...

The Last Dance

In the end, I am grateful for all this book has had to teach me. I offer these stories and rituals, not as rigorous academic research, not as audacious declarations of truth, but in hopes they may inspire and invite you too to know yourself as one with the Evolutionary Dancer.

Dance, remember, is not random movement. It is conscious, cosmic, holy creativity in motion. It is the energetic vibration of Universe. Sometimes the dance is a Tango, a dance of passion. Sometimes a ballet of great tragedy. Sometimes, as in the Canadian square dance, it is a dance of letting go, moving on, and coming back to where you started in a new way. In the end, may this book be an invitation into the dance of becoming. Becoming what – the new storyteller, the Universal Human, co-creators, dancing evolutionaries – the possibilities are infinite.

Evolutionary Wisdom for Evolutionary Dancers

- Know yourself part of a vulnerable planetary family and cosmic communion.
- Pray not to a supernatural deity beyond but to the Infinite Potential within.
- Grieve the terrible death and dying.
- Forgive our species' short shortsightedness.
- Own your creative powers.
- Embrace your future spiritually ethical, socially just, ecologically responsible self.

Making this journey, writing this book, telling this story – may it play a part in our species' evolutionary dance.

Resources and Rituals for Evolutionary Spirituality

AUTUMN EQUINOX

The Dance of Immensity

What. When. Where.
Meditation. Equinox, Personal or Social Turning Point. In, out, or on the fringe of the church.

Evolutionary Moment
The sun shines directly on the equator between September 22-24. Day and night are of equal length. In the northern hemisphere, Earth's energies shift from producing to relinquishing. Not only part of an annual cycle, also part of Solar System's dance in space and time. Global warming signals it is time society shift its energies, relinquish the pursuit of an ever-increasing Gross Nation Product, and participate in the cosmic dance of ever-expanding consciousness.

Intention of Evolutionary Ritual
To show society's emergence from the present phase of overpopulation, overlproduction, and pollution as part of the ongoing evolution in human consciousness which reflects the expansive nature of the Universe.

Preparations
In the pew, on your yoga cushion, or at home, ready yourself for prayer or meditation with deep breathing.
Familiarize yourself with the Universe Story diagram. Place a finger at "Start here."
Following directions, begin the meditation. Take time between spirals to pause for reflection.

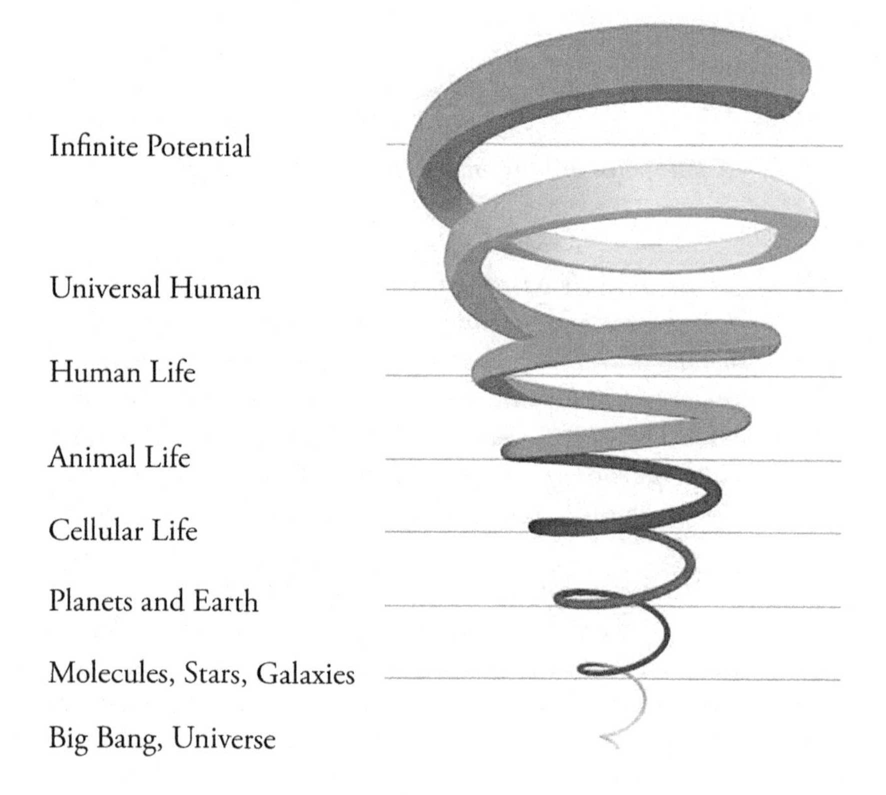

The Dance of Immensity starts here.

1 Flaring Forth of Universe *(start)*
The Originating Power births time, space, light, and particles out of the quantum vacuum by the first law of Universe, Expansion. Inhale the immensity of Originating Power in and around you. Exhale any idea your power is too small. *(move)*

2 Molecules, Stars, Galaxies
Primordial atoms of hydrogen and helium fabricate great sheets of galaxies, an estimated 2 trillion to date. Inhale the elemental potentiality in a cosmogenetic, ever-expanding, infinite Universe. Exhale fears of finite endings. *(move)*

3 Solar System
Around one Star in a disc of colliding gases, the elements of titanium, argon, iron, neon, fluorine, calcium bond into grains of matter to become 9 planets. Only Earth achieved an elegant balance able to give rise to continents, oceans, and life. Inhale resilience. Exhale hopelessness. *(move)*

4 Biological Life
Cells, ignited by lightning, reproduce, populate, and mutate. Through memory and genetic mutation, life evolves and expands. Inhale gratitude for cells that photosynthesize Sun's energy into plant energy. Exhale gratitude for cells that respirate and purify the air. *(move)*

5 Animal Life
Bacteria, our first ancestor; the Protists, Fungi, Plants, and Animals. The 10-30 million species that exist may be but 1% of the billions that have gone extinct. Inhale in wonder at the fecundity of the animal kingdom. Exhale fear of the 6th mass extinction. *(move)*

6 Human Life

Humans emerged with a sense of wonder and celebration, the ability to refashion its environs for its own purposes and self-reflection. Inhale in awe of your ever-expanding consciousness. Exhale forgiveness for your species that has used its creativity in destructive ways. (*move)*

7 Universal Human

The emerging genus is awakening: I'm not *on* Earth but *within* Earth-community. Every being's integral to the whole. Spiritual, social, scientific, technological capacities are integrated. Inhale air breathed by those who carried fire. Exhale any idea of the human as all it can be. *(move)*

8 Infinite Potential

A cosmic pattern, Infinite Potential, is coded in all that is. Evidence includes nanotechnology, cybernetics, artificial intelligence, the new cosmology, and growing consciousness. Inhale the infinite potential of Originating Power. Exhale despair at breakdown of civilization. Step into the dance of immensity.

Journal

The new origin story inspires me to relinquish ...
Coded within me, the Originating Power invites me to participate in the Dance of Immensity by ...

WINTER – ADVENT

The Dance of Radiance

What. When. Where.

A candle-lighting practice. Throughout December.
In, out, or on the fringe of the church.

Introduction

In the darkening days of the sixth mass extinction, evolutionaries light candles of transformation, detachment, creativity, and gratitude to remind us of the four paths by which all creation evolves.

Preparations

Beeswax or soy candles. Table / altar. Light one candle each week of December.

1st week
In the season of growing darkness
may the light of this flame highlight
the injustices to the lithosphere, atmosphere,
hydrosphere, and biosphere.
May it dance me to the path of transformation
and into a coming age of compassion for our planet home.
(reflection, journal, prayer)

2nd week
In the season of growing darkness
may the light of this flame show how
Earth's winter ways of emptying is into fecund nothingness.
May it dance me to the path of detachment
and into the Advent'ure of living within Earth's means.
(reflection, journal, prayer)

3rd week
Releasing the season of darkness
may this flame warm
the seeds of loving consciousness into new life.
May light dance me on life's path of creativity
and into the coming Gaia-centred humanity.
(reflection, journal, prayer)

4th week
In the season of growing darkness
may the light of this flame reveal
the wonder of the Earth-community.
Let it dance me along the path of awe to gratitude
and into the coming Ecozoic era.
(reflection, journal, prayer)

Evolutionary rituals have this intention – to co-create a new humanity.

SPRING – EASTER

The Dance of Transformation

What. When. Where

Evolutionary alter building. Easter or New-life event. In, out, or on the fringe of the church.

Evolutionary Moment

When asked what he thought was the solution to the planetary crises, cosmologist Brian Swimme said, "It would be to reinvent ourselves, at the species level, in a way that enables us to live with mutually enhancing relationships – not just with humans but with all beings – so that our activities enhance the world."[xlix]

Intention of Evolutionary Ritual

To celebrate Easter or a new-life event within the present context of the environmental crisis and the new sacred story of the Universe; to show resurrection as a cosmic pattern of transformation, to embrace our own cosmic power and response-ability for transformation so to cooperate with the evolution of human consciousness.

Preparations

Circle of chairs round a table. Copies of the 3 questions. Black or navy table cloth. Green table cloth. Candle and matches. Potted plant. Packet of seeds. Rabbit figurine. Cross (not crucifix). Potted Lily. Narrator. Presenters.

Narrator: It is Easter (*or* 1st of Spring). A day to celebrate. Yet, surely our celebration must be different in such times.

Presenter: 1st Question: Why must our celebration be different this year?
Narrator: Sixty percent of Earth's species may be extinct by mid-century. We must celebrate in ways that honour these times of great loss.

Presenter: 2nd Question: Why must our ritual be evolutionary?
Narrator: The human species too is threatened. We must celebrate in ways to help us evolve.

Presenter: 3rd Question: Why must the evolutionary story become our sacred story?
Narrator: Science tells us there has been birth, death, and resurrection since the beginning.
Presenter spread dark cloth on table.

Narrator: Everything is a transformation and form of Universe – stars, galaxies, planets, Earth.
Presenter spread green cloth over dark cloth.

Narrator: Sun's energy transforms the darkness to light.
Presenter place and light candle.

Narrator: Plants transform light to life.
Presenter place potted plant on the table/altar.

Narrator: Seeds of Summer's blossoms, Autumn's fruit, Winter's preserves, and a new year.
Presenter sprinkle seeds into pot.

Narrator: The Hare, messenger of the goddess Eostre, symbol of Spring and new life.
Presenter place rabbit figurine on the table/altar.

Narrator: The empty cross, sign of the risen Jesus who transformed death into eternal life.
Presenter place empty cross on the table/altar.

Narrator: In the bulb there is a flower. In the stardust, a planet. In the molten magma, a human. In the *Homo sapiens sapiens* is the *Homo Amore Universalis. In* the sixth mass extinction is a new age. Transformation is the way of the Universe.
Presenter place potted lily on the table/altar.

Time of Reflection

Conversation.

What does Easter, resurrection, transformation, or evolution mean in a planetary crisis?
Do you agree our rituals must be different in these times?
What difference does knowing ourselves as part of an evolving universe make?
Where do you see humanity evolving from its destructive to its co-creative phase?

SUMMER SOLSTICE

The Dance of Intimacy

What. When. Where.
Meditation or Body Prayer. Summer Solstice.
In, out, or on the fringe of the church.

Evolutionary Moment
At the Summer Solstice. Earth's north-south axis is tilted 23.5° toward the Sun. The northern hemisphere enjoys the longest day of the year. The beginning of the season of fertility, bio-dynamic/organic farmers plant their crops. Industrialization, however, has sped the melting of glacial ice. Earth's rotations are slowing. Days are shortening by fractions of milliseconds.

Intention of Evolutionary Ritual
To evoke a shift in human consciousness from reality as independence to reality as interdependence.

Preparations

Narrator, or recording of the ritual. Find an open space, preferably in nature. Scribe an imaginary circle five feet in diameter all around you. Acknowledge your bio-region. e.g. The Canadian Shield, the Algonquin Highlands, the Muskoka Watershed, etc. Locate and mark north, east, south, and west. Practice steps of the dance: turn, step forward, bow, gather (arm movement), bend to touch the earth, and rise. Begin facing the centre of the circle, focusing on the breath.

Turn to the east, your arms opening like tulip petals to sun's rays.
Step into a love story. Sun gives away 4 million tons of itself per second to its solar family.
Bow acknowledging Sun is 330 thousand times the size of Earth.
Gather your day-star's energy into mind and heart, digestive and reproductive organs.
Bend to touch the humus, once leaves, now summer's seedbed.
Rise as a child born of Earth and Sun, offspring of a dance of intimacy.

Turn to the south, arms reaching like rivers to the ocean.
Step into Earth's love affair with water. As heat rose from the young planet it mingled with the cold air of space bringing forth the first rains which pooled as oceans.
Bow honouring oceans as the womb of primal life.
Gather in raindrops from the thirteen billion cubic metres that fall each year.
Bend to touch the planet that is more than three quarters water.
Rise knowing you are 70% water and grateful for the dance of intimacy.

Turn to the west, arms spreading like wings of the Eastern Tiger Swallowtail.
Step into a bio-region kissed, tasted, and impregnated by planetary pollinators.
Bow to the jet stream air currents bringing the Arctic's cooling air.
Gather into your lungs, heart, and belly air's gifts – nitrogen, oxygen, and argon.
Bend hands to soil that, aerated by sister worm, is half air.
Rise as a child of the air and co-creator in a dance of intimacy.

Turn to the north, arms wide open to the 5 million square kilometres of Precambrian Shield.
Step softly on soils that are but a fraction of what was laid down by the glaciers.
Bow to North America's bedrock that rose out of the sea.
Gather rock's micro-organisms into your care, and its magnetic power into your soul.
Bend to put hands to star-dust become Mother Earth.
Rise as a child of rock and rain, sun and soil.

Turn to face the centre then turn again to face outward.
Bow to Sun's dance of intimacy.
Rise into summer, your time to shine and be fruitful.

Study Guide for Evolutionary Dancer

Introduction:
Having read of Kilby's dance with the church, w*ould you describe yourself as in, out, or on the fringe of Christianity?*

Chapter 1: Dancing Like Evolutionaries
Kilby introduces us to the wisdom teachers who challenged and inspired her to step out of her comfort zone into a wider cosmic consciousness.
Which teachers did you find alluring or problematic?

Chapter 2: Work Like Earth Depends On It
Lynda, Doug, Lisa, and Kate reinvented their work on the four paths of creation: a) affirmation of life, b) relinquishment, c) transformation for all, d) creativity.
Which reinventor's story did you relate to? On which path are you spending most of your life energy? On which path(s) would you like to spend more time?

Chapter 3: I Spy with My Evolutionary Eye
To reverse the paradigm of pollution, new frameworks of awe, ecology, and evolution are needed.
What shapes your outlook on life - religion, science, economics, convenience, health, other?

Chapter 4: Stories from Grandmother Universe
As a manifestation of Universe, Kilby's self-awareness shifts from individual to storyteller.
What shifts, if any, happened for you in Grandmother's Outlandish Love Affairs?
What personal powers did you discover in Grandmother's Power-Full Treasures?

Chapter 6: Stepping Back In
Kilby resists returning to the church, but makes many discoveries by doing just that.
What are you resisting? What is your church, society resisting? What's waiting to be discovered?

Chapter 7: The Advent'ure
From new science, Kilby finds new meaning for Advent – the nature of Universe is *becoming.*
Do you feel it's beneficial to revisit our traditions in light of the environmental crisis and new science?

Chapter 8: Conner's Cosmic Christmas
Christianity emerged very recently in deep time.
What difference does it make to place Christianity on the evolutionary time line?

Chapter 9: Evolutionary Epiphanies
By welcoming Greek, Jew, slave, free, male, and female, the early church reflected an evolution in social and religious consciousness.
Could the call for love of Earth be another evolution of consciousness? Is this an axial moment?

Chapter 10: Lent's Prison of Contentment
Reframing Lent as a dream of freedom changes our ideas of sin, sacrifice, atonement, and the cross.
What freedoms did you appreciate and why? What concerns did this chapter raise?

Chapter 11: Freeing Resurrection
Christianity holds no monopoly on the term resurrection.
Does this claim detract from your celebration of Easter?

Chapter 12: Discoveries in the Stable
Kilby was surprised to find Kinmount Church open to the new cosmology, new sacred story, and new ways.
Does this surprise and/or encourage you?

Chapter 13: Evolutionary Rituals for Every Season
Rites have the power to create, preserve, or change culture.
Are rituals important to you?

Glossary for an Evolutionary Spirituality

Our challenge is to create a new language, even a new sense of what it is to be human. It is to transcend not only national limitations, but even our species' isolation, to enter into the larger community of living species. This brings about a completely new sense of reality and value. Thomas Berry

When I was growing up, a web was woven by a spider, a footprint was what a muddy shoe left on the kitchen floor. Today the web is a system of immediate global communication and my footprint is the amount of carbon I add to the atmosphere driving to town. And since burning a gallon of petrol produces enough of the stuff to melt four hundred gallons of ice at the North Pole, my footprint is dirtier than anything my mother could have imagined. And certainly bigger than Mother Earth can bear.

From new consciousness comes new words. From new word comes new language. From new language comes new societies. New language is vital to communicate the rapidly changing reality of our planet. And so new words must become part of our parlance.

Cosmogenesis – Always in a state of genesis, the cosmos is still expanding and growing.

Cosmogenetic – Cataclysm and emergence are cosmogenetic powers by which cosmos creates more cosmos.

Cosmology – A branch of science and a framework for seeing ourselves as part of the Universe story.

Deep time – Coined in 1981, the term helps us describe cosmic events on a timeline that reaches back more than thirteen billion years.

Divine Feminine – Why do we talk of Mother Nature? Because the life force at the heart of the planet that nurtures life is feminine energy. Long denied, repressed, undervalued, it's having a resurgence when the planet most needs ecojustice and unity.

Earth – We capitalize Earth as we capitalize Mercury and Venus. Also because it is a living, intelligent being and a revelation of the sacred Originating Power.

Ecozoic – Coined by Thomas Berry and Brian Swimme, authors of *The Universe Story,* the Ecozoic is the future geological era in which humans will live in a mutually enhancing relationship with Earth and its community.

Evolutionaries – Those who accept evolution as the nature of all reality and reinvent their lifework to align with the Great Work, that is, the evolution of the next species of humanity and the emergence of a new Ecozoic age.

Evolutionary Impulse – Barbara Marx Hubbard, mother of the Conscious Evolution movement, used this to refer to the Divine Intelligence at the centre of the evolutionary story. I use it synonymously with Originating Power or God.

Gaia – The name for a Greek goddess that dwelt in the Earth nurturing and sustaining all life. The word implies that the planet, being home of the sacred, is sacred.

Gaia Hypothesis – The theory was developed by scientist James Lovelock: the planet, as a result of the interrelated and interdependent relationship between atmosphere, biosphere, aqua-sphere, is an intelligent and dynamic being.

G'awed – A term to say where there is awe, there is the divine presence.

Homo sapiens sapiens – Subspecies of genus *Homo* in which modern humans are classified.

One World Mind – A worldview, it sees all species, as well as the human and non-human, as parts of a dynamic and interdependent relationship governed by an intelligence that has a bias for more life and more future. Also expressed as the Gaia Mind or One-Earth Mind.

Universe – The newest science contradicts old images of Universe as a random, cold, dark soup! It is instead ever-expanding and composed of 70% dark energy, 25% dark matter, 4% invisible atoms and 0.5% invisible matter. The remaining 0.5% consists of atoms. All things being composed of atoms, all Earth beings are manifestations of Universe. Implicate in Universe is an intelligence, a Consciousness. Universe is becoming conscious of itself in the human species at this time.

Spirituality – Not a system of belief, a sense of sacred interconnectedness, a way of living in relationship to the larger whole.

Eco-Spirituality – Eco means home. An Eco-Spirituality holds life to be one of sacred relationship within our planetary home. Knowing that that relationship is threatened by climate change, many are seeking to follow the ways of nature to live within the planet's means; many experience a sacred presence in and with nature. This new consciousness is a return to Indigenous wisdom. The hope is it will lead the species to become better citizens of the planet.

Creation Spirituality – A new system of belief that honours all Creation as our Original Blessing. A young tradition, it cites the wisdom of Eastern and Western spiritualities, global Indigenous cultures, and emerging scientific understandings of the Universe. It celebrates mystics, prophets, and agents of social change from every age and culture. See Chapter 1 - Matthew Fox.

Evolutionary Spirituality – This worldview is just now emerging from ongoing developments in science, psychology, sociology, technology, philosophy, and theology. It is based on the belief in evolution as a process in which there is an implicate intelligence, undeniable connection, and intentional direction towards ever-expansive consciousness.

About Carol

Learning the Universe Story at age 55 pushed Carol further outside the box. But that, she discovered, is her place in life.

Adopted, Carol grew up in what, for the '50s, could be called an unconventional home. The girls went to Trinity United Church with Mom while Dad and brother attended St. Mary's Roman Catholic. Home was an apartment over Al's Lunch. On Main Street, things weren't quiet until after the hotel crowd had been fed and gone home, about 2 am. Compared to those schoolmates whose dads worked at the Nestle's plant and moms kept house, her childhood was out-of-the-box.

A therapeutic recreationist in the '70s, she worked for holistic healthcare. Introducing gardening, rabbits, and dogs into chronic care homes, she pushed the envelope and a few buttons.

Church and faith were always important. But she was more interested in doing liturgical dance than teaching Sunday School. When she was ordained in 1991, it was still remarkable for women to become clergy. Declared too feminist by her first congregation, she welcomed calls to more out-of-the-box ministries. But still, she didn't quite fit.

Drawn to Creation Spirituality and the environmental crisis, she left congregational ministry to found the Gaia Centre for Eco-spirituality and Sustainable Work. Surrounded by new-thought teachers and their students, she found herself at home among folks she came to recognize as Evolutionaries.

After fifteen years at the Gaia Farmhouse, Carol and her husband Paul Irwin now reside in Toronto, Ontario where they live in, out, and on the fringe of the church.

Meet Carol Online

1. "Reclaiming the Cosmic in Holiday Rituals." Deeptime Network (dtnetwork.org) Click courses. Nov. 14, 2019

2. Revolutionary Advent and Lenten series 2019 on YouTube.com

3. "Are you still a Christian?" Interview – TheOneNetworkTV (https://www.youtube.com/watch?v=AqnFZhgYk9w), 2012

Next Steps

Contact Carol Kilby *fb.me/EvolutionaryDancer*

[ ] **Explore Study Guide to "Evolutionary Dancer"**

[ ] **Join Facebook Group for blogs and more**

[ ] **Register for Online Ritual Community**

[ ] **Invite Carol, speaker, storyteller, ritualist to your community**

[ ] **Ask about Evolutionary Church Leaders Workshops**

Evolutionary Ritual Community

Join our monthly online gatherings here

fb.me/EvolutionaryDancer

Register to receive notices and dates for the following celebrations via Zoom.

January	*New Year's*	*Dance of Identity*
February	*Ash Wednesday / Lent*	*Dance of Cataclysm*
March	*Spring Equinox / Easter*	*Dance of Transformation*
April	*Earth Day*	*Dance of Communion*
May	*Mother's Day*	*Dance of Synergy*
June	*Summer Solstice*	*Dance of Intimacy*
July	*National Holidays*	*Dance of Differentiation*
August	*Labour Day*	*Dance of Emergence*
September	*Autumn Equinox*	*Dance of Immensity*
October	*World Wide Communion*	*Dance of Inter-relatedness*
November	*Advent*	*Dance of Becoming*
December	*Winter Solstice / Christmas*	*Dance of Radiance*

Workshops for Evolutionary Church Leaders

fb.me/EvolutionaryDancer

- **Advent or Advent'ure. What's the church's role in the Great Work?** At 415 parts per million of carbon dioxide, will we prepare for Jesus' coming again or becoming a new human species? Explore what Thomas Berry called the Great Work and the tools – cosmological science, evolution of consciousness, and the teachings of Jesus.
- **A Cosmic Christmas. What time is it?** Midst social and ecological distress of the sixth mass extinction, will we celebrate Jesus' birth or ask what's being born? Explore why ours is called another axial age, and how God and the cosmogenetic powers of creativity, cataclysm, and emergence are creating a more compassionate society.
- **Evolutionary Epiphanies. What are the gifts to this evolutionary moment?** In, out, and on the fringe of the church, modern magi tell us there are three gifts waiting to be opened: Humanity's Evolving, Religion's Evolving, God is evolving.
- **Lent. What does the Evolutionary Dancer require of us?** Breaking through the theological bars of personal salvation – sin, sacrifice, atonement, death, and the cross – we can find freedom for the holy work of sustainability.
- **Easter in the Ecozoic. What else does resurrection mean?** Raised up by Science, this important Christian theme has many meanings. More than our destiny, it is our mission within the Earth community.

Contact Carol gaiafarmhouse@gmail.com to plan how these workshops can serve you and your congregation, conference, or leaders' group.

Endnotes

i Pierre Teilhard de Chardin, "*Building the Earth, Human Energies*," p.67, teilharddechardin.org/index.php/teilhards-quotes

ii www.statcan.gc.ca/eng/help/bb/info/religion

iii Brian Swimme & Thomas Berry, "*The Universe Story*," Harper Collins, 1992.

iv Thomas Berry, "*The Great Work - Our Way Into The Future*," Random House, New York, 1999, page 3

v Drew Dellinger, "*love letter to the milky way*," a book of poems, Poets for Global Justice Press, Mill Valley, CA 2007

vi Swimme & Berry, p. 58

vii Swimme & Berry, p. 1

viii MacGillis, Miriam, "*The Next Exodus, A Ritual For Passing Over Into the Ecozoic Era*," a handout.

ix http://www.biologicaldiversity.org/programs/biodiversity/elements_of_biodiversity/extinction_crisis/

x Brian Swimme in interview with Brian Wright on meaningoflife.tv, 2013 (Video)

[xi] Dawn James, "*Raise Your Vibration, Transform Your Life*" https://www.youtube.com/watch?v=9uulL8gdLPM

[xii] Barbara Marx Hubbard, "*52 Codes For Conscious Evolution,*" Foundation for Conscious Evolution, 2011, p 84

[xiii] www.narcity.com/news/ca/canadas-environmental-ranking, *Global Wildlife Travel Index*, study by True Luxury Travel

[xiv] David Feinstein and Stanley Krippner, "*Personal Mythology*," Jeremy Tarcher Inc. LA, St. Martin's Press, 1988, p X1

[xv] http://prairieclimatecentre.ca/2017/10/seeing-is-believing-historical-records-prove-canada-is-warming/

[xvi] United Nations http://www.un.org/en/events/desertificationday/background.shtml

[xvii] Hubbard, "*52 Codes,*" p. 25

[xviii] https://www.paulallen.com/how-artificial-intelligence-could-save-the-planet/#dbelbzlV2hcB0sIe.99

[xix] Carl Sagan, "*Cosmos*," Ballantine Publishing, 1980, pg.1

[xx] Diarmuid O'Murchu, "*Quantum Theology,* "The Crossroad Publishing Company, New York, 1997, p.52

[xxi] Matthew Fox, "*Meditations with Meister Eckhart*," Bear & Company, 1983, p. 14

[xxii] Matthew Fox, "*The Coming of the Cosmic Christ*," Harper and Row, San Francisco, 1988, p. 135

[xxiii] Hubbard, "*52 Codes,*" p. 8

[xxiv] Andrew Cohen, quoted in "*Gateways to Conscious Evolution*," Foundation for Conscious Evolution

[xxv] Alanna Mitchell, "*Sea Sick*," McLelland & Stewart Ltd., Toronto, 2009, backcover

[xxvi] https://lop.parl.ca/sites/PublicWebsite/default/en_CA/ResearchPublications/201004E#ftn13

[xxvii] Yaacov Agam & Bernard Mandelbaum, "*AGAM-Art and Judaism,* "Keter Publishing House, Jerusalem, 1985, p.183

[xxviii] Diarmuid O'Murchu, "*Evolutionary Faith*," Orbis Books, Maryknoll, NY, 2002, p.181

[xxix] Jean Gebser, "*The Ever-Present Origin*," 1949

[xxx] http://www.greenmountainmonastery.org/become-a-sister/

[xxxi] www.orderofthesacredearth.org

[xxxii] http://creationspirituality.info/experience/ordination-in-csc/

[xxxiii] Thomas Berry, "*The Dream of the Earth, The New Story,*" Sierra Club Books, San Francisco, 1988, p.137

[xxxiv] Vandana Shiva, "*Stolen Harvest, The Hijacking of the Global Food Supply,*" South End Press, 1999

[xxxv] Hubbard, "*52 Codes,*" Code 13, p. 25

[xxxvi] Matthew Fox, "*Original Blessing,*" Bear & Co. Santa Fe, New Mexico, 1983, p. 85

[xxxvvii] Allen Lane, "*Essays of Michel de Montaigne in The Tibetan Book of Living and Dying,*" London, 1991, p. 95

[xxxviii] Darrell Bricker & John Wright, "*What Canadians Think About Almost Everything,*" 2005, Doubleday Canada, p. 86

[xxxix] Adrienne Rich and Claudia Rankine, "*Collected Poems: 1950-2012,*" W. W. Norton & Co, NY, p. 498

[xl] Irving Stone, *The Origin,* p. 462

[xli] Swimme & Berry, p. 48

[xlii] Lynne McTaggart, "*The Intention Experiment,*" Free Press, New York, 2007, p. 13

[xliii] R. J. Strassman, "*DMT, The Spirit Molecule,*" Park Street Press, 2001

[xliv] Sid Kirkpatrick, "*Edgar Cayce: An American Prophet,*" Riverhead Books, 2000

[xlv] Ervin Laszlo, "*Science and the Akashic Field,*", Inner Traditions, Rochester, Vermont, 2004, p. xi

[xlvi] Seth's transmitted manuscripts are held in The Yale University Library of History.

[xlvii] "*Thank God For Evolution,*" Michael Dowd, Viking, Penguin House, New York, NY, 2008, p. 203

[xlviii] Barbara Marx Hubbard, "*52 Codes,*" p. 9

[xlix] Brian Swimme, https://storyoftheuniverse.org/press/excerpts/

Made in the USA
Monee, IL
12 April 2021